BOLLINGEN SERIES XLIV

Victor Zuckerkandl

SOUND AND SYMBOL

Music and the External World

TRANSLATED FROM THE GERMAN
BY WILLARD R. TRASK

BOLLINGEN SERIES XLIV

PRINCETON UNIVERSITY PRESS

Published by Princeton University Press, Princeton, N. J.

First Princeton/Bollingen Paperback Printing, 1969

Second Printing, 1973

THIS IS THE FORTY-FOURTH IN A SERIES OF WORKS
SPONSORED BY BOLLINGEN FOUNDATION

Library of Congress Catalog Card No. 55-11489

ISBN 0-691-01759-X

Manufactured in the United States of America
by Princeton University Press, Princeton, N. J.

DESIGN BY ANDOR BRAUN

CONTENTS

TIME

SPACE

SOUND AND SYMBOL

Music and the External World

First and above all, an explanation must do justice to the thing that is to be explained, must not devaluate it, interpret it away, belittle it, or garble it, in order to make it easier to understand. The question is not "At what view of the phenomenon must we arrive in order to explain it in accordance with one or another philosophy?" but precisely the reverse: "What philosophy is requisite if we are to live up to the subject, be on a level with it?" The question is not how the phenomenon must be turned, twisted, narrowed, crippled so as to be explicable, at all costs, upon principles that we have once and for all resolved not to go beyond. The question is: "To what point must we enlarge *our* thought so that it shall be in proportion to the phenomenon . . ."

Schelling, *Philosophie der Mythologie*

FOREWORD

AT NO PERIOD of man's existence upon this earth does he appear to have been without music. The harps that have been brought to light from the royal graves of Ur are silent but eloquent witnesses, six thousand years after they were buried with their royal masters, that a highly developed and highly esteemed art of music flourished at the very beginning of history. Concerning prehistoric music, a music whose power and effect we of today should have to call supernatural, we have testimony in the mythologies of many peoples, both in the East and the West. Modern anthropology tells of the far from primitive music of the so-called primitive cultures. Many investigators assume that human speech was originally a sort of chant, and that it was only in the course of evolution that the two branches separated into the language of words and the language of tones. The world of man has never been a world without tone.

Among the various experiences of our senses, tone is the only one that belongs exclusively to life. Light and color, sound, odor, and taste, solidity, fluidity, and gaseousness, rough and smooth, hot and cold—all these are also to be found in nonliving nature. Only life can produce tones. Living beings, out of themselves, add tone to the physical world that confronts them; it is the gift of life to nonliving nature. A scientist, the first man to tread another planet, not knowing if he would find organic life there or not, would only need to hear a tone and his question would be answered.

Sounds are uncrystallized tones, tones that have not yet been realized. May we not assume that it was the sounds in nature—the sound of wind, of water in all its forms, of electric discharges, the rustling of leaves rather than the sight of their growth and fall—which aroused in sensitive minds the idea of a nature alive in all its parts? A completely soundless nature (which is something other than a silent nature—silence is a condition of sound as sleep is a condition of life) could hardly have been felt as alive. The mere contemplation of the motion that accompanies these sounds does not suffice; motion merely seen hardly calls up the impression of life so directly. The image of the soundlessly circling constellations is not an image of life to us. It was not the motion of the spheres but their *harmony,* their sounding together, of which men talked when they thought of the universe as alive. It seemed to them that the universal life must reveal itself as something audible rather than visible. Perhaps it is carrying the antithesis too far if we say that man attains the inwardness of life by hearing and its outwardness by seeing. Yet it seems more than mere chance that it was among a people so deeply anchored in the visible as the classic Greeks that the idea should be conceived of a supreme being which, in absolute immobility, intangibility, and uniformity, represented the direct opposite of everything living. The peculiar melancholy of the Greeks, too, their feeling for the ephemeral, for the element of transitoriness in life, may be connected with their living so much more in the visible than in the audible. In any case, the road to the heart of the living is more difficult, more circuitous, by way of the visible than of the audible.

We are led to similar considerations if we observe certain

differences in the behavior of blind and deaf people. The quietness, the equanimity, the trust, one might almost say the piety, so often found in the blind are in strange contrast to the irritability and suspicion encountered among so many of the deaf. The contrast cannot but be termed strange, because actually we should expect the opposite behavior. After all, it is the blind man —so we should think—he whose deficiency practically cuts him off from the world, who must feel in solitary confinement within himself. Yet it is not the blind man who shows the typical reaction of the prisoner, the man spied upon, who must always be upon his guard; it is the deaf man, whose most important organ of connection with the outside world has remained unimpaired. It seems as if, by the very fact that the blind man trusts himself to the guidance of ear instead of eye, other modes of connection with the world are revealed to him, modes that are otherwise overshadowed by the dominance of the eye—as if, in the realms with which he thus comes into contact, man were less alone, better provided for, more at home, than in the world of visible things to which the deaf man is directed and to which an element of foreignness always clings. Charles Baudelaire, who was exquisitely sensitive to these things, could find no better image to convey final loneliness, the utter absence of all life, more powerfully than the vision in his poem "Rêve Parisien": vast iridescent halls with water flowing everywhere, the height of perfection pictorially—and absolute soundlessness. "Tout pour l'oeil—rien pour l'oreille!" Baudelaire's insight is complemented by Goethe, who wrote (in the introduction to his *Farbenlehre*): ". . . a blind man, to whom the infinity of the visible is denied, can grasp an infinity of life in the audible."

The world in which we usually live, the world of our everyday existence—and not only of our everyday existence—is a world of visible things. The sense of sight has constructed it; the eye is our guide in it. Into it we integrate the impressions of the other senses; our speech, our actions, our thinking, are largely formed and oriented upon its pattern. One might almost suppose, and many do suppose, that the visible world is our entire milieu. We integrate even the audible into the frame of the visible—with one exception: music. Only in music, the art of tone, where the audible is, as it were, alone with itself, comes to itself, is the frame of the visible world broken through. Music does not integrate itself into the world of the eye.

When we open our eyes on the world we see objects: things that confront us, are directed toward us, close in on us. Tones carry outward; lead us away with them. That music is a window opening in the world of objects that closes in on us, a window through which we can look out from our world, men have always felt. The great thoughts that in all times have been thought about music all center upon this point; they are all suggested by this wonderful power of music to be a window. Philosophers of ancient China and classic Greece, mystics of late antiquity, Fathers of the Church, thinkers of the Renaissance, of the Reformation, of the Romantic Period, may differ widely in their speculations as to *where* music leads us. But concerning one thing—that music does cross a decisive frontier; that we find its most essential nature in this crossing, this transcendence—all who have ever thought about music are of one mind, as indeed they are too in finding that this transcendence occurs nowhere else in the same way, with the same directness. It does not happen in the other arts, nor in philosophic thought (all of which somehow remain connected with the world of objects; if not otherwise, then through language), nor in theology; theology, says Luther, begins where music leads to. Even a Herbert Spencer—elsewhere scarcely a decisive witness on such questions—feels himself impelled to combat Darwin's utilitarian interpretation of music as serving the ends of propagation. He pauses in amazement before "our strange ability to be moved by melody and harmony." Confronted with a phenomenon that he can in no way integrate into his picture of the universe, he sees only the possibility of comprehending it as "indefinite expressions of an unknown ideal life" or of letting it alone as "an incomprehensible secret"—both of which are confessions of helplessness.[1]

Spencer's helplessness is not that of a single thinker; it is typical of his own and the following period. When we said that all ages have produced great thoughts about music, we must except one age—our own. It seems that decades of positivist thinking have robbed us of the ability even to see problems of the sort that music raises. It is true that the century which preceded ours was the first to develop a separate science of music; however, like all nineteenth-century science, it was oriented after the pattern of natural science. But the principles and methods of thought, and the intellectual tools, that natural science has developed can be successfully employed only in the marginal provinces of music. Hence modern thought can boast significant accomplishments only on the outskirts of music, above all in acoustics and musical psychology. To approach the central problem of music from the position of natural science is about as hopeless as to attempt to measure air pressure with a thermometer. So it has come about that the very generations that have known more glorious music, and learned to observe it more closely, than any that preceded them have on the whole stopped thinking about music. There have been important exceptions, and we shall return to them later; yet so far they have remained exceptions.

Here we must expect the objection, Has not our training in the school of contemporary thought taught us that thinking had better steer clear of such a subject as music? Prevention of

1. Herbert Spencer, "On the Origin and Function of Music."

epidemic diseases, political economy, epistemology—about these it is possible to think, but not about music. Thinking and music are not made for each other; music is for feeling, not for thought. Hence thinking about music is largely sheer speculation, if not sheer imagination; it is only on the outskirts of music that one has solid matter in one's hands; the inwardness, the essence, of music cannot be thought but must be felt. And this is as it should be. For music is a miracle, and we approach a miracle with reverent wonder; we do not pry into it with thought.

To be sure, music appeals to feeling—to feeling *too.* So does faith; yet we do not allow ourselves to be deprived of the privilege of thinking about faith. St. Anselm of Canterbury called it negligence if one who has come to faith does not through thought also convince himself of the content of faith. To be sure, music is a miracle—shall we therefore refrain from thinking about it? It would be negligence to do so. What miracle wants of us is not that we, as thinking beings, shall capitulate to it, but rather that we shall do justice to it in our thinking. Precisely because music is a miracle, incomprehensible in the framework of the dominant mode of contemporary thinking, impossible to fit into the current conception of the world—a miracle not only in its greatest and most splendid, its most exceptional, manifestations, but in its plain fundamentals, in every simple melody, and indeed in every single tone of every melody—precisely because of all this, it is our duty to think about it. The purpose is not a *rationalization,* a setting aside of the miraculous. Thought that is true to its subject does not annul miracles. It penetrates the fog around them; it brings them out of darkness into light.

How music is possible—to understand this will be our chief task throughout this study. When Kant put his fundamental question, "How is natural science possible?" he did not seek to know *if* it is possible (he saw that it existed); he sought to know what the world must be like, what I must be like, if between me and the world such a thing as natural science can occur. What must the world be like, what must I be like, if between me and the world the phenomenon of music can occur? How must I consider the world, how must I consider myself, if I am to understand the reality of music?

The present volume, as its subtitle indicates, deals in the main with one aspect of this two-faced question; a projected second volume, Man the Musician, will discuss the other.

TONE

I. The Dynamic Quality of Tone

WE BEGIN with a well-known melody of Beethoven's, the theme of the last movement of the Ninth Symphony:

How little of the labor it cost its creator do we hear in this melody! It stands there like the epitome of the self-evident, of the simply and unquestionably valid. What should there be to understand in it beyond the direct auditory experience; what question should it raise? Does it not itself say everything that is to be said about it? The questioning intelligence finds no more points of application here than does the grasping hand on the surface of a crystal ball.

Yet a question must be put if our study is to get under way. A first question is generally a risky step, pregnant with consequences. The step is often taken without much reflection, in obedience to usage, to a traditional schema. Are we always aware how many unexpressed and unadmitted preconceptions such a first question introduces into a study? We think we are still investigating without prejudice, when in reality our thought is set in a definite direction from the very start; the course and the goal are predetermined before the study has really begun.

Four branches of learning provide us with what we may call ready-made questions with which we might begin our study. They are theory of music, acoustics, psychology of music, aesthetics. Let us briefly consider what unacknowledged preconceptions we should bring into this study with these four branches of learning.

The musical theorist looks at his subject above all from the viewpoint of the technique of musical composition. This is not the place to say in more detail that "theory of music" is improperly so called; with a few notable exceptions it has been concerned not with understanding music but with making it. It has become chiefly instruction in the practice of composition (generally a superannuated practice, but that is another question); the few scholars who have been concerned with a real theory of music have remained outsiders. To put it in a rather crass comparison: the problems of the musical theorists are the problems of the electrician, not the problems of electricity. What musical theory, in regard to our Beethoven melody, would have to say on the tonal material and its use, on key and time, on phrase and form, would be directed to the interests and needs of a person who wished to acquire a difficult technique. This is in no sense intended as blame or reproach. Doubt begins to enter only when musical theory behaves as if its questions and answers sufficed to attain to understanding the thing itself, its nature, its essence. The inevitable disillusionment of all those who have hoped to gain a deeper insight into music from current musical theory would alone be cause enough not to entrust our investigation to the questions propounded and the orientation adopted by this branch of learning.

Melodies consist of tones. Tones are events in the external world, natural phenomena, parts in the great whole of external nature, to investigate the general laws and connections of which is the task of natural science, especially of physics. Acoustics is the branch of physics that is concerned with tones as natural phenomena. Vibration and frequency, wave and wave forms, medium and manner of propagation, and the special and general natural laws that these phenomena obey—these are the things concerning which acoustics formulates questions. Concerning our Beethoven melody, the acoustician has all sorts of interesting things to say. He can enlighten us concerning that which, in such a melody, is nature or, to put it more accurately, nature as physics knows it, physical nature. But to expect enlightenment from him concerning that in our melody which is not physical nature but art would be tacitly to equate art with physical nature, music with physics.

Nor does the psychologist inquire into music as such. He is predominantly interested in what takes place in the person who hears music. The origin of tone sensations, the functioning of the infinitely complex physical apparatus of ear-nerve-brain, the nature and structure of simple and complex tone sensations, their relations to other sensations, the partly conscious, partly unconscious physiological and psychic reactions that the hearing of tones and music produces in us, our motor responses and, above all, our emotional responses—these and the like constitute the field in which the musical psychologist works. Some of these problems are of great interest; their investigation has yielded valuable insights into the functioning of the human organism and psyche. Yet we must not forget that the psychologist's field lies mainly inside the skin of the living being he is studying; the world of psychology, in the proper sense, is an *inner* world. If we take the questions formulated by psychology as our starting point in a search for insights into the essence of music, we tacitly postulate that the arena of music is the inner world. No musical psychologist believes otherwise. But it is clear that we must guard against making a decision so fraught with consequences *before* we begin our investigation.

(Here an objection may be raised: If music does not belong in the external world, which physics investigates, nor yet in the inner world, which is the subject matter of psychology, where does it belong? That is the very problem. It is obvious how little we are aided by disciplines that implicitly solve this problem merely through their formulation of a first question.)

There still remains the road of traditional aesthetics, of the philosophy of art. One would indeed suppose that the philosopher was just the man to inquire into a thing as such, without preconceptions, to seek out its essence. Actually, however, no other discipline formulates its problems with such a burden of tacit preconceptions as does the traditional philosophy of art. Philosophy has taken up its abode in three houses: Logic and Epistemology is inscribed on the first—here Truth is discussed; Ethics on the second—here the subject is the Good; Aesthetics on the third—here the subject is the Beautiful. In consequence of this tripartite division, which one is obliged to accept at the outset, together with the entire philosophy that stands behind it, music falls under the jurisdiction of the third house and is dealt with in accordance with the basic concepts that obtain there. Ideal of beauty, aesthetic value, judgment of taste, feeling of pleasure and pain—these establish the point of view from which the problem is approached. To inquire into music with the traditional aesthetician means, then, to assume that beauty, aesthetic value, taste, feeling, pleasure-pain, and so forth are the categories in the light of which music must be viewed if it is to be properly understood. This book as it progresses will show, however, that these concepts, rooted in philosophical systems and their requirements, are not indigenous to the tonal world; the musical experience nowhere suggests them. Under their guidance our questions will forever remain external to the musical phenomenon; our answers will not point to its inner core. Students of aesthetic literature will agree that, in general, thinking about art has produced genuine results to the extent that it has discarded the conceptual framework of traditional aesthetics and has met the artistic phenomenon immediately, with no prepared questions, but, instead, waiting for the phenomenon to suggest the kind of question which should be asked of it and to which it might in turn be willing ultimately to furnish an answer.

Let us now return to our Beethoven melody.

The last sentence sounded insignificant enough, yet something significant was said because the word *melody* was used. Why did we not say simply "succession of tones," or "series of tones," which would have been even more innocuous?

Not every series of tones is a melody. What we hear when a cat runs over the keyboard is a series of tones; presumably it is not a melody. Not because it does not come up to the mark in beauty, in pleasingness, in artistic value—there are ugly, unpleasing, worthless melodies, which are still melodies—but simply because it is nonsense. A melody is a series of tones that makes sense.

Someone talks in a language that we do not know. We hear articulation, vowels and consonants—and nothing more. If we understand the language, we do not hear vowels and consonants but words and sentences. Successions of articulated sounds are words if they have a meaning: *art, rat, tar* have meaning, they are words; *tra* is nonsense, mere sound. Successions of words are sentences if they express a meaning. It is the meaning that turns vowels and consonants into words, words into sentences. The same is true of tones and melodies. What we hear in melodies is not tones but tone words, tone sentences.

How can tones have meaning? Words have meaning because they relate to things; sentences, because they express something about things. Pictures have meaning if they represent something; symbols, if they betoken something, indicate something. Tones do not relate to things, do not express anything about things, represent nothing, betoken nothing, indicate nothing. What is it, then, that is meaningful in tones, that allows us to distinguish sense from nonsense in successions of tones?

Most people understand the language of tones without further ado; they are capable of hearing successions of tones as melodies, of distinguishing between sense and nonsense in tones. The lack of this ability, so-called tune deafness,[1] is a very rare anomaly. (Tune deafness has nothing to do with lack of musical sense; a person may hear melodies, hear the meaning in tones, and remain completely indifferent.) When a tune-deaf person listens to a melody, he hears tones succeeding one another; he does not hear melody. He hears music as we hear a lecture in a language we do not understand. The tones themselves, the sound, he perceives exactly as the normal person does; he lacks the organ for the *meaning* in the tones. To him our Beethoven melody is a succession of tones, what the cat produces on the keyboard is another succession of tones; the distinction between sense and nonsense, between music and nonmusic, escapes him completely. Were we in a position to demonstrate exactly what it is that the normal person hears in a melody and the tune-deaf person does not hear, we should presumably have isolated the

---

1. Cf. Géza Révész, *Introduction to the Psychology of Music,* ch. XVI; also his *Grundlegung der Tonpsychologie.* [See List of Works Cited.]

factor that makes tones meaningful and makes music out of successions of tones.

Let us assume that we hear our Beethoven melody in a distorted form, perhaps thus:

The tune-deaf person will likewise hear that something has been changed; if he has good tonal memory—which is not at all incompatible with his anomaly—he will perhaps even be able to point out the places where the changes were made. Yet he will not find that the change has much significance. For him the result in both cases is about the same: a series of tones without meaning. To a person who does not understand Italian, it does not matter in the least whether he hears *in questa tomba oscura* or *in tesqua bomta ucsora*. To the Italian it matters a great deal. The first version says something; the second is nonsense. The alterations in our melody are not radical enough to change sense into sheer nonsense; but one certainly need not be a professional to distinguish between the right and the wrong version, in other words, to be aware that one version makes better sense than the other. The change in the tones, then, is heard equally by the normal person and the tune-deaf person; but, in addition, the normal person hears something quite different, something that escapes the tune-deaf person: the change of meaning that goes hand in hand with the change in the tones. Once again we can turn to language for a comparison and for clarification: bull and Bill, for example, differ in their vowels, but also, let us say, in the number of legs each possesses—the bull has four, Bill only two. The first difference, the difference in sound, is perceptible to anyone; the second difference, the difference in meaning, is perceptible only to someone who understands English. What is it, then, that changes in a melody when the tones are changed, in the same way as the meaning of a word changes when a sound in it is changed?

That our melody does not proceed to its end in a single non-periodic sweep, like a long sentence without punctuation, anyone, even the tune-deaf person, will observe without further ado. On the contrary, it is clearly divided into subsections, after every fourth measure, by caesuras—we shall call these subsections *phrases*. (The caesura between the third and fourth phrases is concealed by the anticipation of a tone that is actually not due until the beginning of the next measure.) Of these four phrases, the first and second are very similar, the third is different, and the fourth is the repetition of the second. What would happen if this fourth and last phrase, instead of repeating the second, repeated the first, which sounds almost the same, and the melody ended thus:

Again, even the tune-deaf person would hear the change, but that would be all; he would have no fault to find with it; it would be a matter of indifference to him which phrase ended the melody. The normal person, on the other hand, would react to the change with a determined "No!" Asked why he rejected it, he would explain, more or less: "It's not finished; there's something still to come; you can't end like that." The tune-deaf person will have no notion of what the other is talking about. In order to determine where the hearing of the tune-deaf person differs from that of the normal person, what one hears and the other does not, we must, then, accurately describe what it is that prompts us to accept the one version of the end of the melody and reject the other.

We say, then, that the first phrase of our melody cannot be used as an ending, but the second can. The two phrases are exactly alike until their last measure; it is  in the first phrase,  in the second. If we change the last tone of the first phrase, thus,  , it can at once be used as an ending. It is, then, the last tone alone that in this case decides between usability and unusability as an ending. We accept ; we reject . Why?

Suppose that we hear the tone , just the single tone, and ask ourselves whether it is a usable concluding tone. The question would have little meaning. Listen to the tone as intensely as we will, we shall discover nothing in it that could either especially qualify it or disqualify it as a concluding tone. The situation is, however, basically changed if we hear the same tone at the end of the first phrase of our melody and then ask ourselves the same question. The tone we hear is the same; everything that we heard before, we hear now. But we hear something more, something new, of which there was not even a trace in the single tone. A new quality has accrued to it—we must call it a dynamic quality. The single tone was simply a tone; the same tone at the end of the phrase in our melody is a *tone that has become active,* a tone in a definite state of activity. We *hear* this state, we hear it clearly and directly, in the tone itself. What we hear in this way we can best designate as a state of disturbed equilibrium, as a tension, a tendency, almost a will. The tone seems to point beyond itself toward release from tension and restoration of equilibrium; it seems to look in a definite direction for the event that will bring about this change; it even seems to demand the event. It is clear that such a tone cannot be used as the concluding tone of a melody.

Let us go through the same process with the other tone, , and ask the same questions. Again we shall not fail to observe that the tone, heard alone, exhibits not the slightest characteristic that could determine its usability or unusability as a concluding note. In this respect the two tones, e and d, are wholly alike. But if now we hear at the end of our melody, and compare this tone with at the end of the first phrase, another difference, entirely apart from the difference between the two tones as such, from their difference in pitch, is at once strikingly perceptible: a difference in dynamic quality. Once again we now hear not simply as a tone but as a tone that has become active—active in an entirely different way from that in which we found to be active. Instead of the disturbed equilibrium, the tension and dissatisfaction which we registered there, we here receive the impression of perfect equilibrium, of relaxation of tension and satisfaction, we might almost say of self-affirmation. If the other tone pointed beyond itself in a definite direction, if it demanded an event that would restore the state of equilibrium, relax the tension, it now becomes clear that it was precisely the tone to which it pointed, which it demanded. What takes place here between the two tones is a sort of play of forces, comparable to that between magnetic needle and magnetic pole. The activity of the one is a placing itself in a direction, a pointing toward and striving after a goal; the activity of the other is a dictating of direction, a drawing to itself. The one wants to pass beyond itself, the other wants itself; hence the one cannot be used as the concluding tone of our melody, whereas the other makes a good conclusion.

We now know what distinguishes the hearing of the tune-deaf person from that of the normal person. The tune-deaf person is deaf precisely to the dynamic quality of a tone, to the quality that accrues to a tone in the context of a melody, as part of a musical whole. The result would have been the same, no matter what tone of this or any other melody we had chosen; as we shall see later, there is no tone in music without a specific dynamic quality. If the tune-deaf person is incapable of distinguishing between sense and nonsense in tones, it is because he hears only differences in pitch, not dynamic differences. It is, then, the dynamic quality that permits tones to become the conveyors of meaning; that makes melodies out of successions of tones and music out of acoustical phenomena. The dynamic quality is the properly musical quality of tones.

A tone is a phenomenon of the external world. A physical process, the vibration of air, produces it. We encounter it outside ourselves; our attention, when we listen to it, is directed outward. To be sure, the act of hearing, together with the physiological mechanism that comes into play with it—the mechanism of ear, nerve, central nervous system—belongs to us; what we experience in the act, however, the thing heard, is not in us. The difference between heard and merely imagined tone is unequivocal to the mentally normal person. Science has described in detail what we hear when we hear a tone; has distinguished various properties of tone, such as pitch, intensity, color, volume; and has above all demonstrated the closest correspondence between tone perception and the physical state that corresponds to it. Everything we hear in the tone is, so to speak, prefigured in the physical process, in the length, breadth, shape of the sound wave. If something changes in the tone heard, something must have changed in the physical process. The two stand to each other in the strict relationship of cause and effect.

What we have thus described is tone as everyone hears it, the normal person as well as the tune-deaf person, as every apparatus registers it: the single tone removed from any musical context, tone as an acoustical phenomenon. It is not tone as a musical phenomenon. Precisely the quality that characterizes the tone as an element in a musical context, that makes it a musical phenomenon, its dynamic quality, was absent from our description. And there was reason for its absence. Among the qualities that belong to the tone as an acoustical phenomenon there is none that is not determined by a particular element of the physical process and only changes, and always changes, if something changes in the physical process. This does not hold for the dynamic quality of tones. Nothing in the physical event corresponds to the tone as a musical event.

Tones can be made visible. The oscilloscope, through electrical processes, transforms vibrations of the air into a picture that appears on an illuminated screen. It is the picture of a wave line. The different tones appear as wave lines of different dimensions and shapes. Everything that characterizes the tone as an acoustical phenomenon is represented in a particular feature of the picture. An experienced observer can accurately read the acoustical qualities of the tone from the outline of the curve. Looking at the picture of the curve, he could accurately represent the tone to himself—pitch, loudness, color, everything. The one thing he could not in any way deduce from the picture is the dynamic state of the tone. Suppose that our Beethoven melody were made visible in this manner, first with the wrong ending, on , and then with the right one, on . The picture would faithfully convey the difference between the two tones and all the characteristics that belong to them as acoustical phenomena; concerning the difference in their state of equilibrium it would show as little as the hands of a clock do concerning the significance of the hours they indicate. There would be no way to draw a conclusion from the picture about the usability or unusability of these tones as concluding tone; the dynamic, the musical difference, does not appear in the curve. If we play the melody on the piano, first in D major, then in C major, the tone D will sound perfectly balanced in the first case, and sharply unbalanced in the second (just like the tone E before). Yet the curve that represents the tone D will be exactly the same in both cases, although the difference between the two D's that we actually hear is hardly less than the difference between standing and falling. While even the slightest difference in the acoustical event instantly appears in a corresponding change in the curve, even the most basic difference in the dynamic state leaves the picture wholly untouched. The dynamic event leaves no trace in the physical process. When we hear a melody, we hear things that have no counterpart in physical nature.

Let us pause for a moment to reflect on what we have said. Since modern science has rid us of any kind of belief in spirits, we no longer doubt that the external world that we perceive is, without any exception, a material world. What we find in it, what our senses permit us to see, hear, feel, are material things and material processes, or at least their direct effects—a color, if you insist, is not a thing and not a process, but it is a property of a thing, and its basis is a physical process. What our senses show us is a part of the outside world and, as such, belongs in the closed context of physical nature. The nonphysical—thoughts, for example, or feelings, convictions, decisions—exists only in a consciousness, in an inner world, my own or that of some other living creature; it can never be the object of direct sensory perception. Now, however, we say that we hear—that is, perceive in the external world through the sense of hearing—something in in the tones of a melody to which nothing in the context of the physical world corresponds. Are not these precisely the words in which one would conventionally characterize an auditory hallucination, a delusion? If one wished, one could call the dynamic quality of tones a hallucination for the very reason that no material process can be co-ordinated with it; but all that this would accomplish would be to leave us faced with the additional difficulty of comprehending the nature and effect of music as the result of vast mass hallucinations, of a mass delusion. No one as yet has seriously proposed this solution. It appears, then, that the very first result of our investigation brings us into sharp conflict with a basic principle of the modern view of the universe: the observation that we hear something in the tones of music which does not fit into the general context of the physical world is irreconcilably opposed to the assertions that our senses are organs for perceiving the physical world and that the world perceived through the senses is physical throughout.

Two theories have been devised to clear this stumbling block from the road: one claims to have discovered the link that after all connects the dynamic qualities of tones to physical processes; the other undertakes to show that in these qualities we are not dealing with processes in the outside world at all. Since this question is of basic importance for the development of our investigation, we must discuss the two theories in greater detail. We shall begin with that which undertakes to demonstrate a physical basis for the dynamic qualities of tones: the Pulse Theory, originally proposed as the theory of tone-rhythms by the psychologist Theodor Lipps.

II. The Pulse Theory

FROM WHATEVER PRECONCEPTIONS men have set out to reflect upon music, it was inevitable that they should soon encounter the problem of tone relations. The knowledge that numerical ratios are concealed in tonal relations has long formed a part of man's intellectual patrimony. Pythagoras is credited with discovering that the lengths of the vibrating strings that produce the individual tones of our musical system conform to the simplest arithmetical rules: one string always measures exactly one-half, two-thirds, three-fourths, four-fifths, five-sixths of another; the series 1:2:3:4:5:6 appears to govern all tone relations. There is only a minor difference between ancient and modern science in this matter: in modern acoustics we do not measure string lengths; we count frequencies, the number of vibrations per second. Frequencies and string lengths are inversely proportional: if the string lengths of two tones have the ratio 2:3, their frequencies have the ratio 3:2.

Granted that nothing in the physical phenomenon of a tone corresponds to its musical quality, could not the relations between tones, and particularly the precise mathematical order of these relations, still cause the dynamic tone qualities, in the same sense in which vibration differences cause pitch differences? This the Pulse Theory sets out to prove. Air begins to vibrate;

the waves strike our ear: we hear a tone. In the case of the very lowest tones, where the vibrations are still comparatively slow, e.g., sixteen per second, we almost believe that we feel the impact of the individual waves. Within the normal range of tones, where the vibrations are in hundreds and thousands per second, there can of course no longer be any question of sensing the individual impingements. Yet they are there, they strike our ear, one after the other, in swift and regular succession, and something in us receives them and responds to them.

We listen to the ticking of a pendulum clock: the sound stimuli, which strike our ear in a long-continued, regular succession, and in which, as we listen, we gradually lose ourselves, are exactly alike, just as the intervals between them are exactly alike. Yet if we were asked to count with the ticking of the clock, presumably we should not count 1-2-3-4-5- and so on, which would seem the natural thing to do, nor yet 1-1-1-1-; instead, the individual stimuli would automatically group themselves in pairs: 1-2, 1-2, tick-tock, tick-tock—not tick-tick-tick-tick. It is as if a certain rhythm, a duple rhythm, took possession of the process and forced itself upon us; we oscillate with it, unintentionally give it expression in our counting. If the ticking becomes faster, and finally very fast, the counting will presumably no longer keep pace with the individual ticks; but the 1-2 count, the oscillation in a duple rhythm, will not stop for that reason: all that happens is that the counting unit is no longer one tick but, with increasing rapidity, will comprise a larger number of ticks—normally jumping from 1 to 2, then to 4, 8, 16 beats per counting unit. The phenomenon is not observable only in connection with the ticking of a clock; it presents itself whenever we are subjected to a long-continued, regular succession of equal stimuli, be they sound, light, or touch stimuli. We shall have occasion to discuss this curious phenomenon in detail in a later context.

We shall now assume that, when we hear a tone, we react in a similar manner to the regularly succeeding stimuli, the impacts of the individual air waves upon the eardrum—although of course in this case there can be no question of a conscious perception of the individual stimuli. We assume that, somewhere inside us, the air vibrations set in motion a 1-2 rhythm, a pulse, with which we unconsciously oscillate.

If upon such a tone there now follows another, which vibrates exactly twice as fast as the first, the pulse set up in us by the first will take the pulse of the new tone into itself without friction. We shall hardly believe that we hear another tone; it still sounds like the same tone, only at a different pitch. (This is the peculiar phenomenon of the octave.) But if the frequencies of the two tones do not have the ratio of 1:2 but, let us say, that of 2:3 or 4:5, the pulse of the second tone will be far from fitting into the first with such absence of friction. What we hear now is another tone, and, more than that, a tone whose pulse, in relation to the first, appears to be a sort of disturbance—disturbance of an established order, disturbance of an equilibrium. "In every disturbance of equilibrium, lies the tendency to return to the position of equilibrium." From this follows the principal law of the Pulse Theory: When the frequencies of two tones are in such a ratio that on one side we have 2 or a power of 2 (i.e., 4, 8, 16) and on the other side 3 or 5, or 3 × 3 or 3 × 5, "there exists a natural tendency on the part of the 3's, 5's, etc., to move toward the powers of 2 . . . to come to rest there. The former 'seek' the latter as their natural base, as their natural center of gravity."[1]

We have observed the different dynamic qualities of the tones d and e in the Beethoven melody. The frequencies of these tones have the ratio 8:9. According to the law of the Pulse Theory, there must be a tendency from the note e to the note d, with d

1. Lipps, *Psychological Studies.*

representing the state of equilibruim, e the disturbance of equilibrium. e must "seek its natural base" in d. This is what actually happens. Thus theory and observation appear to be in the best possible agreement. Modern science seems to corroborate Leibniz' idea that unconscious mathematical operations of the soul are the basis of our enjoyment of music.[2]

We might now proceed to look more carefully into certain presuppositions of this theory—such, for example, as the assumption of an unconscious or subconscious counting; we might investigate what the state of the case is with respect to the application of the theory to other simple musical situations and to more complex ones. We shall do nothing of the sort. We shall suppose that all the assumptions of the theory prove to be well founded and that the theory everywhere yields the same favorable result as it did in the one situation that we cited as an example. We put another question: Is the theory really able to explain what it professes to explain? Do observation and explanation really agree so well in our example as appeared at first sight? Can disturbances in the relationship of pulsations, and the removal of disturbance, really be causes of the states of activity that we hear in tones?

Let us call to mind other cases of conflicting rhythms, the disturbance of one pulse by another. Men are marching in a parade. A band plays; all keep the same step. The march time will be conveyed to the spectator, who will sway in the characteristic 1-2 rhythm of the march. Now the beat of the music changes. Let us assume that the paraders have been carefully prepared, that the change of beat is anticipated by all the participants, so that the change of step takes place instantaneously. Will the spectator, beyond experiencing the new rhythm as new, bring it into any direct relation with the previous rhythm? And

2. Leibniz' definition of music is from *Leibnitii epistolae*, ep. 154.

even if, in the first instants after the change, he has the sensation of a disturbance, will he therefore sense in the new rhythm anything like a *pointing,* a *striving,* toward the previous rhythm? But perhaps this is too simple an example. So let us assume that one of the paraders has fallen asleep as he marched. He has not heard the change of beat and marches on in the old step. The spectator, to be sure, will see this step not simply as a different one, but as one to be suppressed, because it is contrary to an order, disturbs an equilibrium. But he will certainly not see, in the disturbing step itself, a pointing toward the step of the others or even a tendency to fall in with it. The case will be the same in all instances where a process that communicates its rhythm to us is replaced by or combined with another that brings a different rhythm with it. The disturbance will be there, the discrepancy, the contradiction, but not the pointing, the drawing and striving, the directional demand of the one for the other, which we hear so clearly in the tones of a melody. Still, if a rhythm that is in conflict with a previously established rhythm is experienced not merely as different or disturbing, but quite definitely as a thing to be eliminated, the reaction has the quality of a directed drive, of a will bent upon removal of the intrusive factor. If this is accomplished, and order is restored, something more than a mere zero point has been reached; something positively satisfying has happened. Are not these the same sort of phenomena as those we hear in tones? Are not the No and the Yes with which we accompany the disturbance and restoration of the orderly march related to the No and the Yes with which we reject and accept the notes e and d in our melody? The similarity is undeniable—but so is the difference. In the case of the marchers, the Yes and the No come from *us;* in the case of the melody they come from *the tones.* The wrong step disturbs *me, I* want it eliminated; it would be nonsense to claim that the step

I see wants to eliminate itself. The note e, on the contrary, says No *to itself;* and if I cannot be satisfied with it, if I want to eliminate it, the reason is because *it* wants to eliminate itself: e wants to go to d; that is, I hear in the note e the wish not to continue sounding, and to let the note d sound in its stead. The dynamic qualities that the Pulse Theory explains are not qualities of the tones; they are qualities of the hearer's response. If the theory were adequate, musical experience would, in the last analysis, be an experience of bodily states, of sympathetic vibrations ordered according to the mathematical relations among the vibration rhythms, of disturbances created and disturbances removed, and of the accompanying feelings of dissatisfaction and satisfaction. Who recognizes music in this?

Strangely enough, a few people would—namely, the deaf. That deaf people are capable of enjoying music seems, at first thought, a nonsensical assertion. Yet the fact has been established beyond any doubt. The musical enjoyment of the deaf person can have only one source: an unusually highly developed sensitivity to vibration, which permits him to feel air vibrations as such. We know, from the results of other investigations, that it is possible to translate tone sensations into sensations of vibrations. If we lightly touch vibrating tuning forks, we not only feel difference in tone as difference in vibration; we also feel, from the relation between the vibrations, whether two tones are more or less in harmony with each other—exactly as the frequency ratios would indicate. It is, then, upon sensations of this nature, sensations of conflict and agreement, of roughness and smoothness, friction and conformity, and the accompanying feelings of tension and relaxation—it is upon such sensations and feelings that the musical enjoyment of the deaf person must be based. But he who "hears" these various states in this manner perceives and enjoys them as pertaining to his own person, not as something occurring in the external world. The psychologist Géza Révész, to whom we are also indebted for the keen analysis of tune deafness cited on page 16, has studied the phenomenon in detail. He reports what he himself feels when he "hears" music with his ears completely closed: "One becomes conscious of a remarkable transposition. Whereas musical tone is always localized in outer space, the localization of sensations of vibration takes place in our own body: the tones are, so to speak, drawn into the interior of the body." [3] Here, then, we in fact have a music that is made up of nothing but vibrations, relations between vibrations, and the corresponding sensations of a "listener." This is the music to which the Pulse Theory legitimately applies: music as the deaf hear it, music without tones.

It was the aim of the Pulse Theory to resolve the sharp contradiction between the simple facts of melodic hearing and the commonly accepted principle that the external world and the material world, sense perception and perception of material processes, are one and the same. Starting from the valid position that the basis of the dynamic qualities of tone is not to be sought in the individual tone but in the relations of the individual tone to other tones, it got no further than explaining how certain highly refined bodily sensations correspond to mathematically ordered air vibrations. The basic facts of music, tones acting and being acted upon, remain unaccounted for; the dynamic qualities of tone *as events of the external world* are as much of a problem as before. Indeed the problem has become more accentuated, since the attempt to find a physical counterpart to the dynamic tone qualities proves equally futile both when tones are considered in relation and when they are considered individually.

3. Géza Révész, "Gibt es einen Hörraum?"

III. The System of Tones

TWO TONES of a melody are the narrow basis upon which our study has so far been built. Before we proceed, and turn our attention to the other theory we proposed to discuss, we shall broaden our basis a little.

The melody of our first example was in the key of D major. If for some reason we should choose to play or sing the same melody in another key—say, in F major—the dynamic qualities we observed in the tones e and d will reappear; but they will have shifted to other tones, in this case to g and f. On the other hand, if we play any other melody in the key of D major (or D minor), the tones e and d will show the same dynamic qualities as in the Beethoven melody. From this we conclude that the dynamic quality of a tone is a function of the key.

What is a key? The tonal basis of Western music is a system of seven tones arranged in a particular way. (A different number of tones, a different arrangement, characterize the music of other civilizations.) Arranged according to pitch, these seven tones produce the scale, the *diatonic* scale of our music. The eighth tone, which concludes the scale, is always a replica of the first, its octave, frequency relation 1:2. That is, if we begin, for example, with a d, the eighth tone is again a d. Here the scale begins anew;

it repeats itself in both directions, upward and downward, to the limits of pitch sensation.

The distinguishing characteristic of the system is the way in which the tones are arranged. They are not placed at equal intervals; on the contrary, there is an alternation of larger intervals, *whole* tones, with smaller intervals, *half* tones, so that after every two or three whole tones there is a half tone—as the following schema shows:

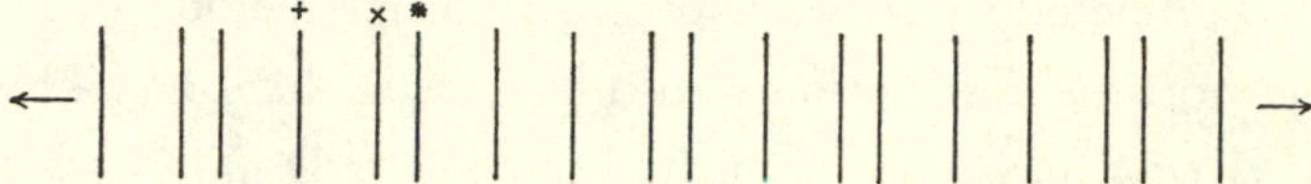

Of every seven successive intervals in this arrangement, five are always whole tones, two always half tones. The sum of five whole tones and two half tones gives an octave. According to which point we choose as starting point, as tone 1 of the scale, different series are produced: these are the ecclesiastical modes of medieval and early modern music. For example, the series beginning at +, | || | | || |, is the Dorian mode; at ×, the Phrygian begins, schema || | | || | |; at *, the Lydian, | | | || | ||; and so on. Of the ecclesiastical modes only two survived the musical revolution of the seventh century to become the *major* and *minor* modes of our music. The schema for major is the following: | | || | | ||; for minor it is | || | || | |. *Key,* as distinguished from mode, usually refers to major and minor only; the different keys of our music result from taking different *tones* as starting points of the major or minor schema (C major, C minor, D major, etc.)

Musical scholars, physicists, and philosophers have exerted themselves to find a rational basis for the fact that the arrangement of the tones in our music is precisely this and none other. Their speculations have not been particularly fruitful. In this study we shall follow a different line of questioning. We do not ask, *Why* is the tonal system of our music this and none other? We ask, What does the fact that its tones are arranged thus and not otherwise *do* for music; what does our music *possess* in its tonal system?

The following considerations will be confined to the seven-tone system in the major and minor modes. What do we hear in these tones?

We have described what is heard in the tones d and e of the Beethoven melody; had we chosen any other melody in D major or D minor, the description would have been the same. The tones d and e are tones 1 and 2 of the D major or D minor scale. Had the melody been in C major or C minor, the same description would have fitted the tones c and d, which are tones 1 and 2 of the C major or C minor scale. What we described, then, was the dynamic qualities of tone 1 and tone 2 of the scale. The directionality, the pointing beyond itself, the gravitating of the one tone toward the other, was precisely the gravitating of a tone 2 of the seven-tone system to a tone 1 of that system; the attraction, the giving of direction, the pointing toward itself, of the other tone was precisely the action of a tone 1 of that system. What we hear, then, at the two places in our melody is not simply two tones of definite pitch, d and e, but these two tones in particular places of a seven-tone system: $d = \hat{1}$, $e = \hat{2}$. (We shall employ these symbols henceforth.) The musical difference between the two tones is, strictly speaking, not a difference of pitch but of position in the tonal system.

The same is true of all other tones in the system. Each of them, exactly like the tone $\hat{2}$, points beyond itself, to $\hat{1}$; indeed, this pointing toward the same directional point, toward a common center, is precisely what makes them elements in one system. But each of them, again, points to the common center from a different locus, and so each does it in its particular, one might almost say personal, way, with a gesture that is its own, a tonal gesture. It is this different way of pointing to $\hat{1}$, this different gesture, which gives each tone its particular and distinctive dynamic quality, which sounds in it and which we hear in it, when we hear it as a tone in a melody. This and nothing else is the content, the meaning, of its utterance, its musical meaning. Thus, though we speak of the tone c or g or b, we actually hear c = $\hat{1}$ or c = $\hat{6}$, g = $\hat{7}$, b = $\hat{3}$, and so on. Every tone of a melody, as it sounds, directly announces at what place in the system we find ourselves with it. Hearing music does not mean hearing tones, but hearing, in the tones and through them, the places where they sound in the seven-tone system.[1]

It will be expected that we shall now undertake to do for the remaining tones of the system what we did for $\hat{1}$ and $\hat{2}$; that we shall describe their dynamic qualities. That, however, would not take us very far. Speaking first of the major mode, we could say that the tone $\hat{7}$ gravitates toward $\hat{8}$ just as $\hat{2}$ does toward $\hat{1}$, but even more urgently. We could further single out two tones and distinguish them from the rest: $\hat{3}$ and $\hat{5}$. The tendency toward $\hat{1}$ is clear in them both; yet the striving seems less outspoken here. Unlike $\hat{2}$ or $\hat{7}$, these tones are not, as it were, torn from their places; they are more firmly rooted in themselves. Their condition might perhaps be described as outer equilibrium together with noticeable inner tension. Owing to their greater stability, $\hat{3}$ and $\hat{5}$ serve their more unstable adjacent tones, especially the higher, as the nearest points of support. Thus $\hat{4}$ gravitates to $\hat{3}$, $\hat{6}$ to $\hat{5}$, in the same way as $\hat{2}$ to $\hat{1}$; $\hat{4}$ points toward $\hat{1}$ across $\hat{3}$, $\hat{6}$ across $\hat{5}$. Speaking of the minor mode, we could remark that the

1. Experiments with animals reveal the extent to which musical tone is not mere tone, an acoustical phenomenon. Conditioned reflexes, which are otherwise infallibly produced when a certain tone sounds, are not produced when the tone appears in the context of a melody. See James L. Mursell, *The Psychology of Music,* p. 81.

contrast of the two modes, major and minor, the "hard" and the "soft" (in the sense in which light can be hard or soft), appears concentrated in the two versions of the tone $\hat{3}$; that $\hat{7}$ in minor, so to speak, turns its back to $\hat{8}$ whereas major $\hat{7}$ looks toward $\hat{8}$; that minor $\hat{6}$ leans more heavily toward $\hat{5}$ than major $\hat{6}$. But with this, the extent to which these phenomena can be described in words is reached and perhaps overpassed. True enough, expressions like stable and unstable equilibrium, tension, attraction, gravitation, and the like, can give a *general* conception of the phenomena with which we are dealing. But what it is, for example, that differentiates the unstable equilibrium $\hat{3}$ from the unstable equilibrium $\hat{5}$, the attraction $\hat{2}$-$\hat{1}$ from the attraction $\hat{7}$-$\hat{8}$, the gravitation $\hat{4} \rightarrow \hat{3}$ from the gravitation $\hat{6} \rightarrow \hat{5}$; in short, what the particular dynamic quality is that characterizes the individual tone and represents the basic material in which and through which music expresses itself—all this eludes description. To those unfamiliar with the phenomena, words can convey little; and anyone familiar with the phenomena does not need to have them described in words. This is so, not because the phenomena are so complicated, but, quite on the contrary, because they are so extremely simple and elementary, purely auditory experiences, only to be known through hearing. Any schoolboy who has learned to sing by solmization knows them as familiarly and effortlessly as he does the letters of the alphabet. There is immediate recognition of one tone in a melody as $\hat{3}$, another as $\hat{7}$—an eloquent indication of the fact that, besides itself, a tone also expresses its personal relation to the tone $\hat{1}$, its place in the tonal system as a whole.

A system in which the whole is present and operative in each individual locus, in which each individual locus knows, so to speak, its position in the whole, its relation to a center, must be called a dynamic system. The dynamic qualities of tone can only be understood as manifestations of an orderly action of forces within a given system. The tones of our tonal system are events in a dynamic field, and each tone, as it sounds, gives expression to the exact constellation of force present at the point in the field at which the tone is situated. Musical tones are conveyors of forces. Hearing music means hearing an action of forces.

In the seven dynamic tone qualities we have the material out of which melodies are built. When we speak of the "material" of an art, the word usually suggests a kind of building stone, dead matter, disconnected individual parts, out of which the artist builds up the living whole of his work. This interpretation cannot be applied to music. A tone does not need to enter into the context of a melody in order to acquire relation to a whole. Simply as an element of a key (and it is only with tones as elements of keys that music has to do, even atonal music, greatly as the concept of key has been altered in it), the individual tone carries within itself relation to a larger whole. Such a thing as "mere matter" does not exist in music; its very material is permeated with relation to wholeness. This explains why we can hear the very first tone of a composition as dynamically active, as a musical tone, although dynamic quality is manifested as a relation *between* tones. We hear in it the *promise of a whole* that it bears within itself. Musicians will call to mind what unique effects the masters have been able to achieve on occasion by *not* fulfilling this promise.

Everybody knows that a piano keyboard has white and black keys, and that between a tone and its octave there are not seven but twelve tones. How does this agree with the statement that our music is a seven-tone system? Even at an early period in the development of Western music, it proved desirable and logical, for various technical reasons, to raise or lower the pitch of a tone of the seven-tone system on occasion by about (not exactly) a half tone—c, for example, would become c sharp, b would become b flat, and so on. When each tone is given its higher and lower variant in this fashion, the schema of the seven-tone system assumes the following appearance:

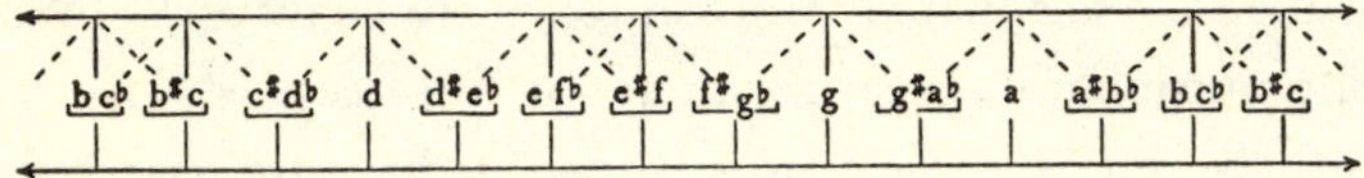

The grouped tones are very close together in pitch; a tone lying between them could hardly be distinguished from either by the ear. The builders of our pianos, organs, and wind instruments have made good use of this situation, by making available at each of these points only one tone, which, consequently, has to play two roles; thus, for example, on the piano the black key between c and d has to serve both as c sharp and d flat. To the violinist, who makes his own tones and thus is very well able to distinguish between c sharp and d flat, this somewhat crude simplification is, so to speak, a thorn in the ear. On the other side, however, we must set the fact that a Johann Sebastian Bach championed this acoustical compromise, that the excessively refined musical ear of a Chopin was satisfied with an instrument so acoustically unrefined as the piano for the formulation of his ideas—a clear indication that acoustical perfection is not a prerequisite of musical perfection.

The result of this simplification, as is apparent from the figure, is the division of tonal space (as the totality of all possible pitches is called) into equal intervals, half tones, twelve in every octave: the chromatic scale. It is very significant that the rationally sound system, equal distribution of tones throughout tonal space, represents, musically considered, the dissolution of all order: between the tones of the chromatic scale there are no relations of pointing and being pointed to, of gravitating and attracting—no dynamic relations; every tone is as good as every other. Rapidly played chromatic scales remind us of the screeching of a siren—the result is tonal chaos. (The chromatic scale owed its popularity among the older school of cinema composers to its ability to serve as an unfailing means of representing a chaotic wallow of emotions.)

Of the many gains that the enlarging of the tonal material brought to music we shall mention only one. So long as there are only seven tones, it is impossible for the tonal system to change place, as it were; on a piano without black keys we can never play in anything but one key, in C major (or A minor). We see from the following sketch that in the strict seven-tone system the schema for major can only be applied at one place; if we try to do it at another, there will always be tones lacking.

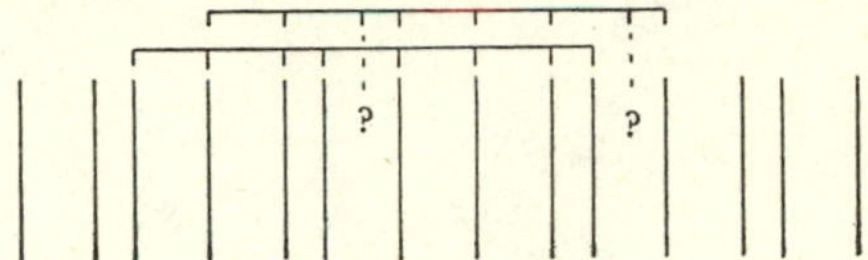

(The same, of course, holds true for minor.) On the other hand, if tonal space is equally divided into half tones, the schema can be applied at any point. Any tone can at any time become $\hat{1}$ of a

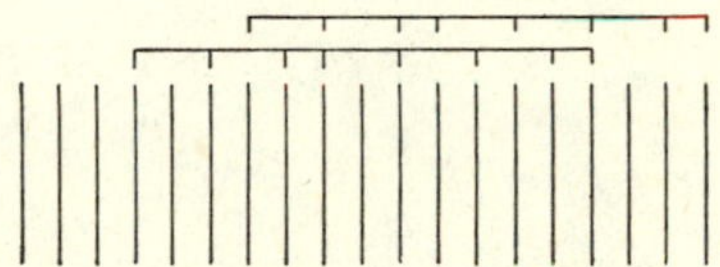

seven-tone arrangement; it becomes possible to change key in the course of a composition. We can imagine what an enrichment this brought to the tonal language. The change of key itself became a principal theme of later music. The dynamic qualities no longer remain attached to the same tones throughout a composition; each tone can change dynamic quality, and vice versa. Furthermore, at each change there can be a moment during which the key itself, and with it the musical quality of the tones, is in suspense. The state of suspense can be prolonged, it can, even when it seems to be resolving itself, be drawn into a new change, a new state of suspense, until we finally reach a state of perpetual change, of perpetual suspense. In crudest summary, this sketches the course followed by the evolution of music from the seventeenth to the twentieth century.

IV. Associationism

Obviously, with the enlargement of its means of expression, music became more and more complex and presented increasing difficulties to the listener. Yet the fact has little to do with the language of tone as such. One may have a thorough understanding of the French language, and still not understand a poem by Mallarmé. What creates difficulties for the uninitiated in the late Beethoven, in Bruckner, in Stravinsky, is not the language but the person, the personal nature of the thoughts formulated in the language. New means of expression are always quickly seized upon by popular music without detracting from its intelligibility. In and for itself, then, each tone of the enlarged system, in accordance with its particular dynamic quality, is as directly understood as the tones of the seven-tone system. To be sure, it will no longer be easy to *name* the place of any given tone in the system correctly; but for *hearing* there is no real difficulty even here. Every change in the dynamic quality of a tone is unmistakably comprehended by the ear as what it is; every substitution of one of its higher or lower variants for one of the seven tones is faithfully interpreted with perfect clarity. The same organ that reacts to acoustical stimuli so crudely that one and the same tone can be presented to it now as C sharp, now as D flat (although strictly speaking it is neither), will not have an instant of doubt as to whether C sharp or D flat is *meant*—unless the composer has left the meaning of the tone indeterminate, either purposely or from inability to express himself clearly. And not only the "musical" person hears these things, but everyone for whom music is not simply audible nonsense. That the person who is not a musician is not aware of them intellectually has little to do with the case. If his attention is drawn to them, he will notice what happens. There would simply be no music if the human ear were not an organ capable of perceiving dynamic tone qualities in their most delicate distinctions. And now let us realize once again that this manifold play of forces takes place without any corresponding occurrences in the physical world—as if we were exposed to an infinite variety of most finely graduated contacts without ever being able to discover what it is that touches us. Yet there is no vagueness, arbitrariness, delusiveness about these phenomena; they are as precise, clear, reliable, and trustworthy as any phenomenon of the tangible and visible world.

The startling discrepancy between such observations and our beliefs regarding the nature of the external world and the function of our sense organs resolves itself if we accept the explanation of *associationism.* In briefest summary, its solution is as follows: nothing in the physical world corresponds to the play of forces in tones, for the reason that these forces are not active in the tones at all, but *in us,* in us who hear. They have their origin in us—in the feelings that hearing tones arouses in us and that we then project out of ourselves into the tones.

Let us take a simple musical phenomenon, such as the previously described dynamic difference between the tones $\hat{2}$ and $\hat{1}$, and attempt to interpret it in accordance with this theory. Are we not guilty, the associationist will ask, of a sort of primitive tonal animism if we ascribe a striving, an attraction, a will, to *the tones?* What really takes place, he will tell us, is something quite different and far less mysterious. It is simply that we have so often heard the sequence $\hat{2}$-$\hat{1}$ as the conclusion of a phrase or a melody that, in our consciousness, the idea "preceding $\hat{1}$" is most closely associated with the perception of $\hat{2}$, as the concept "following $\hat{2}$ and concluding" is with the perception of $\hat{1}$. Hence it is only natural that when we hear the tone $\hat{2}$ under these circumstances, we understand it as announcing a coming $\hat{1}$ and connect (associate) the expectation of this latter tone with it; what we have called the tension, the trend, the unstable equilibrium of the tone $\hat{2}$ is nothing but *our* tension, *our* trend toward the expected event, *our* disturbed equilibrium. The like is true for the tone $\hat{1}$, which, in the same way, we have learned to connect with fulfilled expectation, relaxation of tension, restored equilibrium. One has only to play our Beethoven melody to a Chinese who has never heard Western music; he will not detect the slightest trace of the dynamic qualities of the two tones. He is without the *experience* that alone has taught us to relate the two tones to each other in the manner described. If, however, the Chinese has lived for some time in the Western world and been exposed long enough to musical experiences, his hearing will no longer differ from ours. If the dynamic qualities really lay *in* the tones, anyone should be able to discover them there, even without previous experience.

The same point of view can be applied to all the tones of the tonal system. It is simply, we are told, because we have heard these tones so often in typical connections and sequences that we continually accompany them with the corresponding sensations of tension and relaxation, expectation and fulfillment. In this manner the entire tonal system is understood by most psychologists as a projection of variously oriented and graduated expectations and fulfillments. The musical tone thus falls into two components, one coming from without, the acoustical phenomenon, the other coming from within, the state that the hearer, as conditioned by his experience, connects with the tone—whether one thinks in the more old-fashioned terms of states of mind and feelings or, more modernly and scientifically, in terms of internal bodily sensations of pressure and tension. The quality of tone that we have designated as properly musical is, in any case, made out to be something added by the hearer to the physical phenomenon: *it is the hearer who makes the music.* "The unity, then, which marks the difference between a mere succession of discrete tonal stimuli and a melody, arises not from the tones themselves: it is distributed by act of the listener." [1] Psychologists therefore refer to the mental processes involved in the hearing of a melody as *produced representations:* we enjoy what we have ourselves created.

There is something so plausible and attractive about this interpretation—it settles so many vexing questions and fits the refractory phenomenon of music so neatly into the current system of ideas—that it is understandable how it has succeeded in making itself generally accepted without any very close scrutiny, and that there has been no demand for another explanation. Since we are here at the source of far-reaching misunderstandings concerning the nature of music—and of art in general—we must subject the theory to a more thorough examination. We shall show (1) that the theory makes assumptions and leads to conclusions which are contrary to the facts, and (2) that if the theory were correct, the evolution of music could not have followed the course it has in fact followed.

1. Let us return once more to our two tones e and d, $\hat{2}$ and $\hat{1}$, in the Beethoven melody. The pointing-beyond-itself of the one, the goal nature of the other, are, then, held to be nothing

1. William VanDyke Bingham, *Studies in Melody,* p. 87.

more than my own inner states, which I, as auditor, project out of myself and into the music. Into the manner and cause of such a feat of projection we do not inquire; they are the concern of psychology. We inquire into the material conditions. I must, then, have learned through experience, under similar circumstances (i.e., when a melody is in D major or D minor), to connect the expectation of a d with the hearing of the tone e and to connect *no further* expectation with the hearing of the tone d—otherwise I should be dealing with two expectations, and not with expectation and fulfillment. In order for such an unfailing connection between tones and feelings to arise in my consciousness, one of two things is necessary: either, in melodies in D major and D minor, the tone d always, or in the overwhelming majority of cases, actually follows the tone e, and the tone d is actually followed by nothing (really nothing, or nothing in the sense in which nothing follows the last word of a sentence); or else the sequence "e-d-nothing" must have impressed itself upon my consciousness as a striking phenomenon independently of the frequency of its appearance.

That the first condition does not hold is self-evident. Let us see what the situation in this respect is in our melody. The tone e appears there 14 times; 6 times it is followed by d, 7 times by F sharp, once by a. The tone d appears 10 times; only twice is it followed by "nothing," at the end of the eighth and sixteenth measures; twice it is followed by another d, six times by another tone, which indeed is precisely e. We see, then, that upon the basis of this experience we should have to connect expectation of e with d as much as expectation of d with e. The expectations cancel each other; the result is zero. The example is typical; we can count all tonal sequences in all melodies, and the result will always be the same, zero.

It is somewhat different with the second condition, the striking phenomenon. Of the two places in the melody where d in fact follows e and "nothing" follows d, one coincides with the strongest caesura in the melody (why this is so, we cannot yet discuss; it has to do with meter), and the other coincides with the end of the melody. Now in this respect, too, the example is typical. Since the close of a principal phrase and the close of the entire melody are certainly striking phenomena, which particularly impress themselves upon the listener, the persistent connection "e → d: end" could well establish itself in his consciousness, the more so as we are dealing with a typical formula. And such would be the associationist's line of argument. Thus, to return to our starting point, in a melody in D major, d would be usable as a concluding tone, and e unusable, not by reason of an alleged dynamic quality of these tones but simply because d is preponderantly used as concluding tone and the succession e-d as concluding formula, and we have become accustomed to them. The alleged dynamic qualities are the result, not the cause, of this practice. Is this logic to be accepted as valid? But if so, then how would the usage ever have become established? After all, a thing must first be present, then I can grow accustomed to it; the sequence can hardly be reversed. How are we to understand that a typical concluding formula could develop at all, and that precisely $\hat{2}$-$\hat{1}$ came to have that significance? May a sort of natural selection have taken place, in the course of which $\hat{2}$-$\hat{1}$, for one reason or another, gradually came to preponderate? The facts show the contrary: the earlier the music, the more *exclusively* $\hat{2}$-$\hat{1}$ is employed as concluding formula. If, further, associationism were correct, the expectation we connect with the tone e would never be simply that of the tone d, but always of d as *concluding* tone; so that whenever e-d was not followed by "nothing" but by another tone, we should register it as a kind of shock, a disappointment. Nothing of the kind occurs when, for example, at the beginning of the third measure of our melody, we hear e-d followed by another e.

The difficulties for associationism increase considerably if we go on from the simplest musical phenomena, such as the relation $\hat{2}$-$\hat{1}$, to others more complex, and finally contemplate the full extent of the activity of tonal dynamic qualities. The pointing-beyond-themselves, with all its variations in direction and gesture, that can be heard in tones, and heard with such unparalleled precision and clarity—how can this be attributed to feelings of expectation that experience has allegedly taught us to connect with tones, when, as a matter of fact, experience teaches nothing except that in general the probability of the tone *x* being followed by the tone *y* is just as great as that of the tone *y* being followed by the tone *x*? Anyone who has become familiar with the activity of tonal forces in music and with the expressions of that activity will regard such an assumption as ridiculous. Music would indeed be in a sad plight if, in order to make sense, it had to rely on the precision of the expectations that habit had taught us to associate with individual tones.

2. Incapable as associationism is of doing justice to the elementary data of the language of music, it is equally incapable of doing justice to the historical development of music.

We have mentioned that the exclusive use of $\hat{2}$-$\hat{1}$ as concluding step belongs to an early period of our music. The development of polyphony necessitated the use of other steps for conclusions, among which $\hat{7}$-$\hat{8}$ was the most important. In the process, something momentous happened to that step—momentous because it opened the way for the enlargement of the tonal basis of our music, for the introduction of new tones, chromatic tones, into the diatonic system of the modes.

When we compare the schemas of major and minor we notice a difference of pitch distance between the tones $\hat{7}$ and $\hat{8}$: it is a half tone in major, a whole tone in minor. The musical result of this difference is evident when the two scales are played in their diatonic form; the sense of conclusion that so distinctly marks the step $\hat{7}$-$\hat{8}$ in major is lacking in minor. On the other hand, if the minor scale is played with $\hat{7}$ raised in pitch so that the distance between $\hat{7}$ and $\hat{8}$ becomes the same as in major, one half tone, the sense of conclusion emerges with full force.

In all but one of the medieval modes the pitch situation between $\hat{7}$ and $\hat{8}$ is the same as in minor. It is most interesting to observe how the need for a strengthening of the concluding effect of the $\hat{7}$-$\hat{8}$ step gradually prevailed against the resistance of a traditionally fixed tonal material, until the raising of $\hat{7}$ whenever $\hat{7}$-$\hat{8}$ is supposed to convey a sense of conclusion became the rule that must not be broken.

It is this kind of development which no association theory, and no theory which seeks the origin of tonal meanings in conditioning, in habit, can possibly explain. Taking the situation as of today, it is easy to assert that the half tone step $\hat{7}$-$\hat{8}$ has a concluding character because it has been heard innumerable times as a concluding step. But there was a time when this step was new, a revolutionary departure from the habitual $\hat{7}$-$\hat{8}$, which, in three cases out of four, was a whole tone. If it is habit that gives a certain tonal move its meaning, how can departure from habit strengthen that meaning? The associationist might answer that probably the meaning of the new step was not understood at first and had to be learned through repeated experience. But, then, why was the change attempted in the first place, and insisted upon? If repeated experience is all that matters, what difference does it make whether the step is a whole tone or a half tone? Such a development makes sense only when we recognize that at certain times composers *discover new meanings in tones* and gradually persuade the change-resistant ears of listeners to accept and understand them. If habit *created* these meanings, no such events could ever occur, and the history of Western music would resemble that of the religious arts of certain nations, which remained static for centuries; whereas, in fact, it is a history of stormy developments and revolutionary changes.

With another of the revolutionary events, which marked an epoch in our music, and particularly in the development of harmony, we will now briefly concern ourselves. Since our discussion has as yet been confined to melody, a few preliminary remarks are necessary.

Western music is distinguished from the music of all other cultures by the fact that in it tones do not only follow one another but also sound together. A completely new world, full of prodigious tonal phenomena, arises from this: the world of chords, the world of harmony. Chords are produced by tones sounding together. Harmony is chords in succession, as melody is tones in succession. Acoustically, chords are characterized by the peculiar merging of the component tones into one complex sensation, and by the properties, familiar to all listeners, of *consonance* and *dissonance.* Musically, chords are characterized, as individual tones are, by dynamic qualities. The acoustical phenomenon of the simultaneous sounding of different tones, for example, $\left\{\begin{matrix} c \\ a \\ f \end{matrix}\right\}$, becomes a musical phenomenon when the tones, as elements of a musical context, acquire dynamic quality, for example, $\begin{matrix} c=\hat{5} \\ a=\hat{3} \\ f=\hat{1} \end{matrix}$ or $\begin{matrix} c=\hat{2} \\ a=\hat{7} \\ f=\hat{5} \end{matrix}$, and so on, according to the place of the tones in the system. In an important respect the dynamic quality of a chord is different from that of a tone: in general the chord does not express the *direction* in which it points as clearly as does the tone of a melody. There is audible, in every chord, in accordance with its place in the tonal system, a particular state of tension that belongs to it alone; yet this goes no further than a general will to pass beyond itself; no definite point of direction or goal crystallizes for the ear.

From this general characterization two chords must be excepted: first, the central chord itself, the *tonic chord,* the simultaneous sounding of the tones $\left\{\begin{matrix}\hat{5}\\ \hat{3}\\ \hat{1}\end{matrix}\right\}$, which announces itself to the ear, with complete clarity, as the center of action; then the so-called dominant seventh chord, the combination $\left\{\begin{matrix}\hat{4}\\ \hat{2}\\ \hat{7}\\ \hat{5}\end{matrix}\right\}$. The dominant seventh chord is distinguished from all other chords by the fact that its sound makes audible, distinctly and unmistakably, not only a pointing-beyond-itself but at the same time the goal of that pointing. It strives toward this goal, the tonic chord, as unmistakably as does the tone $\hat{2}$ to the tone $\hat{1}$, the tone $\hat{7}$ to the tone $\hat{8}$ (the tones $\hat{2}$ and $\hat{7}$ are elements of this chord). Thus the chordal succession dominant–tonic is the harmonic equivalent of the melodic steps $\hat{2}$-$\hat{1}$ and $\hat{7}$-$\hat{8}$; it has the same character, that of attaining a goal, and produces the most definite effect of a conclusion. It turns out that in the majority of cases the dominant seventh chord is in fact followed by the tonic and that comparatively strong caesuras—momentary or final points of rest—are generally expressed by this succession. The importance of this succession of chords becomes so preponderant in eighteenth-century music that the tonal language seems to be entirely under its spell. During the nineteenth century, however, composers began to challenge this rule with increasing audacity. The revolutionary outbreak came in Wagner's *Tristan.*

In the opening measures of the *Tristan* Prelude—probably the most discussed measures in the entire literature of music—

—the dominant seventh chord suddenly appears, no longer as pointing toward the goal, but as the goal itself! The same chord with which we have been positively forced, by countless repetitions of experience, to associate a particular state, that of concentrated tension immediately *before* the attainment of the goal, now expresses the opposite state, the comparative relaxation of attaining a goal. The associationist will again reply that this was the very reason why the music of *Tristan* was not at first understood by the public. But, for one thing, it *was* understood by a not inconsiderable number of people; and, for another, according to the presuppositions of associationism, how could all those who did not understand this music at first have *ever* come to understand it? After all, people did not thenceforth hear nothing but the *Tristan* type of music, but continued to be deluged, at concerts, at the opera, at dances, with old-style dominants. It must be completely incomprehensible, and indeed preposterous, to the associationist that such an idea ever arose in the mind of the composer; that in his imagination the familiar chord of tension could, for the first time, assume the meaning of relaxation. Certainly the relaxation of tension attained in this way is by no means complete; but such is not the intention of this music. Nor is it simply the composer's purpose here to break off the music at the moment of highest tension, before fulfillment, and thus to make it proceed from one unfulfilled expectation to another. Such an explanation is refuted by the testimony of the ear. Let us only try having one of these dominant seventh chords followed by the appropriate tonic: it certainly does not sound like a fulfillment that the music had denied us. Rather, it sounds senseless, stupid, like a bad joke, or like a sound imported from a foreign idiom. After this dominant chord we have no expectation of a tonic—what we expect is *nothing*.

We have discussed this instance at some length because it so typically represents the fact before which associationism and all related theories come to grief: the fact of creation. It is clear that any theory which attempts to refer the possibility of the artistic experience back to conditioning, repetition, habit, learning, to sequences that have become mechanical, cannot but leave the element of creativeness out of account. Since every work of art is essentially creation—more accurately, creative discovery—no associationist or behaviorist theory can ever give an adequate interpretation of artistic phenomena.

V.

The Three Components of Sense Perception

IT MIGHT BE ASKED why we are so intent upon refuting a theory whose psychological premise, the central importance of association in mental life, psychologists themselves are abandoning more and more. For one thing, this abandonment is so far only a matter of individual pioneer groups, not of the science as a whole; and, for another, we are here dealing, as I have said, less with an opinion held by specialists than with a mode of thought that has penetrated deep into the general consciousness and is not so easily to be uprooted by the proofs to the contrary adduced by a few professionals.

In our thinking about music, about art in general, in any case, this mode of thought continues to wreak havoc unimpeded. It is all the more stubbornly adhered to because important intellectual interests, so to speak, are bound up with it; after all, it affords the welcome opportunity to avoid certain logical consequences that we should otherwise have to draw from the elementary data of the arts and that threaten to endanger the basic tenets of our common understanding of the external world. It is therefore necessary to block up this way of escape, to make this emergency exit really impassable. Not until it has so become part and parcel of us that it is no more reasonable to look for the sources of the elementary phenomena of art in the person of the recipient than it is to attribute them to some sort of daemons of art or to definite intervention on the part of God; so sunk into our very flesh and blood that we compromise ourselves when we practice this sort of mythology in reverse—not until then shall we resolve to look the facts squarely in the face; resolve not merely to accept such a phenomenon as music for what it is but also to draw the required logical consequences from the fact that it exists.

Let us once again summarize the principal features in which the result of our observation of elementary musical processes runs counter to the common understanding of the external world.

At the beginning of our study we discussed to what a great extent our world is a *visible* world. Opening one's eyes, closing one's eyes, are the symbols for entering the world and leaving the world. Yet we do not only look, we also act; eye and hand are the two organs to which we chiefly owe the building up of our world. Thus to visibility is added tangibility: our world is a visible-tangible world, a corporeal world. The experiences of the other senses, our speech, our thinking, are all fitted into this frame; words like *grasp, comprehend, clarify, illuminate, indicate,* sufficiently demonstrate this.

To acquire status in this world, a thing has to make good its claim by showing that it is tangible and visible. If I see something that I cannot touch, if I touch something that I cannot see, if I hear a sound without discovering a tangible-visible source for it, I know that I am deluded. Our senses, even our hands and eyes, are subject to delusion; hence we have created artificial hands and eyes, incomparably farther reaching, incomparably more sensitive, and unqualifiedly reliable—our instruments, the telescope and microscope, photographic plates, thermometers, micrometers, and electrometers, Geiger counters, and what not, which tell us what belongs in our world and what does not.

Sense perceptions that are valid, that are not delusions, are, then, perceptions of phenomena in the corporeal world. Now often enough, to be sure, we think that we perceive things and processes that certainly do not belong in the corporeal world; as when we dream, imagine, are under the influence of hypnosis. In such cases it is not possible to speak of the senses being deluded, because the senses do not come into action at all. That, however, does not trouble us; we know that the scene of these phenomena is not the world to which we are otherwise directed by our senses, but our own self, our mind, our soul—use whatever word you please. Dreams leave no traces, then, in the corporeal world. In doubtful cases they can be recognized by this characteristic.

Thus we arrive at separating the outer world and the inner world. The outer world is the world of bodies and of the unbroken connection between them; it is the world we meet in our sense perceptions. The inner world is the world of the mind and its states, the world of thoughts, feelings, imaginings, decisions of the will, an immaterial world. Of these things—so far as they are conscious—we have immediate experiences. The perceptions of the so-called inner senses, the muscular sense or the sense of equilibrium, for example, are nothing but perceptions of corporeal phenomena, save that in this case their place is our own bodies.

But in the outer world there are not only bodies; there are also forces. It is forces, indeed, that hold the corporeal world together. Body and force are dependent upon each other: without forces, no bodies; but, equally, without bodies, no force. What would a force be that should not act in and on bodies? After all, we know of forces only through their material effects. The talk of immaterial or supermaterial forces, that is, of forces whose action is not manifested in a continuous material trace, we can accept only as fantasy or at best as poetic metaphor. To be sure, we speak of perceiving the action of a force, as when we say that we feel the weight of a burden, see the flash of a signal lamp, hear the crash of an explosion. But these are linguistic short cuts; what we actually perceive in these cases is never anything but the material consequences of the action of a force. Precisely because everything that we see, touch, or otherwise perceive through our senses is of a material nature, force itself can never be directly perceived; it can only be deduced from material traces of its action.

Now, we have said that in the tones of music we *hear forces*—and this was not meant as a linguistic short cut; the phrase meant exactly what it said. We have encountered an action of forces which not only does not coincide with its material consequences but with which no material phenomena can be correlated at all. To be sure, the deployment of this action presupposes material phenomena, acoustical phenomena: without tones, no music—which, however, means no more than without walls, no mural paintings. To be sure, tones involve actions of forces that do produce material effects—the forces, namely, that set the wave-generating bodies, the wave-propagating air, in motion and stimulate the auditory apparatus. But these forces have no more to do with those which manifest themselves in the dynamic qualities of tone than a man's physical powers have to do with his intellectual power, his power of faith, his power of artistic creation. It is simply not true that if we know all the material and physiological processes which occur when music is heard, we shall know everything about the forces active in it. On the contrary, even the most accurate description of everything that goes on in the material world in connection with the hearing of music would not give the least indication even of the elementary phenomena upon which music is built. And precisely because the forces active in musical tone, which indeed actually create it, leave no traces whatever in the material world, they cannot be deduced but only directly perceived.

So long as the outer world and the material world were not synonyms, so long as the outer world was not held to be an exclusively physical whole, it was possible for man, when confronted by phenomena that would not fit into the physical whole, to posit their source in God or in the world soul. A few centuries of scientific thinking have driven God and the soul, if not from the world, at least from the outer world; have relegated these immaterial principles to a habitation in the inner world. So it is only logical if we, the heirs of this intellectual tradition, confronted by phenomena for which no source in the material world is discoverable, view them as derived from our feelings, as native to the inner world. To give this view scientific sanction has been the endeavor of associationism. That is why it was so welcome, why it has taken such deep root in the general consciousness.

But what if in a specific case, in the case of music, this way out is no longer practicable? What if it can no longer be denied that the phenomena which appear in the simple musical tone are genuine phenomena of the outer world and not projections of phenomena of the inner world? We shall be all the less inclined to go back to God or the world soul as source or explanation since, in that case, we should have to assume the co-operation of sublime entities even in the melody of the commonest street song. Still, certain conclusions force themselves upon us as soon as musical experiences are admitted as sources of evidence in matters concerning the outer world: the current equating of outer world with physical world, sense perception with perception of physical data, is not confirmed by the evidence of music. The outer world is not exclusively a world of physical occurrences; sense perceptions are not exclusively perceptions of physical phenomena. In the outer world there are forces active whose activity transcends the physical, and at least one of our senses is an organ capable of directly perceiving nonphysical occurrences.

At this point it is important to draw a clear distinction between the dynamic qualities that appear in musical tones and the *emotional tone,* which more or less observably accompanies all our sensations.

The existence of so-called pure sensations, the mere registering of an elementary datum of the outer world by the sense organ, is no longer credited by psychologists.[1] Sensations that are not in some way colored by feeling have no existence in reality. The bull that becomes enraged at the sight of a red cloth is the extreme representative of a universally valid pattern. We differ from the bull not only in possessing less violence of feeling (and hence greater self-control), but above all by the fact that the bull, unburdened by any tradition of philosophy, ascribes the cause of his behavior directly to the irritating quality of the red color, whereas we, in similar cases, are more inclined to ascribe it to a particular irritability in ourselves. We do not deny that red has something exciting about it, as blue has something calming, yellow something exhilarating; but we have learned to separate the color as such, the "objective" datum, from our "subjective" reaction to the sight of the color. What we actually *see* is a red, a blue, a yellow, and nothing more; excitement, calm, exhilaration are entirely our own, the observer's contribution to the phenomenon. If sensations absolutely uncolored by feeling do not exist, this means that every sensation is made up of two components, one coming from without, physical, one coming from within, psychic—a conception thoroughly in harmony with the distinc-

1. For a thorough discussion of the different theories of sensation, cf. Charles Hartshorne, *The Philosophy and Psychology of Sensation.*

tion "outer world = physical world," "world of feeling = inner world."

Recent investigations, however, seem to be more in accord with the bull's view. Careful research and reflection have brought out the fact that the element of feeling is more closely bound up with the outer-world component than had been assumed. If the emotional tone is removed from the sensation, these investigations hold, what remains is not a changed, a purified, a neutralized sensation, but no sensation at all; what remains is a mere thing of thought, an abstraction. When the emotional tone of the color disappears, concrete color disappears too. So it would seem that the emotional tone is not a contribution on the part of the perceiver after all, but an original quality of the thing sensed itself. "The 'gaiety' of yellow . . . is the yellowness of the yellow," [2] as a keen formulation expresses it. But with this the old intellectual schema of physical outer world and psychic inner world is shattered. We hear of "objective feelings"—feelings whose locale is no longer the inner world, a consciousness; the outer world itself is revealed as permeated with feeling, and the purest form of sensation is supposed to exist where the emotional coloring can appear most openly: in artistic experience.

If these views have, in the words of the author quoted above, "proved hopelessly incredible to most persons," the reason is doubtless that, though the strict separation of the two worlds is abandoned, the two components, physical and psychic, are still maintained. The nonphysical element that is found in the outer world, although it is no longer imported into it from an inner world, is yet, so to speak, an "external psychic." Even the vocabulary—feeling, excitement, gaiety, and so on—is wholly drawn from the psychic realm. (In this connection we must not forget that our language, which conforms to our mode of thought,

2. Hartshorne, p. 7.

provides a vocabulary for physical phenomena and for psychic phenomena, but none for phenomena that belong to neither class: a source of frequently insuperable difficulties in all investigations that do not readily fit into the traditional pattern of thought.) But how, without falling back upon the old belief in the world soul or in a God in nature, we are to conceive feelings outside of a consciousness, and a seeing, hearing, and touching of feelings (to say nothing of other complications), we cannot at first see. In this situation, music shows us the way out.

Tone sensations, of course, are subject to the same law as all other sensations: they too are always colored by feeling. We do not hear flute tones or trombone tones; we hear charming flute tones, solemn or threatening trombone tones. Low tones sound serious, high tones gay, and so on. Now, whether we interpret the emotional tone as something contributed by the hearer or as a quality of the tone itself, one thing is certain: the *musical tone* cannot be adequately described in terms of these two components, the physical and the psychic. Let us think of the Beethoven melody of our first example. When it appears for the first time in the Ninth Symphony, it is played by the lower strings. The tones of the celli and double basses in this passage—especially by contrast with what has preceded—have a very definite emotional character: it could be called a character of solemn repose. The two components, then, are present—the physical, the acoustical tone, and the psychic, the emotional tone; but the *melody,* the *music,* as we know, is in neither of these. What we hear when we hear melody is simply not F sharp, G, A, etc., plus "solemn repose," tone plus emotion, physical plus psychic, but, with that and beyond it, a third thing, which belongs to neither the physical nor the psychic context: $\hat{3}$, $\hat{4}$, $\hat{5}$—a pure dynamism, tonal dynamic qualities. It is not *two* components, then, which make up musical tone, but *three.* The words we use to describe this third component—words such as force, equilibrium, tension, direction—are significantly such as neither of the two sides claims for itself alone and, consequently, may well refer to a separate realm between the two, a realm of pure dynamics. What makes tone musical tone is so much the work *not* of the physical and *not* of the psychic component but of the third, a purely dynamic component, that, compared with the latter, the two others appear to sink to the function of trigger and aftereffect: a physical process sets off the dynamic phenomenon; the latter reverberates in a psychic process. It is hard to understand how the musical psychologists have never been able to see anything here but a bipartite structure, have jumped from tone to emotion, from emotion to tone, in an effort to explain the relation between the two, but have entirely missed what is produced by the trigger action and produces the aftereffect, the dynamic process, the properly musical phenomenon. Even the philosopher among the musical scholars of our time, Ernst Kurth, who never doubted that in music we have essentially to do with dynamic processes, nevertheless finally interpreted this dynamic factor as a psychic factor, and even as a creation of the listener's.[3] So greatly is our thinking under the spell of the two-worlds schema! Perhaps the sterility of traditional aesthetics is owing to the fact that it has never escaped from this schema; that it continually swings like a pendulum between a physical and a psychic component of art work and art experience, in a vain attempt to comprehend the phenomena of art from the narrow viewpoint of the trigger action and the reverberation.

With this last observation we have extended the result of our investigation beyond the realm of music to all art. It seems that an even more far-reaching generalization would not be entirely unjustified.

That we *see forces in colors,* in the same sense in which we

3. Kurth discusses the problem in *Musikpsychologie;* cf. also his *Grundlagen des linearen Kontrapunkts.*

hear forces in musical tones—and in colors as such, not only as elements of works of art—is the bold statement made by the psychologist Gustav von Allesch in his book *Die aesthetische Erscheinungsweise der Farben,* and shown to be valid with a thoroughness that leaves nothing to be desired. Arguing from the results of experiments carried on over many years, he was able to state that "the essential element in the impression of color is dynamic in nature, based upon a movement toward a definite goal or a movement away from a goal." To see colors means to see *directions, intentions.* "In any case the apprehension of a color is an event in which a direction, a drive, a will, becomes perceptible." The parallel to hearing tones in melody is unmistakable. There can be no question of seeking the source of these phenomena in the observer. The observer's share in the impression of color, whatever he contributes to the impression from himself, from his inner world, is carefully isolated and taken into account. The conclusion drawn is, "The intention always appears as an intention *of the color*"; the drive is "a drive of the color itself." Associations are inadequate to explain this. Red is not fiery because fire is red, but because, from a certain point of view, this particular red and fire are one and the same; no precise word to express this is available. There are innumerable other things, aside from fire, which are the same color as this red and of which one does *not* think when one sees this red. "Associations are countless channels that serve the purpose of opening the way to the one meaningful connection that establishes identity of intention. They are something completely secondary." Every color is seen from a specific *niveau,* as departing in a specific degree from a *niveau;* accordingly it has a specific *fall.* Its intentionality, its dynamic character, has its origin in the tension between color and *niveau;* we see that, among colors, the function of the *niveau* is related to that of the tone $\hat{1}$ among tones. Hence similar dynamic characters sometimes appear in different colors. "No case is identical with another, but the forces at work are always the same. The given colors are, to a certain extent, only the material in which the action of the forces reveals itself. Hence too we find that colors physically very different are often completely equivalent in respect to intention. It is, then, a matter of indifference whether one looks at a green or a red. The dynamics of the total phenomenon comprehend both colors in such a way that the same configuration develops from both of them." Again the parallel to musical phenomena imposes itself. Nor did it escape the scientists who undertook these investigations.

We see, then, that in the phenomena which we have observed in tones in melody, we have not to deal with isolated manifestations occurring only in music and not perceivable by other senses than that of hearing. It appears, rather, that the tripartite structure belongs to other sensations too. Could it be that the third component, the dynamic component, represents the core of all that is manifest to the senses? The "external psychic" would then prove to be something purely dynamic, not feeling but force—a force for which the physical would be as it were transparent, which would work through the physical without touching it. That it required so great and complex an effort to make clear for the eye phenomena immediately apparent to the ear in the hearing of simple melodies seems to indicate that the ear is the organ particularly capable of perceiving the dynamic component of external events. Precisely because the eye has such an important part in the construction of the world of material things, fulfills its chief function there, it will penetrate only with great effort to the perception of nonmaterial, purely dynamic phenomena.

VI. The Dynamic Symbol

THE VIEW here maintained cannot be considered really established so long as we have not disposed of the weightiest argument against it. How do we explain the fact that a Chinese, an Indian, totally unfamiliar with Western music, can no more distinguish between sense and nonsense in our tones than can the tune-deaf person; that he takes the tuning of the orchestra for the beginning of the symphony, has not the most remote idea of what we are talking about when we refer him to the dynamic qualities of tone —but then, years later perhaps, as the result of accumulated experiences and growing familiarity, may reach the point of hearing our music with a comprehension equal to our own? Does not this finding—original incomprehension, comprehension as the result of a process of learning and habituation—seem to justify the associationists and put us in the wrong? If the dynamic qualities were really *in the tones,* then anyone to whom they were pointed out must needs find them there, and immediately, not after long practice, habituation, experience. Perhaps it requires a certain practice to *discover* the outlines of the figures that are hidden in puzzle pictures; but to *see* them, when they are pointed out, requires neither particular practice nor particular experience but simply two good eyes. Thus everyone whose attention is drawn to it hears the difference between high and low, loud and soft, steady and vibrato tones, between the sound of a trumpet and the sound of an oboe—all of them characteristics that are really in the tones and belong to the tones. But when people with good ears and normal minds simply hear *nothing* where we, pointing out certain tones, speak of a distinction between attracting and being attracted, between tension and relaxation, the only conclusion that can possibly be drawn is that the phenomena we cite are not where we are pointing, not *in* the tones themselves.

This conclusion owes its force simply and solely to the inadequate attention we pay to the little word *in*. It tacitly presupposes that there is only one kind of "being in," of being contained: the material, the physical. Sunspots are *in* the sun, the coffee is *in* the cup, the sugar is *in* the coffee, the chemical element C is *in* the sugar, or sweetness is *in* the sugar; for this kind of "being in" it is true, to be sure, that what one person finds, another must find, and the impersonal measuring instrument must find it too. Whether there are other kinds of "being in," and whether the same conditions of discoverability and demonstrability hold for them as for physical "being in," we do not, at first sight, know at all; one would, rather, tend to deny it. That the dynamic qualities of tone cannot be *in* the tones because no instrument finds them there, because a Chinese or an Indian or indeed an infant, to whom we play our Beethoven melody, will simply hear nothing of a striving of the tone e toward the tone d, however much we may exhort him—the conclusiveness of this dictum rests entirely upon the assumption that physical "being in" is the only possible way of "being in."

It demands no particular subtlety to show how unfounded and indeed arbitrary an assumption this would be. After all, our daily life has made us familiar with various ways of "being in," or being contained. Ideas are in the sentences that we hear or read, and they are certainly not in them physically. Often, for example in a book by a difficult author, the idea is deep in the sentence and hard to extract: a sentence can be understood in various ways, different ideas can be read from it—although, taken physically, it always contains exactly the same letters and groups of letters. We say of a man that there is something sly in his movements; another carries a secret about with him; it is in him, but certainly not physically. The way in which the future organism is contained in the egg can hardly be understood in a purely physical sense. And so on—examples can be multiplied at will.

If we ask ourselves with which of these various kinds of non-material "being in" we have to do in music, the comparison with language will immediately impose itself. Instinctively, when we think of music we think of a language. Like the words of a language, the tones of music are not meaningless sounds and signs; they make sense. We have already emphasized this relationship; we have attempted, by a comparison with words and their meaning, to make it comprehensible how there can be meaning in the tones of a melody.

Music has often before been interpreted as a language. Since it is of the essence of a language to say something, the question arose: What does music say? The usual answer was: As the words of language have factual meaning, the tones of music have emotional meaning; music is the language of feeling. According to this conception, the musical meaning of our Beethoven melody would lie in its expressing the feeling of joy, with a power far exceeding that of Schiller's poem and of all words. This interpretation cannot be ours. The key to understanding the processes that make the tones of this melody a melody at all, a piece of music, we found not in the relation of the tones to any particular feeling but in the relation of the tone e to the tone d. That the dynamic qualities of tone, in which we recognized the genuine musical element, have nothing to do with the expression of feeling, or with the expression of anything whatsoever, follows from the mere fact that they clearly appear even where absolutely nothing is meant to be expressed or stated, namely, when a scale is played.

Music and language, then, have one thing in common—that tones, like words, have meaning and that the "being in" of the meaning in the word, like that of the musical significance in the tone, is of a nonmaterial nature. But beyond that, the relations that connect the word with its meaning, the tone with its musical significance, are quite different. The word and its meaning are independent things. *Here* is the word—a complex of sounds or signs; *there* is what it means. The two are separable; each exists by itself, the word without the thing, the thing without the word. The same thing is designated in different languages by different words. We can refer to a thing otherwise than through a word—through a symbol, for example, or a sketch. The tone and its meaning, on the other hand, are connected in a far more intimate way. The acoustical event and its musical meaning are in no sense two independent phenomena, existing by themselves. They cannot be imagined separate. To be sure, it is possible to imagine a tone that means nothing, that is a simple acoustical phenomenon; but it is impossible to imagine the musical meaning of a tone, its dynamic quality, without the tone. The particular state of tension, for example, which we designate by $\hat{2}$ does not exist outside of a tone. What tones mean musically is completely one with them, can only be represented through them, exists only in them. Except in the case of creative language (in the biblical sense of Adam's "naming" things) and of poetic language, where other, more "musical" relations come into play, language always has a finished world of things before it, to which it assigns words; whereas tones must themselves create what they mean. Hence it is possible to translate from one language into another, but not from one music into another—for example, from Western into Chinese music. Hence too the number of words, of the smallest meaning units of language, corresponds roughly to the number of things: languages are rich in words; whereas twelve tones suffice to say everything that has ever been said in our music.

In what sense, then, is the meaning *in* the word? In much the same way as the curve is in the sign ⓢ that warns the motorist of it. Words are signs that refer to particular things; if I understand them, they bring to my knowledge the things they signify. Here we have to deal with three components: the physical sound or written sign, the function of indicating, the thing indicated. Strictly speaking, only the indicating is actually *in* the word, not the thing indicated, the thing meant. Tones too indicate, *point to* something. The meaning of a tone, however, lies not in what it points to but *in the pointing itself;* more precisely, in the different way, in the individual gesture, with which each tone points toward the same place. The meaning is not the thing indicated but the manner of indicating (otherwise all tones would mean the same thing, namely, $\hat{1}$). In words, the indicating is no more than a neutral connecting process between physical sound or written sign and thing signified; in the musical tone the indicating is itself all. In the strictest sense, then, what the tone means is actually and fully contained in the tone itself. Words lead away from themselves; but tones lead into themselves. Words only point toward what they mean, but, beyond that, leave it, so to speak, where it is: the nonmaterial "being in" of the meaning in the word is a mere "being signified." Tones, on the other hand, have completely absorbed their meaning into themselves and discharge it upon the hearer directly in their sound. The nonmaterial "being in" of the meaning in the tone is no mere "being signified"; it is complete, actual presence. The force that gives meaning is in the tone as life is in a face; we see it, we cannot touch it; nonphysical, it is yet one with the physical appearance and cannot appear save through a material medium, which it nevertheless infinitely transcends. When meaning sounds in a musical tone, a nonphysical force intangibly radiates from its physical conveyor.

We find a similar kind of "being in" in the religious symbol. The symbol is the representation of a supermaterial—that is, physically indemonstrable—force in a material form. (We expressly refrain from saying a supersensual or supernatural force, our chief concern being to let music show us that supermaterial is not necessarily also supernatural or supersensual.) The religious symbol is not a sign that merely indicates the divine being to the believer. Rather, the deity is directly present *in* the symbol, is one with it, and is also directly beheld in the symbol by the believer. The believer in the presence of the symbol does not *think* of his god; he does not associate religious *feelings* with the image—association does not enter in at all, otherwise religious experience would be learnable—he apprehends his god in the symbol in a direct perception. He cannot but see him there. Great as the difference between musical tone and religious symbol may be, in this one essential point they are alike: in both, a force that transcends the material is immediately manifested in a material datum. In this very special sense, then, we can speak of the tones of music as *dynamic symbols*. We hear forces in them as the believer sees the divine being in the symbol.

Let us now think back to the objection that the forces cannot be in the tones because many people with normal ears do not hear them there. Do normal eyes suffice to see the god in the symbol? The believer sees him; the unbeliever sees nothing—who is *right?* The believer himself says that the unbeliever can see nothing there. What does disbelief prove against belief? To hear the dynamic qualities of tones requires no particular belief. That they are not physically in the tones, that no instrument would register their presence, is no argument against their existence; it is rather the distinctive character of their existence. To him who opens himself without reservations to symbols, their meaning will gradually become clear of itself. The Chinese who hears mere noise in our music has not yet given the symbols sufficient opportunity to impart to him the significance they contain. But if the opportunity has been present, and still nothing happens, the only conclusion that can be drawn is that, as the result of some obstructive circumstance or other, this one person, although physically his hearing is unimpaired, cannot share in the community of those who hear musically. His musical deafness says neither more nor less against the existence of the dynamic qualities than blindness says against the existence of light, or an absence of metals against the reality of magnetism.

At the beginning of this book we briefly referred to the particular nature of the *audible* in comparison with the data of the other senses. To this we now return.

We do not simply see colors, or light, but colored, illuminated things. We do not touch hardness, smoothness, we do not feel warmth; we touch hard, smooth bodies, feel warm bodies. We do not taste a flavor but a food; do not smell an odor but a gas. We do not hear tones but—what?

In seeing, touching, tasting, we reach through the sensation to an object, to a thing. Tone is the only sensation not that of a thing. In the case of color, hardness, odor, we ask, *What* is it that possesses the color, the hardness, the odor? Even in the case of noise we ask, *What* is making it? It is not so with tones. Language makes a very subtle distinction: we say, The leaf is green, the wall is smooth, the honey tastes sweet; but we do not say, The string is g, or the flute sounds d-ish.

Sensations are our answer to the world as given. Seeing, touching, smelling, tasting, we respond to its physicality, its materiality. To what datum of the world do we respond in hearing? Is hearing only a sort of seeing around the corner, seeing in the dark? If noises were all that we heard, hearing could be so interpreted; could be regarded as an auxiliary sense, added to seeing and touching. But there are tones, and there are tones because there is music, not the other way around. Only in tone is the true nature of sound revealed; in the hearing of tones the sense of hearing fulfills its destiny and discovers the side of the world that is its counterpart. Which side is it, since it is *not* the material-factual side? Whatever the answer may be, we know now that the question itself is reasonable; that there is something real to be inquired into in this direction. Because music exists, the tangible and visible cannot be the whole of the given world. The intangible and invisible is itself a part of this world, something we encounter, something to which we respond.

To quote the biologist Jakob von Uexküll: "Where there is a foot, there is also a path; where there is a mouth, there is also nourishment."

MOTION

PREFATORY NOTE

THE AIM of the remainder of this study will be to make clear how three of the foundation pillars of our picture of the external world, the concepts of *motion, time,* and *space,* look in the light of the experience of music.

To this end, we shall proceed as follows. In the foreground is always the musical experience: What do I hear? From this experience we isolate a motion component, a time component, a space component, describe them as accurately as possible; compare what we have described with the concepts of motion, time, and space that our intellectual tradition has rooted in the general consciousness. In so far as disparities between experience and concept are brought to light in this way, our investigation will become a critique of these fundamental concepts on the basis of musical experience: music makes us revise these concepts to bring them into agreement with our experience. In this procedure we can appeal to the precedent of the natural sciences, which, for their part, are constantly summoning fundamental concepts before the judgment seat of their observations and descriptions, and which, when necessary, recast them to maintain agreement between concept and experience. Our own twentieth century is well acquainted with this procedure: the shock of the so-called relativization of space and time is still very much with us.

It is not usual to hear the voice of music testify in matters such as these. This is no reason, though, not to accept its testimony. To deny it the right to be heard would be a sign of unscientific dogmatism.

VII. The Paradox of Tonal Motion

So FAR, tones as elements of musical contexts have been the subject of our investigation. We now turn and inquire into the context as such, into that of which the tones are elements. With what sort of context are we here confronted?

Again let us briefly establish what is *not* our aim in putting this question. We do not seek to know how musical contexts are created, composed; this is a question for musical theory. Nor are we interested in whatever moral, emotional, or other effects the hearing of musical contexts may produce in the listener. We simply ask: What is given in musical experience directly as context? What do I hear when I hear context? What do I call the thing that, interpenetrating the multitude of successive tones, connects them together?

Let us again begin from the fundamental experience; let us try to describe the phenomenon of melody. If we permit ourselves no straying into technical matters or into emotional commentaries, we shall inevitably speak of the tones as going up and down, of a rise to a high point, a descent, a lingering, of steps and leaps—in short, of motions. Let us listen, for example, to the beginning of the *Marseillaise:*

What is it—aside from being tonic and dominant, march time, up-beat; aside too from being beautiful, proud, heroic, aggressive, inspiring—but an ascent? And what an ascent! It is beautiful, proud, inspiring, *because* it is that particular ascent. The motion is the primary thing.

Musical contexts are *motion* contexts, kinetic contexts. Tones are elements of a musical context because and in so far as they are conveyors of a motion that goes through them and beyond them. When we hear music, what we hear is above all motions.

When motion in music is discussed, we naturally think especially of rhythm. Rhythm seems to us to be the real kinetic element in music. It is the rhythm of a march or of a dance which, as the expression goes, "gets into our legs"; it is the rhythmic power of the performance of a great interpreter which, if the audience were less civilized, would tear them out of their seats. Later we shall discuss the entire complex of rhythmic phenomena; here for the moment we shall leave them out of consideration. Rhythm is not a specifically musical phenomenon. It is the one element which music has in common with other phenomena and processes. The rhythmical instruments in the narrower sense—the percussion instruments, the various drums, cymbals, triangles—are not properly *musical* instruments, since, with the exception of the borderline case of the kettledrum, they produce noises, not tones. But here we are concerned primarily with tones, with the motion that lies in tones as such—with what we called the *ascent* in the opening of the *Marseillaise.* That was precisely *not* the rhythm, the ever identical rhythm of all marches; it was a motion which, *apart from the rhythm,* we heard in the tones as such. And we must not forget that what *we* call rhythm in music is a comparatively new thing, unknown to antiquity and the Middle Ages. But music has *always* been perceived as motion, entirely independently of whether it possessed rhythm in our sense or not.

It is, in fact, most striking with what uniformity, despite all differences between persons and periods, the idea of motion forced itself upon thinkers and scholars when the question of designating the essential element of music arose.[1] Saint Augustine has little in common with modern experimental psychologists in other respects; but when, in his profound utterances on the subject of music, he describes its nature as *ordered motion,* he and the antique tradition, which he here continues, reach across the millennia to the modern scholars who "hold that, in a study of melody, the focal point must be sought in melodic motion" and to whom "motion appeared to be the essential element." [2] With changing periods, the concept of motion may change its meaning; but nothing changes in the interpretation of music as motion. If in the seventeenth and eighteenth centuries all art is held to be imitation, music is held to be the imitation of *the motions of feeling.* If to the earlier Romanticists music stood highest among the arts, it was because they believed that they perceived the mysterious *flow* of life itself in music—here we have a new motion symbol. Hegel speaks of music's task "of echoing the motions of the inmost self," of its power "of penetrating with its motions directly into the inmost seat of all the motions of the soul." [3] The Scientific Age finds its characteristic form of interpreting music as motion: Helmholtz undertakes to refer the effect of music back to its relationship with physical movements.[4] Edmund Gurney, author of a remarkable book, *The Power of*

1. The philosophical problem of motion in music is discussed, and sources are quoted, in Kathi Meyer, *Bedeutung und Wesen der Musik.*

2. Sophie Belaiew-Exemplarsky and Boleslaus Jaworsky, "Die Wirkung des Tonkomplexes bei melodischer Gestaltung."

3. Hegel, *Vorlesungen über die Aesthetik.*

4. H. L. F. von Helmholtz, *On the Sensations of Tone as a Psychological Basis for the Theory of Music.*

Sound, opposes Helmholtz's view; his musical instinct rejects the attempt to understand music in accordance with the motion of *bodies* but not the use of the concept of motion itself; to him music reveals itself as "ideal motion." Eduard Hanslick's definition of music as "*tönend-bewegte Form,*" as "sounding form in motion," is well known. (He was wrong, though, in claiming priority for this idea, as when he wrote: "Though the idea of *motion* appears to us a most far-reaching and important one, it has hitherto been conspicuously disregarded in all enquiries into the nature and action of music." [5] Can it be that his historical knowledge was as imperfect as his artistic judgment?) While Hanslick connected the concept of motion with a shallow and rigid concept of form, we find a far more fruitful linking of the two ideas, form and motion, in the work of the greatest musical theorist of our time, Heinrich Schenker, who understood the musical work of art as a complex kinetic organism.[6] Ernst Kurth, setting out from a different basis and aiming in a different direction, coincides with Schenker in his conclusion that "all musical phenomena rest upon kinetic processes and their inner dynamics." [7] Not only theoreticians, but creative musicians too, are of the same opinion. "Basically, music is not so much sound as motion," writes Roger Sessions in *The Musical Experience of Composer, Performer, Listener.* To conclude, let us hear a contemporary aesthetician and a contemporary psychologist. "Auditory movement [of a melody]," says Carroll C. Pratt, "as well as visual and kinesthetic, is an immediate fact of direct experience." [8] And in Erwin Straus'

---

5. Eduard Hanslick, *The Beautiful in Music,* p. 38.

6. Heinrich Schenker's principal works are *Neue musikalische Theorien und Phantasien, Der Tonwille,* and *Das Meisterwerk in der Musik.* The most authoritative book in English based on Schenker's theories is Felix Salzer, *Structural Hearing;* cf. also Adele T. Katz, *Challenge to Musical Tradition.*

7. Ernst Kurth, *Grundlagen des linearen Kontrapunkts* and *Musikpsychologie.*

8. Carroll C. Pratt, *The Meaning of Music.*

Vom Sinn der Sinne we read: "The unity of music and motion is primordial, not artificial, not contrived, and not learned."

But it is not only these and similar statements by authoritative thinkers and scholars which we can adduce in support of our contention that music is motion. From a direction whence we should not have expected it, from the side of exact measurement, comes confirmation that we do not deceive ourselves if we interpret the direct musical experience as an experience of motion.

In the first section of this book we spoke of the practical but somewhat crude compromise represented by the tuning of such an instrument as our piano, with its division of the octave into twelve equal half tones. The differences between this compromise, the so-called *equal temperament* and the *just intonation,* which rejects the compromise and which, for instance, a violinist would prefer, are audible to very acute ears, but are so slight that they lie below the threshold of disturbance. Hence the problems involved are of technical and scientific rather than artistic interest. And it was a purely scientific, a psychological problem, in no way connected with the matters that here concern us, which started the experiments we shall now discuss. Their object was to determine if people who sing tend more to equal temperament or to just intonation. To this end, it was only necessary to have the same melody sung by a number of people and to register their tones by a measuring instrument, such as an oscilloscope.

The result of these measurements was highly unexpected. It went so far beyond the limits of the original question as to render it meaningless. What appeared was that the singers sang neither in just intonation nor in equal temperament—they simply sang unimaginably off pitch. And this was equally true of all the singers, trained and untrained, unmusical and highly musical. The scale of measurement employed was as follows: the difference in pitch between each two adjacent tones of the tempered chromatic scale was rated as 100,—so that, beginning with c = 0, we get c sharp–d flat = 100, d = 200, d sharp–e flat = 300, e = 400, etc. For every possible pitch, then, between c and c sharp, the instrument shows a particular number between 0 and 100, and so on. According to this scale of measurement, the difference between the tempered and just intonation of a tone lies within the average magnitude of 10. For example: tempered d = 200, pure d = 204; tempered e = 400, pure e = 386. Translated into the language of the measuring instrument, the questions posed by the investigation were, for example: Does the singer at this place tend to produce the tone 300 or the tone 316, at this other place the tone 500 or the tone 493? The answer given by the merciless instrument, from which there was no appeal, was neither 300 nor 316, but 238; neither 500 nor 493, but 586. Tones which lay far closer to the adjacent tone of the chromatic scale than to the tone actually to be sung! Such facts can no longer be discussed in terms of poor intonation; the singers simply sang different notes from those which the text prescribed.[9]

As an answer to the original question, then, the result was valueless. Instead, it brought a very different and much more interesting situation to light. It became evident, that is, that the great discrepancies always appeared where a rise or fall of the melody was clearly marked, and that, in the majority of cases, the *direction* of the discrepancy followed the upward or downward direction of the melody. The impression is inescapable that the movement of the melody seizes upon the tones and carries them with it. (Exceptions to this norm are always to be explained by the particular situation in each case.) Motion establishes itself

9. Otto Abraham, "Tonometrische Untersuchungen an einem deutschen Volkslied."

as a real factor in music by producing tangible, measurable effects.

But the most significant thing about the result of this experiment is the fact that it required the intervention of the measuring instrument to reveal these grotesque distortions of pitch, these false tones. The audience, which included experienced musicians, had not noticed them at all. So long as one is, so to speak, alone with music, so long as there is simply singing on the one side and listening on the other, there is no consciousness that anything is wrong. It is not until physics intervenes, with its measuring instruments, that the false tones are brought to light—to the surprise of the investigators, to the astonishment of the musicians. But what do "wrong" and "false" mean here—where obviously, so long as the approach is purely musical, so long as no measurements are undertaken, everything is right and nothing wrong or false? For what is musically right, musically wrong, the court of last appeal is the ear of the musician, not the physicist's apparatus. If the same ear, under other circumstances, immediately and unfailingly perceives discrepancies that are mere fractions of those here established, and yet hears nothing wrong here, this means neither more nor less than that right or wrong in music is not a matter of pitch as such but of pitch in relation to the direction of motion. The acoustically wrong tone can be musically right if the deviation is right in the sense of the movement. It cannot, then, be simply tones as such, tones of a predetermined pitch, which we sing or hear in melodies; it is motions represented in tones. Whatever else music may be, one thing it must be: motion.

Thus buttressed by the concurrent testimony of direct experience, of philosophic speculation, and of measurement, we shall now ask ourselves a series of questions that will shake our conviction that music is motion and dispose us to recognize that it was the result of self-deception, of an illusion.

To hear a melody, we said, means to hear a motion. But can one *hear* motion? To see motion, to touch motion, is comprehensible—but to *hear* motion? Certainly we hear the approach and departure of the band playing the *Marseillaise* out in the street. But this—the motion of the musicians and their instruments—is not the motion we have in mind; we mean the motion of the music: the ascent of the melody, for which it is immaterial whether the musicians are marching or sitting down.

Motion always implies something that moves, that is in motion. A bird flies past. A snowflake falls to the ground. To speak of motion makes sense only when something is present that moves. What is it that moves in a melody?

It will be answered: the tones. But is a tone something that can move? What moves is objects, things—and have we not shown that the tones of music are precisely *not* that, are not like things, are not like objects, and have no reference to things and objects? And now are they suddenly to do what only things do—to move?

Something moves—first it is here, then there. This means it is *the same* something, the same thing, which at different moments appears at different places. The thing that remains the same is the indispensable and permanent core of the phenomenon of motion.

What is the permanent core of a tonal motion, the particular something that always remains the same during the course of the motion? To be sure, when we discuss tonal motion we tacitly assume that there actually is such a permanent core of the phenomenon, a real entity "tone" which performs the motion, which, during the course of the melody is to be found first here, then there, and so on. What meaning could the expression "tonal motion" have otherwise? But at every attempt really to grasp this entity "tone," it vanishes in our hands: it is a mere abstraction. We can think it, but we cannot hear it.

Furthermore, motion implies not only something that moves but also something that does not move, or moves differently: a background, a frame. The bird flies through the sky; the snowflake falls past the aperture of the window frame. To talk of motion, then, means to talk of two things and their mutual relation. What may this second thing be in a melody? To hear tones means to hear nothing but tones; besides the tones, there is nothing else, no background, no frame, before which they might move.

But do they move at all? Actually, they standstill! In the *Marseillaise,* for example, we hear the first tone —it does not move; then comes , another static tone; this one is repeated; then comes ; and so on. No tone, so long as it sounds, moves from its place. What has happened to the motion? When we said earlier that a thing in motion is now here, now there, now elsewhere, the essence of the matter was certainly not the being here and being elsewhere but what occurred *in between,* the connection, the transition: motion is the process that *conveys* the thing from here to there, in a continuous and never suspended traversal of the interval. If it stops anywhere, the motion is instantly abolished. But in melody we have nothing but this, nothing but stops, a stringing together of static tones, and, between tone and tone, *no* connection, *no* transition, *no* filling up of intervals, nothing. It is the exact opposite of motion. And if we attempt actually to connect tone with tone, to create transitions, to fill up the intervals completely, taking real motion as our model, the result is the familiar screeching glissade of the siren, in which melody and music are destroyed.

In music, then, there is nothing that can move, nothing in

relation to which anything can move; there is nothing but tones—and they do not move; indeed, when they actually begin moving, the music vanishes. Under these circumstances, how much sense does it make to speak of music as tonal motion?

For various reasons this question has greatly interested psychologists. We shall briefly summarize the essential points that have been brought forward *against* the argument just outlined.

Certainly tones, if only because they are not things, cannot, like things, occupy positions in space and move from place to place. But to conclude from this that it makes no sense to speak of tonal motion is at least overhasty. Rather, we are here confronted with a phenomenon of motion unique in its kind. Different tones are always also tones of different *pitch.* In fact, among sense perceptions, the distinguishing characteristic of tones is that they differ like two colors, green and blue, *and* like two shades of a single color, light green and dark green; like two tactile sensations, rough and round, *and* like a greater or lesser degree of roughness or roundness. Pitch is a characteristic of such a nature that it both *distinguishes* different tones from one another and at the same time *orders* them in a definite way: tones can be arranged in a series according to pitch as people can be according to height. And this is not an abstract or computed characteristic—as, for example, the vibration numbers of colors are—but a characteristic directly given, perceptible to the senses. Just as normally we do not have to compute and measure in order to determine which of two people standing side by side is the taller and which the shorter, so we do not have to know anything about frequencies and string lengths in order to know at once and unequivocally, to know *by hearing,* which of two tones is the higher and which the lower. Every child to whom the difference is pointed out understands what is meant and can immediately apply the distinction correctly to other cases; whereas the statement that violet is "higher" than blue has little meaning for direct visual experience and does not help one to answer other questions, for example, whether blue is higher or lower than green. If, then, tones are not like things, each of which has its particular place in space, every tone nevertheless has its particular pitch, its particular place in tonal space. Differences in tone are always differences in pitch also, and a succession of different tones is always and definitely also a becoming higher or lower, a rise or fall. The quality of motion in music is saved. What we hear as motion in a succession of tones is the rise and fall of the tones in tonal space.

This attempt to save the situation is ephemeral. The counter-argument is that when we speak of a rise and fall of tones as of a real motion, we have simply become victims of a primitive verbal and emotional suggestion.

We say, one tone is higher than another. Why do we use that word "higher" to express the difference? Is there anything *actually* higher about one of the tones than the other? The head of the note is higher on the staff; the singer's larynx is higher in his throat, and often it even draws his whole upper body up with it in a manner unpleasant to behold; the violinist's hand slides up and down (but the cellist's hand slides down and up, the pianist's from side to side); certain bodily sensations of vibration, on the part of the listener, called forth by different tones are supposedly localized at different heights in the body. But in all this we are merely talking about conventional signs in musical notation, about physiological processes connected with the production and perception of tone—not about tones themselves. Is it possible that, misled by the permanent association of tones with spatial symbols and bodily movements, we have simply carried over the spatial meaning of high and low into our distinguishing of pitches? How else are we to understand the fact that other languages make the same distinction by entirely different words—Greek, for example, by sharp and heavy, English, together with high and low, by sharp and flat? (But in no language would it be said that the fourth floor of a house was sharper than the third, the first flatter than the second.) Let this be clearly understood: it is not intended to deny the presence of the characteristic that permits the arrangement of tones in a series, nor that it is a genuine characteristic of tones, directly perceptible to the ear, not an illusion. What is denied is the *true spatiality* of the characteristic, the assumption that the word *height* in connection with tone is anything more than a metaphor. Suppose that children were taught to distinguish tones not by high and low but by thick and thin, or by light and dark—would anything in these words contradict the phenomena? We are here confronted with a unique characteristic of aural perception, which can only be described metaphorically by words from the realms of the other senses. Talking about the rise and fall of tones is using a metaphor, and nothing more.

The argument over the spatiality of tonal motion fills volumes. It has led to many interesting sidelights, but not to any conclusive result. The negative and affirmative statements remain irreconcilably opposed. Many scholars take a sort of middle position and grant pitch differences a spatiality that, though less than real, is still more than merely metaphorical. The most thorough and conscientious scholar in this field, Karl Stumpf, who was greatly concerned to grant tones real spatiality, thinks that he can say no more than that, in the differentiation of tones by high and low, we have "gradation in an absolute direction."[10] That the gradation is spatial in the direct sense, he could not conclusively show. In general, the closer an investigator is to music, the more

10. Karl Stumpf, *Tonpsychologie.*

he will tend to maintain the genuine spatiality of high and low in tones—very probably on the ground that he sees no other possibility of explaining the compelling impression of motion that music conveys to anyone musical. But with this the discussion has become a circle. We set out by asking upon what the impression of motion conveyed by a melody is based; the answer was, on the rise and fall of tones in tonal space. Now we ask what justifies us in calling a succession of tones of different pitches a rise and fall; and we answer, the impression of motion conveyed by melodies demands it! In any case, the reality of tonal motion in music, of which we were so convinced before, has now become wholly problematic.

VIII. The True Motion of Tones

UNEXPECTEDLY, we find ourselves on treacherous ground. What is the difficulty? A direct experience of motion does not stand up under the test of critical thought; it appears that we must write off our original impression as an illusion. But there is something very familiar about these formulas; we can find them elsewhere—in discussions not of music, of tones and their motion, but of motion in general. How was it that the subtle Zeno of Elea, almost two and a half millennia ago, threw his fellow Greeks, and all subsequent generations, into such lasting perplexity? He summoned the phenomenon of motion before the judgment seat of rational thought and demonstrated that it could not survive there. He succeeded in showing, with unexceptionable logic, that the swift-footed Achilles could never overtake that lumbering creature the tortoise. By this and other no less striking arguments, he succeeded in making all motion thoroughly suspect. He unmasked it as self-contradictory, and cogently concluded that it, and with it our whole world of the senses, permeated as it is by motion, could be nothing but illusion. Can it be that the difficulty which tonal motion presents to our understanding is a universal difficulty, rooted not in the particular conditions of the tonal world but in the nature of the process of motion itself? Have we been brought up against the age-old crux of the problem of motion?

To avoid losing ourselves in the complexities of the problem, we shall lay down a course for our investigation to follow. Two separate questions will confront us. First, are we forced to abandon the idea of a tonal motion if it cannot be interpreted as a rise and fall of tones in tonal space? Can music be real motion if our talk of tones rising and falling is no more than a metaphor? The second question concerns the problem of continuity. If movement is continuous transition from place to place, how can there be movement in music, where all we have are stationary tones strung together without any transition—a perfect example of discontinuity? To begin, we shall try to clarify the kinetic content of three elementary phenomena of music: the melodic interval, the scale, and the harmonic cadence.

INTERVAL

First, a few technicalities. Interval is the term for the distance in pitch between two tones. The standard of measurement is the seven-tone scale. The interval between every two adjacent tones of this scale is called a *second;* from any tone to the next but one is the interval of a *third;* then, correspondingly, we have the *fourth, fifth, sixth, seventh, octave;* then, beyond the octave, the *ninth* and *tenth.* Larger intervals are only exceptionally of practical importance.

In current usage these names are applied not only to the *distance* between two tones but also to the *connection* between them, whether they sound successively as melodic steps or simultaneously in harmony. Second, third, fourth, and so on, then, mean the succession or the simultaneous sounding of two tones separated from each other by the interval named. In our notation these relations appear as simple visual patterns, which impress themselves on the eye:

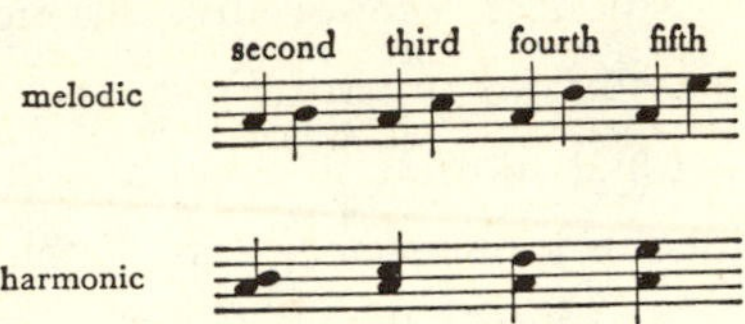

In the following discussion intervals are considered in the melodic sense only, as tonal successions.

A tone, as we said in the first section of this book, is not yet music; it is at best a promise of music. Music actually begins when a second tone has followed the first. The smallest particle of music, then, the musical atom, is not properly the tone but the connection of tone with tone, the interval.

If musical contexts are truly kinetic contexts, if the whole of music is motion, the parts that compose it can in turn only be motions, component motions. Not tones, then, are properly the elements of melodies, but tone-to-tone motions: the interval becomes a *step,* and melodies appear as successions of tone steps rather than of individual tones.

Hearing melodies as motion implies hearing intervals as steps. We have referred to the *ascent* in . It is accomplished in three component phases. First comes , then , then . Only if and as we hear each of these intervals as a step can we hear their succession as motion.

We now ask, What is it, strictly speaking, that makes such an interval, for example, , a step?

The conventional answer is the change of pitch. The succession of tones constitutes a step because it takes us from one place in tonal space to another, from a lower tone to a higher. This is the answer which did not stand up under a more searching analysis of the concept of pitch, with the result that the statement that music is tonal motion appeared untenable.

We question the validity of this answer. Is it correct to say that it is the change of pitches which gives us the experience—or the illusion—of motion? Does this agree with the audible facts? Is it even logical?

Tonal motion is a musical phenomenon. It is only as melodies, as musical contexts, that series of tones are experienced as motions. But pitch is an acoustical characteristic. Have we not established that it is *not* an acoustical characteristic which makes tones elements of musical contexts?

The tune-deaf person hears the differences in the pitches of tones; he does not hear melodies. If the experience of motion were based upon differences in pitch, he could not fail to hear successions of tones as motions, as contexts, as melodies.

Is what we hear in [musical notation] really only the succession of two tones of different pitch, e-a? It is music with which we are dealing—and we have found that in the entire range of music no such thing as "the tone e" or "the tone a" occurs; what occurs is always and only the tone e *with a particular dynamic quality,* the tone a *with a different dynamic quality.* The dynamic quality, not the pitch, makes the tone a musical fact. Hence, whenever we have a succession of two tones, an interval, as a piece of tonal motion—as an element, that is, in a musical context—we must necessarily hear something in it besides different pitches, namely, different dynamic qualities. That we do so in fact, any child who has received elementary musical instruction can confirm for us. One of the first things he is taught is to recognize intervals by ear. He does it not by estimating pitch distances, but by identifying dynamic qualities (in the guise of tone syllables, *do re mi fa sol . . .*). A pupil who, asked what [musical notation] is, correctly answers "A fourth" has not estimated a pitch distance correctly; he has heard something else, namely, $\hat{5}$-$\hat{8}$, *sol-do*! And he knows, he has learned, that *sol-do* is a fourth. This, and none other, is the way in which intervals are heard. The interval actually heard does not extend between two different pitches; it extends between two different dynamic qualities. It is not the difference in pitch but the difference in dynamic quality which generates the interval as a musical phenomenon.

Has this brought us any closer to understanding tonal motion? Our difficulty arose from the fact that we could not establish more than a metaphorical meaning for the difference between high and low in tones. Is there more and truer spatiality in the dynamic qualities of tone than there is in pitches? One would be inclined to assume the contrary, for, with the dynamic qualities of tone, we have moved entirely out of the world of objects.

No, they do not possess spatiality—in any case not in the current sense of the word space—but they have something else, something that pitches do not have: they have *direction*. As we know, musical tones point to one another, attract and are attracted—hearing musical tones is hearing directional forces; is also always an experience of direction. But then, of course, the interval, too, the succession of two tones, always has a perfectly definite content of direction, determined by the mutual directional relation between the two tones. In the case of our melody, for example, is not simply e-a but e $=\hat{5}$-a $=\hat{8}$; a tone that points, in a definite direction, toward another tone, followed by the tone toward which it pointed: a "not there yet" followed by a "there now," an arrival. Then comes , again not simply a-b but a $=\hat{1}$-b $=\hat{2}$; the tone that wants itself, followed by the tone that wants to return to the preceding tone: a "there now" followed by a "no longer there," a departure. In b $=\hat{2}$-e $=\hat{5}$, the tone that wants to return to $\hat{1}$ is followed by a tone that lies in the opposite direction;[1] it is the contrary of a return, a further removal. Finally,  , e = $\hat{5}$-c♯ = $\hat{3}$-a = $\hat{1}$; here, in two stages, what the tone $\hat{5}$ wants actually happens: return home to $\hat{1}$. (It is at the same time the belated fulfillment of what $\hat{2}$ already wanted.) Arrival, departure, further removal, return home; it appears that intervals, if they are heard in accordance with their dynamic meaning—if they are heard musically, that is—cannot be heard otherwise than as phases of a motion, as steps.

Our concern that analysis of the concept pitch might show the direct experience of motion in music to be an illusion thus appears to have been unfounded. The experience of tonal motion has its origin not in differences of pitch but in differences of dynamic quality. The whole argument about the spatial character of pitch differences does not even touch the problem. What we hear in melodies as movement is something basically different from a bridging of distances between higher and lower tones. The talk of "high" and "low" in tones may or may not be metaphorical; the kinetic character of tonal successions in melodies is not affected one way or the other, since only if *something besides pitch differences* comes into play can music be experienced as motion. Far from explaining the phenomenon of tonal motion, the reference to pitch as its basis actually precludes understanding it.

We add the following supplementary observation. The experience of motion in a railway train is different according to whether one sits facing forward or backward. The difference becomes diametric if one first looks from the front of the train in the direction being traveled and then looks back from the rear

---

1. What "opposite direction" means here will be explained on pp. 97-98.

platform of the last car. The one is a driving forward, an anticipation of the coming motion; the other is a recovery of the motion that has been accomplished, a being drawn backward. How does one hear melodies—facing forward or facing backward? There should be no doubt about the answer. We have understood the dynamic qualities of tone as the particular kind of unfulfillment peculiar to each tone, its desire for completion. No musical tone is sufficient unto itself; and as each musical tone points beyond itself, reaches, as it were, a hand to the next, so we too, as these hands reach out, listen tensely and expectantly for each next tone. To be auditively *in* the tone now sounding means, then, always being *ahead of* it too, on the way to the next tone. Inasmuch as we thus continually participate in the transition from tone to tone, we hear each interval as a step, as motion. If the distances between pitches were the decisive thing, we should in each case hear in the interval the distance from the *preceding* tone; for the amount of the interval always becomes evident retrospectively, *after* the step has been taken. In that case, we should be facing backward, not forward, in our hearing of melodies. Our instinctive rejection of this conclusion expresses the fact that we do *not* hear distances between pitches in intervals.

"Pitches, whatever they may be," writes Wolfgang Koehler, "do not deserve the place hitherto accorded to them" [2] What is their proper place? Here we have been primarily concerned (and we shall still be concerned in the next few chapters) to show that they are not, as has been so frequently asserted, the conveyors of the musical phenomena of motion. They are only the external occasion for the appearance of the true conveyors, the dynamic qualities of tone. To put it in Platonic terms: they are not the cause, but that without which the cause could not be cause. We

2. Wolfgang Koehler, "Akustische Untersuchungen."

shall only add that this negative conclusion still leaves unsaid the last word as to their role in music.

SCALE

Motion, as we said before, always implies something that does not move or that moves differently—a frame, a background, against which the motion appears as motion. What is this frame or background in the case of tonal motion?

It is, some have answered, tonal space, the totality of all possible tones arranged according to high and low. Our investigation of intervals has shown that this answer does not accord with the facts. Intervals are steps, not because tones are variously high but because they are variously directed. Successions of tones are motions not in respect to an order based on *pitches* but in respect to an order based on the *forces* in tones. To this order, because it is a dynamic order, we earlier applied the concept *dynamic field.* We now say that the frame, the background, against which such successions of tones appear as motions is not a problematic tonal space; it is a dynamic field. Music is motion in the dynamic field of tones.

To attain a clearer idea of the content of this statement, let us investigate the simplest case of such a motion, motion along the seven-tone scale. We choose the C major scale, ascending. What do I hear when I hear  ? Eight tones, of course, arranged according to pitch, in the familiar succession of half-tone and whole-tone intervals; the eighth tone is the higher octave of the first.

True enough—but it is no answer to our question. Had we asked what eight people hear, each of whom hears a single one of these tones and who then put together their several experiences, perhaps with the aid of an oscilloscope, the answer would have been valid. But our question was, What do *I, one* person, hear, hearing eight tones? We are not inquiring into *eight* experiences but *one* experience, the total experience.

What can be said of the motion that I believe I hear in this case? Am I simply following a random section of a course of motion, as, for example, I follow the motion of an automobile that comes around a corner into my field of vision and shortly thereafter disappears around another corner?

Certainly not. In the random section the motion simply disappears, as if cut off; the motion that I hear in the scale does not simply disappear; *it reaches a goal.* Our ear leaves us in no doubt that the last tone is not simply a last tone but is a goal tone.

We could not hear it as such if we had not heard the immediately preceding phase of the motion as an advance toward a goal. In its latter part, then, the motion follows the general schema: advance toward . . . attainment of a goal.

Does this schema contain the whole of the motion? Again our ear gives us the answer: No. The beginning of the motion, in any case, is not heard as an advance toward . . . but, on the contrary, as a departure from . . . Hence we say that the motion along the scale begins as an "away from" and ends as a "toward" and the attainment of a goal.

Thus far the description agrees with our earlier findings. We know that in the scale of C major we do not hear c-d-e, etc., to b-c; we hear c $=\hat{1}$–d $=\hat{2}$–e $=\hat{3}$, etc., to b $=\hat{7}$–c $=\hat{8}$. Successions of tones are motions in respect to the directions of the tonal forces. The beginning $\hat{1}$-$\hat{2}$ runs counter to the will of the tones; it is a step *against* the forces in operation, "away from . . ." The close $\hat{7}$-$\hat{8}$ does what the tones want to do; it is a step *with* the forces in operation, "toward," a step that leads to the goal. Let us represent these processes in a diagram:

$$\overrightarrow{\hat{1}\quad\hat{2}\quad\hat{3}\quad\hat{4}\quad\hat{5}\quad\hat{6}\quad\hat{7}\quad\hat{8}}$$
$$\longleftarrow \qquad\qquad\qquad \longrightarrow$$

What is the relation between the points of departure and arrival of this motion? Acoustically speaking, the goal is an octave higher than the start. Dynamically speaking, both tones say the same thing, $\hat{1} = \hat{8}$. But this—since the dynamic quality determines the "place" in the dynamic field—means that where we arrive is exactly where we started. The schema must be departure from . . . advance toward . . . arrival at the point of departure as goal.

In the course of this motion, then, the departing becomes a returning. The direction of the motion at the beginning appears changed into its opposite at the end. Is it possible to determine a point at which the reversal takes place, at which "away from" becomes "toward"?

Again our ear is ready to guide us. There is such a point; it is the tone $\hat{5}$. Up to $\hat{5}$, all motion is a departure from . . . ; after $\hat{5}$ it is an advance toward . . . ; $\hat{5}$ is the turning point.

And again what we hear in this case agrees with what we said earlier in respect to individual tones and their dynamic qualities: $\hat{3}$, like $\hat{2}$, points toward $\hat{1}$ (though with a different gesture), $\hat{4}$ points toward $\hat{3}$ and, across $\hat{3}$, toward $\hat{1}$—all motion from $\hat{1}$ to $\hat{5}$ is motion against the forces in operation, is an "away from $\hat{1}$." With the attainment of $\hat{5}$, however, the view opens in the other direction, in the direction of $\hat{8}$. Tone $\hat{5}$ itself points in both directions—hence the "knife-edge balance" characteristic of this tone. Beyond $\hat{5}$ we are already on the way to $\hat{8}$. The tone $\hat{6}$ still plays a double role, since it can be heard both as a state in the succession of $\hat{5}$-$\hat{6}$-$\hat{7}$-$\hat{8}$ and as bound to and pointing toward its comparatively stable adjacent tone $\hat{5}$; the particular circumstances determine whether the meaning "away from $\hat{5}$" or the meaning "toward $\hat{8}$" preponderates in the step $\hat{5}$-$\hat{6}$. Tone $\hat{7}$, on the other hand, is unmistakably and wholly under the spell of $\hat{8}$.

Let us now complete our diagram in accordance with these findings:

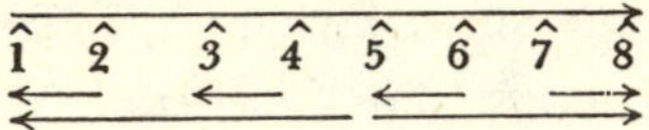

This diagram is inadequate in an essential point. It does not bring out the "arrival at the point of departure as goal" at all, nor "$\hat{5}$ as the turning point" with sufficient clarity. If "away from," "reversal," "back to" are to be made apparent in our representation, the tones must not appear arranged side by side along a straight line. Rather, we must dispose them in a curve, more or less as follows:

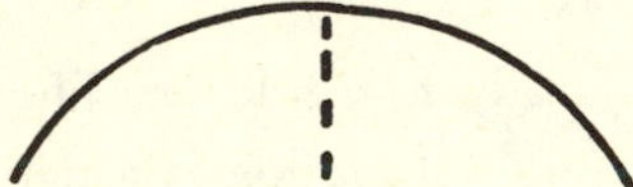

If we also take into consideration the various degrees of stability and instability that we have observed in the individual tones, we get a picture something like this:

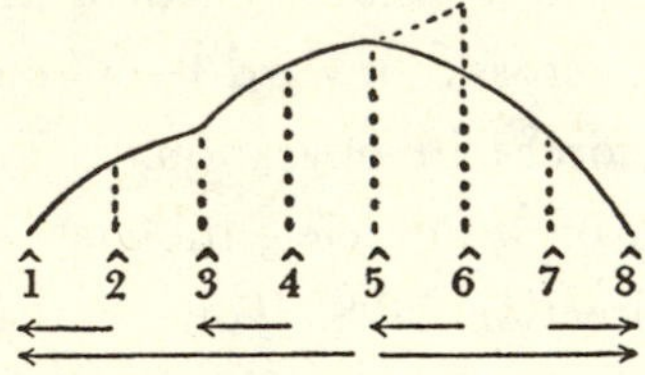

With this curve—which we must imagine repeated on either side as many times as the scale is repeated in higher and lower octaves—the stage is set, so to speak, on which the tonal motions of our music run their courses. It gives us a picture of the organization of the dynamic field as it reveals itself when the scale is traversed. Motion in the dynamic field of tones is essentially motion in terms of this curve. We make the reservation "essentially" because of course tones are not *bound* to this curve; they *can* simply move back and forth along this curve—and many melodies do just that for long stretches—but they are not *obliged* to do so. Melodic motion is *free* motion; the curve, however, is the *norm* that serves this freedom as a standard, gives it meaning, and thus makes it possible at all.

The study of melodies is the study of the freedom, the inexhaustible, miraculous freedom of their motion measured by this norm. Here we can only give a superficial indication of what is involved. The "ascent" at the beginning of the *Marseillaise* has that sweep because $\hat{1}$-$\hat{2}$ is not continued by a normal $\hat{2}$-$\hat{3}$ but by a $\hat{2}$-$\hat{5}$, which, skipping the remaining steps of the rising curve, suddenly brings us to its peak. This is the first and obvious freedom of tones—freedom from following the scale step by step. But they have other and very different freedoms. Of the tones as they succeed one another in the scale we may truly say that each of them exists beside all the others as what it is, with equal rights. Tone $\hat{2}$ says "$\hat{2}$!" with the same weight as $\hat{1}$ says "$\hat{1}$!" In music, this quality of equal weight in the individual tones of a melody occurs almost exclusively in folk songs; in art music the opposite is the rule—there are far-reaching differences in weight. In art music we do not simply have one tone following another of equal rank, one step following another of equal rank; we find that stronger tones have subordinated weaker tones to themselves. The motion does not proceed, as it were, in a straight line but as if in flourishes and circuits, with the weaker tones playing around and connecting the stronger tones. Hearing such melodies is not just a simple hearing of motion; it is a stratified hearing, which groups and classifies: the ear understands as it follows; distinguishes between the principal and the subordinate elements of the motion. If the theme of a Bach fugue, for example, begins thus

, we do not hear seven tones of equal rank, $\hat{8}$-$\hat{7}$-$\hat{8}$-$\hat{2}$-$\hat{1}$-$\hat{2}$-$\hat{5}$; we hear something like  , a principal movement $\hat{1}$-$\hat{2}$-$\hat{5}$, and minor movements in which $\hat{1}$ and $\hat{2}$, each for itself, exercises its vitality, as it were, for a moment in a little private away-from-and-back-to. The second tone of the second group,  , is thus not $\hat{1}$ but "tone next below $\hat{2}$"; we hear in it not "having arrived" but "being away," that is, from $\hat{2}$. Or take the conventional ornament of the so-called "turn," e.g.,  . Here the five small notes are not $\hat{7}$-$\hat{8}$-$\hat{7}$-$\hat{6}$-$\hat{7}$ but $\hat{7}$, next tone above $\hat{7}$, next tone below $\hat{7}$. And as such it is infallibly heard, not as a succession of tones of equal value, but as motion around a principal tone, as subordinate motion within the principal motion. The second tone of the group, , is not $\hat{8}$, goal, at all; on the contrary, in it we are on the way to a tone, $\hat{7}$, which is itself on the way to a goal.

This sounds complicated when we read it. But when we hear it, there is no problem at all. The tones never leave the listener in any doubt as to how they are meant. And this is not true only of the simple cases that we have cited, cases which go beyond the bare norm by only a single step. Complex organization of the kinetic structure by no means always results in increasing difficulty of aural comprehension. Melodies that enchant by their inexpressible simplicity—melodies of Mozart, Schubert, Verdi—are often the very ones that, upon a more searching examination, disclose a marvelously intricate kinetic structure as the token of their artistic rank and their high origin.

Let us return to our curve. The "rise and fall of tones in tonal space" may or may not be more than a metaphor. But now our curve brings us the picture of a genuine, actual rise and fall, a rise and fall not in tonal space but in the tonal dynamic field, in relation to a given audible center of force. Tones on the curve rise as a weight rises in an upward-moving hand, and fall as a stone falls. The seemingly metaphorical rise and fall and the real rise and fall, the phenomenon in tonal space and the phenomenon in the dynamic field, cut across one another in a peculiar way. In relation to tonal space, motion from left to right in our diagram is a constant increase in elevation, an "up"; in relation to the dynamic field, in terms of the curve it is an up *and* down. The reverse motion, which, in relation to tonal space, is a constant "down," is again an up *and* down in the dynamic field. This situation gives rise to paradoxical manifestations.

Let us examine the phenomenon more closely. If we proceed from left to right, the so-called rise in tonal space is at first also a rise along the curve. But after a time, that is, from $\hat{5}$ on, the further rise in tonal space becomes a fall along the curve; the acoustical "up" becomes a musical down. The reverse procedure at first (until $\hat{5}$, that is) exhibits opposition between the acoustical "down" and the musical up; then, in the second half, there is parallelism between the metaphorical and the actual case. Of both procedures, then, it holds that as the scale is traversed the distance in pitch from the point of departure becomes increasingly great, so that we get farther and farther away from the starting point. But the motion in terms of the tonal forces each time represents an "away from," a departing, only in its first half; in its second half it is a "toward," an approaching. Rectilinear departure in tonal space turns into a reversal of direction in the dynamic field. If we continue the movement, through higher or lower octaves, the same thing repeats itself as far as tonal space extends. In tonal space we shall always get farther and farther from the point of departure, can always increase the distance; in the dynamic field we must always reverse direction. Here there is no "away from . . ." beyond $\hat{5}$; with $\hat{5}$, so to speak, the greatest possible distance from $\hat{1}$ is reached; after $\hat{5}$ it is an approach again. Approach to what? The tone toward which we look in the descending segment of the curve is always the same tone we left behind us in its ascending segment. We go toward a tone by going away from it. The distance in pitch from the point of departure increases with every step, but with the eighth tone we are again at the point of departure. Leaving has become returning; start has become goal.

This is the phenomenon that has fittingly been called "the miracle of the octave"; Ernst Kurth characterizes it as "one of the greatest riddles . . . the beginning of irrationality in music, a thing unparalleled in all the rest of the phenomenal world." Let us consider what, precisely, is unique and miraculous in it.

If I light a candle in a dark room, the room becomes light; if I light a second, it becomes lighter. If I load an infantryman with a forty-pound pack, he will walk heavily; if I load him with sixty pounds, he will walk still more heavily. What should we say if lighting the second candle made the room dark again, if imposing the greater weight took the burden from the bearer's shoulders?

If I have myself shot from the earth to the moon in a habitable projectile, the journey begins as an ascent, an "away from"; it is pursued counter to the direction of gravity. As we near the moon, the "away from" becomes a "toward," the ascent a descent: motion and gravity now point in the same direction. Here, then, with increasing distance from the starting point, a departure becomes, dynamically speaking, an approach. But the point that we thus approach and reach as our goal is not the starting point; it is the moon, not the earth. The going away becomes *an arrival, not a return.*

As an example of a motion in space that could be likened to the motion of tones along the scale, ascent in a spiral is often cited, because it keeps bringing us back to a point that is *exactly above* the point of departure. But this image is appropriate only to the *acoustical* phenomena, to the constant rise in pitch and the return of the same tones from octave to octave; it shows nothing at all of the dynamic, the musical processes. That motion along the scale is not a constant rise in relation to pitch but a rise *and* fall in relation to tonal forces, a departure from . . . and approach to . . . ; that the eighth tone is not simply the higher repetition of the first but the attained goal, an event that strikingly stands out in the whole process and is marked as such for the listener by the characteristic sensation of something clicking—none of this appears in the spiral image.

If I walk out of the front door of my house and keep going on straight ahead in the same direction, I shall eventually re-enter my house by the back door. This is so because the earth is spherical, and if we go straight ahead on a sphere, we actually go around it. Is not this the spatial counterpart of motion along the scale? No, because in space we are not *obliged* to proceed in a circle; but in the tonal field of force—and only there does tonal motion occur—*all* paths always lead back to their point of departure. From the earth, even though at present only in thought, we can set out into the cosmos, and go on and on, to the point of no return. In tonal space we can do nothing of the sort, either actually or in thought. We cannot, precisely because no tone appears only once, but each tone is repeated with every octave; because the center of the dynamic field is not present merely in one place but is reproduced with every new octave, to the limits of tonal space. Going away from the center of force, we immediately find ourselves going toward it, toward its repetition at the next octave. It has anticipated the issue, it is always ahead of the motion; always we have before us what we have left behind us. As infallibly as in winter we go toward that from which we have gone, toward summer; as infallibly as, in our breathing, every expiration is a departure from a previous inspiration and at the same time an approach to the next inspiration—just so infallibly does all tonal motion always return to its beginning. The primordial symbol of motion, the straight, pointing arrow, here takes the form of a wave. Thus the phenomenon of the octave reveals the structure of the world of tone: a rhythmical structure, we might call it, which stamps the form of back-and-forth, with-and-against, hither-and-thither, up-and-down, on all tonal motion—the form of the wave, then, of the pulse, of respiration. Formulations that in the world of space are paradox, indeed nonsense—wherever we go, we return; start and goal are one and the same; all paths travel back to their own beginnings—are in the world of tone, simple statements of fact.

HARMONIC CADENCE

Our investigation of the elementary musical phenomena of interval and scale has shown the connection between tonal motion and tonal forces. Tones in succession constitute movement on the basis of their dynamic qualities and against the background of the dynamic field. The most revealing manifestation of tonal motion, however, is not found in melodic processes; it is found in harmony, in the motion of chords.

In an earlier context we mentioned the epochal discovery that European musicians made at the beginning of our millennium and that started Western music on its unique course. It was the discovery that not only the succession but also the conjunction of tones could yield music; that tones could not only follow one another but could also sound together. The decisive force that brought about this development was at first not concerned with these tonal conjunctions as such at all. Music was preoccupied with, as it were, extending itself from a line to a surface, from a thread to a woven fabric—with ceasing to be a *single* stream of melody and becoming a *combination* of several streams of melody pursuing their courses at the same time, not ∽∽ but [≋.

During this transition from one voice to several voices, from monophony to polyphony, the peculiar acoustico-psychological phenomenon that we today call "tonal coalescence" came to light. In general our senses react to a number of simultaneous stimuli by a number of simultaneous sensations. Thus the eye is able to make a clear separation between several simultaneously appearing colors; they are present to consciousness as so many different color sensations. On the other hand, several tones sounding in conjunction produce one sound sensation; the ear is incapable of making a clear separation between them, they flow together, coalesce into a complex sound. The usual comparison with chemical transformation is not entirely appropriate, because in chemical transformation the separate elements vanish, so far as perception goes, without a trace, whereas a trained ear can still hear the separate tones in the conjoint that they produce. Yet the product of the coalescence remains so in the foreground, so greatly absorbs the individuality of the separate tones, that we are completely justified in referring to the conjoint as *one* sensation.

In polyphonic music, then, as the several melodic lines pursue their courses together, this sort of coalescence, or short-circuiting, between tones sounding simultaneously must continually and automatically be produced:

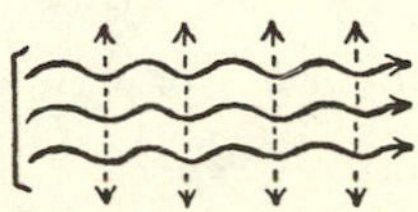

In themselves, these "vertical" relations have nothing to do with the "horizontal" intentions of melodies; they can even become a disturbing influence. It turns out that the process of coalescence does not always take place without friction and produce a smooth conjoint; it is often accomplished over the heads of the tones, so to speak, audibly against their will; the tones seem to resist it. The result is a harsh sound filled with inner frictions and tensions, a *dissonance,* which stands in sharp contrast to the smooth frictionless sound of the *consonance.* The consonance is unobtrusive, transparent; the ear can listen through it unimpeded to what is going on horizontally. The dissonance forces itself on the ear almost tyrannically and draws all attention to itself, that is, to what is going on vertically, and away from what is going on horizontally. Hence the first commandment of polyphonic music, which was above all concerned with melodic-horizontal contexts, was to seek consonance as good and to avoid dissonance as evil, or at least to admit it only with extreme caution and only to the end that consonance should be revealed all the more gloriously by contrast.

With all this the history of harmony has not yet begun. So far tonal conjunctions have appeared only as the unavoidable by-products of polyphony, by-products whose best virtue was unobtrusiveness. Half a millennium passed before music discovered the intrinsic value, the intrinsic life, of these vertical relations. Then threads unique in character began to spin themselves between tonal conjunctions as such. Of themselves, and out of their own energy, conjoint attached itself to conjoint; a completely new phenomenon of motion appeared: a motion based not on tones, like melody, but on the products of tonal coalescence, and the elementary conveyor of which is not the individual tone but the individual conjunction of tones, the chord.

The chord, the conjunction become conscious of itself, is, then, not simply the sum of the individual tones as they sound together; it is something above and beyond that sum, something new as compared to the individual tones, something that radiates from their union, that hovers about them like an aura—inconceivable so long as only individual tones were known, indescribable in words. This new thing in the universe of tone has been referred to as a third dimension, added, as a sort of tonal depth, to the linearity of monophonic music and the plane juxtaposition of polyphony. We have already mentioned the comparison with chemistry; yet in chemistry it is always a case of substances becoming another substance, whereas the chord is simply *not* another tone. If we insist on a chemical simile, we should rather think of the heat set free by chemical transformations, of fire, the brightness of fire; of what, speaking unscientifically, one could refer to as the immaterial radiations that accompany transformation of material substances. If we were obliged to call tone immaterial, the chord is immaterial to the second power. A tone can still always be represented by a symbol; a note, a syllable, a numeral, can be brought into comprehensible relation to a particular physical process, a vibration of the air; it can be produced by depressing a key or plucking a string, it can be sung. But a chord can, strictly speaking, be neither played nor sung nor written. We can only play and sing and write all the individual tones that go to compose it; and the physical process that corresponds to it is again only a particular vibration of the air, the result of the mixing of the individual vibrations—whereas the chord is precisely not a mixture, a mixed tone, a different tone, but something basically different from individual tone. Its very essence, then, its uniqueness, that which transcends the sum, remains inaccessible to all these approaches. Here even the last frail relations still observable between the individual tone and the world of individual things are severed.

The basic chord, the only consonant chord, the holy chord

of our music, is the *triad,* the conjoint of three tones arranged in a definite pitch pattern: 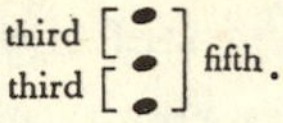 third third [• • •] fifth. In this pattern the interval between the lowest and the highest tone, the fifth, acts as the firm frame, while the middle tone has a choice of two positions. For example, if c and g are taken as the lowest and highest tone, the middle tone can be either e or e flat. As a result we get two kinds of triads, major and minor. (This freedom of the middle tone has its origin in the different position of the tone $\hat{3}$ in the major and minor scale pattern: one half tone above $\hat{2}$ in minor, one whole tone above it in major. There is a corresponding difference in the two thirds of the triad pattern; one of them is always a *major* and the other a *minor third.*)

The most important characteristic of the triad, however, is its inner organization. Its component tones are not merely arranged in a definite pitch pattern; they are dynamically related to one another. If we make them stand out one after the other in the sound of the chord, perhaps by stressing them individually, we encounter a familiar phenomenon: the tones are dynamically active, and in such a way that two of them point to the third as the center and source of the acting forces. This tone, the *root* of the chord, has, then, in the conjoint, the function of a tone $\hat{1}$, while in the other tones we immediately recognize the dynamic qualities of $\hat{3}$ and $\hat{5}$. Thus, within the coalescence, the triad represents a definite dynamic organization, a miniature gravitational system, with the root as sun and the two other tones as planets. To hear a triad means to hear its root as ruler of the conjoint—or better, to hear *the* chord in which a tone presents itself as ruler among simultaneously sounding tones. In this sense the root can be referred to as the *representative* of the triad.

That the triad is not only an acoustico-psychological but

also a dynamic phenomenon has an important consequence for music. Let us look, for example, at the E major triad, . This chord is not only the coalescence of the three tones E, G♯, and B; it also combines the three dynamic qualities $\hat{1}$, $\hat{3}$, and $\hat{5}$. But the dynamic quality of a tone is always the same, no matter in what part of tonal space, no matter in what octave, the tone sounds. If e is $\hat{1}$, then *all* e's in tonal space are $\hat{1}$. If g♯ is $\hat{3}$, then *all* g♯'s are $\hat{3}$; if b is $\hat{5}$, then *all* b's are $\hat{5}$. Hence the triad remains the same no matter how the tones that compose it may be distributed in tonal space. The E major triad is  , but so is or  . A change such as  is no change in the perspective of harmony. All these are merely various acoustical possibilities of making one and the same harmonic-dynamic statement. This independence of the chord from the actual position of its individual tones in tonal space will give us the key to understanding chordal motion.

As a tone in itself is not yet melody, so a chord in itself is not yet harmony, musical harmony. Music is motion—tonal motion as melody, chordal motion as harmony. To grasp the musical meaning of tones, we had to hear them as elements in a melodic context; to grasp the musical meaning of chords, we must hear them as elements in a harmonic context. We can limit ourselves to triads. Our music, of course, has other chords; but the elementary fact of harmonic motion can be fully demonstrated on the basis of triads.

We will examine the simplest example in order to see what takes place. If we hear the E major triad as an isolated phenomenon, as an individual chord, we hear nothing but smooth coalescence, complete equilibrium. The chord is at rest, self-contained, balanced around its center of gravity; it could remain so forever, nothing else need ever occur. Then we hear the same triad played, perhaps, in an accompaniment to the *Marseillaise:*

The rest, the equilibrium, have vanished. The same chord that, just before, had seemed to be so firmly secured in itself is now, as it were, shaken to its foundations, subjected to a strong pressure; what sounds from it is tension, an urgent demand that something happen: the perfect aural image of disturbed equilibrium. Any lingering in it is difficult to imagine. Whence the radical reversal?

The phenomenon is analogous to what we observed in single tones when they became elements in a melodic context: a becoming active, the manifestation of a definite dynamic state, which expresses itself as a will; the chord points beyond itself, appears to be attracted by something. The essential difference lies in the fact that the single tone, considered by itself, exhibited no dynamic quality, whereas the chord, as we found, is in itself a dynamic phenomenon, a result of an action of forces. It appears, then, that the chord as a whole, the miniature closed dynamic system, is subjected, as soon as it becomes an element in a musical sequence, to an additional dynamic influence coming, as it were, from without; is drawn into a new dynamic context. How can this take place?

Our first thought is to make tone $\hat{2}$ in the melody, which sounds at the same time as the chord, responsible for the dynamic state of the sound—as if the unstable state of the tone in the melody radiated over the chord in the accompaniment. There is some truth in this; but it does not explain the phenomenon, because the phenomenon is exactly the same if we omit the melody and play only the chords of the accompaniment.

The root of the E major triad is the tone e. Within the chord, from the "vertical" point of view, this tone acts as a center of gravity, as a $\hat{1}$. But the chord does not occur in a vacuum or in a laboratory but in a musical context, hence in the realm of a particular seven-tone system. This at once raises the question, What is the tone e in this seven-tone system? The tonality of our brief example is A major; we are in a dynamic field whose center is the tone a. So here the root of the E major triad is not $\hat{1}$ but $\hat{5}$—and it is *this fact that its root is* $\hat{5}$ which so strongly affects the chord, which sounds so clearly from it. The dynamic state of the chord, its will, its pointing, is that of its root, a tone $\hat{5}$, transferred to the dimension of harmony.

Let us compare to it the other chord that, in our example, precedes and follows the E major triad,  ; it is the A major triad. Here nothing of disturbed equilibrium is audible; a stable sound rests on a firm base. But we hear something else too: our ear leaves us in no doubt of the fact that this is the sound to whose appearance the will of the other was directed and in which the other can bring its disturbed equilibrium to rest. Between the two sounds play the familiar relations of indicating and being indicated, of attracting and being attracted. And all this is as it is because the root of the A major triad, the tone a, is the dynamic center, is tone $\hat{1}$, not only within the chord but also in the context of the seven-tone system here prevailing.

Generalizing, we may say that on the one hand, a chord is organized *around* its center of gravity; on the other, *through* its root, and in so far as this root, as an element in a musical context, belongs to a particular seven-tone system, the chord is rendered susceptible to the influence of forces acting from the center of the seven-tone system. Because in a musical context every root is also an event in the dynamic field of a seven-tone system, every chord, in its particular language, also expresses the dynamic state that corresponds to the place of its root in the field. Chords as events in such a field are called *harmonic degrees.* The chords of the I, II, III, etc., degree (Roman numerals are employed) have, respectively, a tone $\hat{1}$, $\hat{2}$, $\hat{3}$, etc., as root. It is not properly with chords and successions of chords that we have to deal in music, but with harmonic degrees and successions of harmonic degrees. And, like the succession of individual tones, the succession of harmonic degrees becomes *motion* solely upon the basis of the differences in dynamic qualities that sound from the various chords. In the case of our example, it is only because the chords are not simply A major triad, E major triad, A major triad, but I chord, V chord, I chord, that we hear more in their succession than merely one sound following another. I-V says "away from . . . ," it is a step; V-I says "toward . . . ," a step in the opposite direction; the whole, I-V-I, says "away from . . . and back to . . . ," a succession of steps, a course of motion such as we have also found in melodic motion. The "vertical" phenomena have of themselves become elements of a "horizontal" context.

Let us recall with what purpose we entered upon this entire excursion into the realm of harmony. We expected to obtain additional information concerning the nature of musical motion. We are now in a position to understand this information correctly.

We will put the following question: What is the mutual relation between chordal motion and change of pitch, the rise and fall of tones in tonal space? In the case of melodic motion, the question was meaningful. We were able to show that ascent and descent in tonal space, and on the curve that represents the situation in the tonal dynamic field, can be either in the same direction or in opposite directions. The step $\hat{7}$-$\hat{8}$, for example, an ascent from the point of view of tonal space, is a descent from the point of view of the curve. Here, then, there is still a demonstrable relation between tonal motion and change of pitch. But what is the situation in harmony? To put the question concretely: Does the step V-I, for example, correspond to an ascent or a descent in tonal space? We grasp the nature of harmonic motion when we see that this question is *pointless.*

What are the conveyors of harmonic motion? Not simply tones, but coalescence products of tones, chords—an aura, we said, something that hovers about tones, that radiates from their union. Just as the chord is not a sum of tones, so chordal motion is not a sum of motions of individual tones. We cannot find it even in the succession of roots: the root *represents* the chord, the succession of roots represents the succession of chords—but that is all. If a step from root to root were a piece of genuine tonal motion, a real step from one tone to another, we could meaningfully ask if V-I is directed upward or downward. Is the step from the root of the V chord to the root of the I chord—in our example it was the step from the root e to the root a—an ascending fourth, 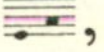 , or a descending fifth, ? Can the question be asked? A root, as we have found, is not bound to a particular locus in tonal space; it is wherever the same tone is repeated from octave to octave throughout the extent of tonal space. The root of the E major triad is not this e  or this  . It is no particular e at all; it is all the e's in tonal space. The same is true of the root a of the A major triad. So the step from the root e to the root a is, if you like, a step from all the e's in tonal space to all the a's in tonal space—from what is common to all the e's to what is common to all the a's. Is this step in tonal space directed upward or downward? Which is higher, all e's or all a's? We see that the question has no meaning. As we know, the other tones of a chord are no more bound to a particular locus in tonal space than is its root; they too are wherever the same tone is repeated from octave to octave. Thus every chord in a sense extends over the whole of tonal space; no chord can be "higher" or "lower" than another. The chord is, so to speak, a sound-state of all tonal space. Chordal steps lead from one sound-state of all tonal space to another sound-state of all tonal space. Such steps are no more directed upward than downward in tonal space; they seem steps of tonal space rather than *in* tonal space.

The chordal step V-I is called the *cadence,* the "fall." It is so called in all languages. Does this not, after all, contain an explicit statement of its direction—specifically, that it is a step directed downward? We understand to what this statement refers: to the dynamic meaning of the chordal succession, the "going to . . . ," the reaching the goal, the arrival at the center of gravity. But this dynamic meaning remains exactly the same, whether the individual tones actually move downward, as here,

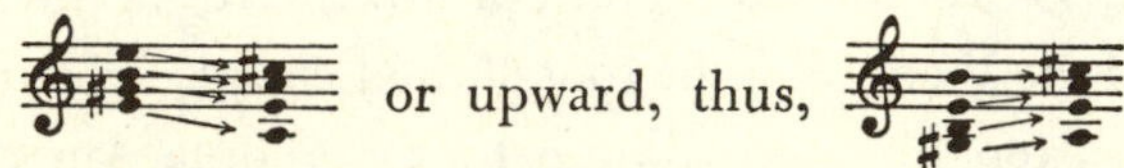

Obviously we are here dealing with an event in which the plane of pitches has been left behind. It is meaningless to think of chordal motion in terms of a rise and fall of tones in tonal space.

Thus, to a certain extent, harmonic motion represents the most extreme and purest case of musical motion. As, in the chord, the last feeble threads that still connected the world of tones with the world of things are severed—the external correlation of individual tone and individual symbol, of musical and acoustical phenomenon—so the motion of chords, a motion from sound-state to sound-state, is no longer to be understood even metaphorically after the manner of a motion of things, of things changing place in space. It represents the pattern case of a nonspatial and nonmaterial motion. And it does not have to pay for this loss of materiality by a loss in definiteness and effective power. On the contrary, in definiteness of intent, in force of tension, one might almost say in physical impact, certain effects of harmonic cadence have no equal in all the rest of music. Music is of such a nature that it attains the maximum in precision and concentration of its dynamic charge at the farthest remove from the world of things.

"Real motion is rather the transfer of a state than of a thing." [3] For the truth of this statement, music throws the whole weight of its evidence in the scale.

To meet possible objections, we repeat: with all this, the last word on the subject of high and low, up and down, in tonal space is not yet said. If we were obliged to deny that pitch differences deserved the role which is generally accorded them in producing the experience of musical motion, this is not to say that they cannot have other musical functions. The praying voice in Bach's cantata *Gottes Zeit* says:

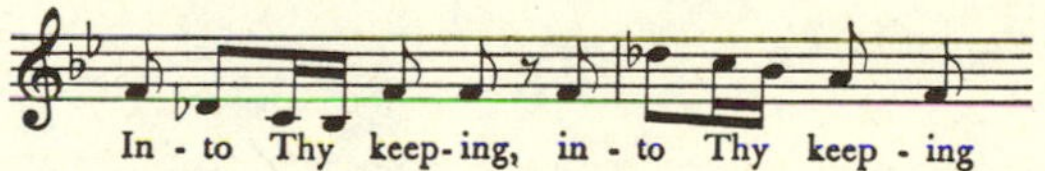
In - to Thy keep-ing, in - to Thy keep - ing

Who would deny that the difference between $\hat{5}$-$\hat{3}$ downward and $\hat{5}$-$\hat{3}$ upward, between and , means something here? Is there a different meaning in the bowing and raising of the head in prayer? To be sure, it is not a matter of above and below in a spatial sense, of a difference in spatial directions, but rather of a difference between planes of existence: "where I am"—"where

3. Bergson, *Matière et mémoire.*

God is." If it is nothing spatial, nor even anything resembling space, which we call "height" in tones, feel as height, and, in the passage from lower to higher tones, as motion upward, it could still signify something entirely different, something like "nearer to God"—and where God is, is "above."

IX. The Continuity of Tonal Motion

THE FIRST STAGE of the road that we hope will lead us to clarifying the concept of musical motion lies behind us. We have saved tonal motion from being identified with "up" and "down" in tonal space and from being rejected when it appeared that these terms could not be interpreted literally. We are now at the beginning of the second stage, in which a more formidable obstacle remains to be overcome: the problem of the continuity of tonal motion.

We use the term continuous in reference to a process that leads from one state to another in an uninterrupted transition. In contrast, the discontinuous process takes place in jumps; we can find gaps in it. The rise and fall of temperature is a continuous process; in the transition from one degree of heat to another all the intervening degrees of heat are traversed. The transition can be gradual and even, or sudden and uneven; but in no case will it exhibit gaps. We have an example of discontinuity in the process of biological mutation, the appearance of new species or subspecies; this takes place suddenly, at one jump, not as the result of a development that passes through all the intervening stages. The series of all possible tones is continuous—the siren passes through it; the series of overtones is discontinuous.

It is an old article of belief that nature makes no jumps. The principal support of this belief was the conviction that all natural phenomena could be referred back to motions of bodies. For motion, a thing changing place, is obviously a continuous process. One does not get from one place to another without passing through all the intervening places; the motion traverses the space between one place and the other in an uninterrupted transition. The path it follows, the track it leaves behind in space, is an unbroken line—hence the line is the graphic symbol of motion. If a thing changes place without having traversed the interval between its former and latter place uninterruptedly, we have not motion but a miracle.

Not only will a thing in motion from one place to another skip none of the intervening places; it will also halt in none of them. If it did so, the motion would at once be at an end; its contrary, rest, would have appeared. Motion, then, has no gaps and no halts. These are the distinguishing characteristics of its continuity; they belong to it as weight to mass, luminosity to light. Motion without continuity is inconceivable.

How does the case stand with tonal motion?

Let us go back to the melody of our first example: , etc. What do we hear—a progress advancing in uninterrupted continuity or an alternation of skips and halts, a discontinuous progress? There can be no doubt about the answer: we could not hear the melody as motion if we did not hear it as continuous. Casting about for a graphic symbol for our experience, we will instinctively draw a curve, thus perhaps 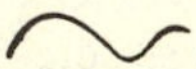 , an unbroken line in any case, such as one would use anywhere to picture a continuous process. Now, does such a line faithfully render what actually occurs in tonal motion?

We know that it does not. Let us look at what takes place in the melody just cited. The tone f sharp sounds: so long as it continues, it does not move from its place, does not change its pitch; it is directly succeeded by the tone g, which, as long as it sounds, shows as little alteration as the preceding tone; in the same manner the tone A follows; and so on. There is no question of any transitions, whether gradual or sudden; tone stands beside tone without connection. A faithful graphic representation of what takes place would have to look like this (line length signifies duration of the individual tone):

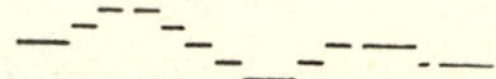

Where is the continuously progressing line, the symbol of continuity of motion? Stasis-gap-stasis-gap; our graph is the perfect image of discontinuity. One is at a loss to understand how *this* can ever be heard as a continuous process.

Similar contradictions between acoustical data and musical experiences, which we encountered earlier, were resolved when it appeared that other than acoustical processes, namely, dynamic processes, were the basis of musical experiences. But, this time, such an interpretation does not help, because the dynamic qualities change, so to speak, in step with the tones, in sudden jumps and without transition. So that, whether our question is directed to pitches or to dynamic qualities, the result is the same: it appears that we absurdly apply the term motion to a collection of stases and gaps.

We are, however, familiar with one case in which this very absurdity takes place, in which stases and gaps compose motion: the case of the moving picture. The individual picture in the film shows nothing but stasis. It is a cross section of a train of motion, and between section and section, close together as they may be, there is a gap in the train. But if the film is unrolled before us at the proper rate of speed, the eye supplies the missing transitions, the gaps are filled, the discontinuous series of static pictures becomes a continuous train of motion. Certainly, the continuity that thus appears is not given in the thing itself, it is simply imagined, is an illusion; the motion we see is an illusory motion. Nevertheless, the illusion is not a matter of choice; it is inescapable, it obeys a law, under certain conditions it necessarily occurs. Is not this exactly the same thing that occurs in our melody: the individual tones that do not move from their places, the gaps between tone and tone, and the impression of motion that necessarily follows when the tones pass before us at the correct rate of speed—discontinuity that produces an illusion of continuity? In the last analysis, then, is tonal motion to be interpreted as an illusion after all?

The parallel holds only superficially. The aim and the accomplishment of the film consist in creating an illusion of gaps being filled. The creation of the illusion depends upon the extent of the gaps between the pictures and upon the tempo of their succession; if the gaps are too great, or if the tempo is too slow, the illusion of motion becomes poorer and finally collapses completely, the deception becomes visible. Can one say the like of melody? Does melody perhaps achieve the impression of motion by creating an *illusion* of gradual transitions between tone and tone, of the gaps between pitches being filled? Do we imagine that we hear such transitions, such sliding connections between tone and tone, when we hear melodic motion? All this is out of the question. Does increasing the intervals between pitches, or slowing down the tempo, perhaps influence the perception of motion? Then the illusion must be better, more complete, in the case of our Beethoven melody, with its flowing connection of tones that lie close together, than, for example, in the following fugue theme by Bach,  , in which there are great gaps between tones and the tempo is exceedingly slow. Nobody would make such an assumption. Experience teaches that the perception of musical motion is (within reasonable limits) independent of the size of the intervals and the tempo. On the other hand, an actual filling of the gaps between tone and tone, a sirenlike glissading up and down, does not produce the most perfect musical motion but no musical experience at all; it produces mere noise.

The result is even more convincing if, instead of pitches, we consider dynamic qualities. Here there can be no question of filling gaps, of continuous transitions, either actually or as illusion. Is a connecting transition conceivable from the state of attraction to that of being attracted? From the pointing gesture peculiar to the tone $\hat{2}$ to that peculiar to the tone $\hat{3}$? The differences between tonal dynamic qualities are not of the nature of gaps that can be filled by transitions. Melodic and cinematographic motion are incomparable, not only because melody neither achieves nor seeks to produce an illusion of continuous transitions but because among dynamic qualities, upon which the experience of musical motion is based, continuity as uninterrupted transition from one state to another is not even thinkable.

The difference between tonal motion and illusory motion is carried to the extreme in an interesting musical phenomenon: the *rest.* We find rests in music not only at caesuras, not only where a longer or shorter context comes to an end and where, as a result, rests actually mean "interruption"; they also appear within continuous contexts, where they function not as punctuation but as real elements in the context, just like tones themselves. Such a rest does not interrupt the continuing motion of the melody; the motion goes on through it: a void, a nothing, becomes the conveyor of motion. If, for example, the theme of another of Bach's fugues begins  , the rest does not separate the first two tones from the third (anyone who plays it thus  talks nonsense with tones); instead, one continuous course of motion runs through tones and rest,  . So little is heard motion an illusion, a conjuring up of something where nothing is, that the frank recognition of the fact "nothing" does not cause the slightest break in the experience of motion.

The last way of escape from the dilemma—and one which is often chosen—we have already closed. It is the association and projection theory. For the followers of this theory there is no difficulty; like the dynamic qualities of tone, they hold, the experiences of motion based upon them are the "subjective" product of the listener, "produced representations," inner events released by outer events and projected back into them. To be sure, these authors write of melodies ascending, hovering, descending; but they never fail to tell us that it is only we, the listeners, who ascend, hover, descend, and not the tones. What we call motion here, they say, is a purely psychological phenomenon, and any contradiction to the data of the external world need trouble us as little as that between our dreams of flying and the conditions for flight that we encounter in our waking state.

We need not repeat the arguments against these theories. The attempt to relegate musical phenomena to the subjective realm must come to grief before the facts of tonal motion as it does before the facts of the dynamic qualities of tone.

(This rejection does not refer to theories like that of the psychologist Melchior Palágyi, according to which "perception of motion is bound up with living participation in the motion; without this there could be no perception of a motion." [1] There is an immense difference between saying that in hearing music we inwardly enact the motion of the tones, accomplish it in living participation, and saying that we first generate such a motion in ourselves, as a reaction product to some outside stimulus or other, and then project it outside ourselves. The one statement does not affect the reality of music; the other dissipates it as a phantom.)

---

1. Palágyi, *Wahrnehmungslehre.*

There is, then, no escape. Every motion is a continuous process; no succession of tones in music is a continuous process; no succession of tones in music can be motion. The unassailable logic of this syllogism stands in complete and preclusive opposition to the definition of music as tonal motion. The concept of tonal motion seems finally to be shipwrecked on the problem of continuity.

PHILOSOPHICAL CONSIDERATIONS

Let us think back: How did we reach this point? It was the certainty of direct experience which caused us to refer to music as motion of tones. Musical experiences had to be admitted to the great group of phenomena that we call motion. There were no difficulties, no irreconcilables; on the contrary, the heard and the seen, tonal motion and material motion, joined for our consciousness in sisterly agreement.

Difficulties began only when reflection entered in. Now contradictions appeared—not between experience and experience but between experience and concept. Our concept of motion, derived from the data of material motion (continual change of place by a thing which remains the same), refused to fit the data of tonal motion. In the case of such a conflict between an experience and a concept authorized by science and generally accepted, we habitually distrust the experience and assume an illusion or an error. This is what has happened in our case. The standard of the generally accepted concept of motion has been applied to the experience of musical motion; since the two could not be reconciled, the assumption of a tonal motion was judged highly problematic if not impossible.

But something essential was overlooked in this. Zeno of Elea had been forgotten. It had been forgotten that there is a *problem* of motion. As a standard, a concept was used that had nothing of the reliability of a standard. The experience of motion in music was held to be highly problematic because it did not correspond to a concept that itself is highly problematic.

Most certainly it did not take music to reveal irresolvable contradictions between reflection and experience in the realm of motion. The difficulty is as old as the search for a conceptual understanding of the universe. The earliest Greek philosophers found themselves faced with it—and did not solve it. "Emancipated thought," writes Oswald Spengler, "was shipwrecked on the problem of motion." [2] Lack of experience in logical training cannot be held responsible for this failure, because two thousand years later such a master of the arts of logic as Leibniz could find no other way of saving the concept of motion except the assumption that the thing in motion is destroyed every instant and created anew by God—an expectation in the face of which one feels inclined to prefer the old Eleatic's solution and hold that the whole universe of motion is an illusion.

Such, then, is the reliability of the standard which it is sought to apply to tonal motion. If tonal motion is problematic, then material motion is certainly not less so. Indeed, it is so on perfectly analogous grounds; it appears that, for reflection, the indigestible kernel in both experiences is the same: continuity.

A discussion of the problem of continuity, even in outline, would go far beyond the limits of this book as well as the competence of its author. The following is an attempt, with the aid of a simple example, to obtain a view of the central difficulty.

A body in motion traverses a certain distance in a certain time. The velocity of a motion is measured by the length of the distance traversed per time unit. We compare two motions at different velocities, that of an automobile and that of a pedestrian:

2. Spengler, *The Decline of the West,* Vol. I, ch. 1.

	Distance traveled in			
	1 hr.	1 min.	1 sec.	$\frac{1}{1000}$ sec.
Automobile	60 km.	1000 m.	16.6 m.	16.6 mm.
Pedestrian	6 km.	100 m.	1.66 m.	1.66 mm.

However small the time interval, and with it the spatial distance, becomes, the one distance always remains ten times the other: the speed of the car is ten times that of the pedestrian.

Both motions are continuous processes; that is, they stop at no point and skip no point in their course. We may therefore meaningfully ask: What distance does the car traverse in the shortest conceivable time, in an instant? The answer must be, the shortest conceivable distance, the distance from one point of its course to the directly adjacent point. For if the distance were only minutely longer, there would be, between the point where it begins and the point where it ends, at least *one* point, which, for the sake of continuity of the motion, could not be skipped and which the vehicle must needs enter *before* it enters the point that marks the end of the distance—that is, after a time shorter than the shortest conceivable time, which is nonsense. But we arrive at exactly the same answer if we put the same question for the pedestrian: of his motion too it is true that, in the shortest conceivable time, he traverses the shortest conceivable distance. Now the difference has vanished: the automobile and the pedestrian traverse the same distance in the same time; they move with the same speed. Like Achilles and the tortoise, the automobile can never catch up with the pedestrian, to say nothing of passing him.

Thinkers of all ages have been concerned to reconcile this contradiction between irrefutable logic and irrefutable observation. In our context Henri Bergson's attempt is of decisive significance.[3] It began a new epoch in the history of the problem of motion. Following Bergson, we should reason thus:

What do we do when we measure the velocity of moving bodies? We observe, for example, 1:15 P.M.—automobile at point A of the street; 1:16 P.M.—automobile at point B of the street; length of the section of the street between A and B, 1000 meters; elapsed time 1 minute. What has become of the *motion?* We have established a time frame. We have measured a distance. Of the thing in motion we have said nothing except that it is first in one place, then in another. To be in one place, to be in another—is that motion? A moving thing is not in this place and not in that place; it is *on the way* from place to place. To be in motion does not mean to be first here, then there; it means to be on the way from here to there. The basic schema of the process must, in addition to providing for "here" and "there," provide for "on the way"—thus, for example, "place | between | place." As we see, we cannot make up motion out of one thing, two places, and "to be at"; the "between" is lacking, the real, vital element of motion. But in our measurement we were dealing only with "thing," "place," and "to be at"; the being on the way, the transition, precisely what takes place in the "between" and which is the flesh and blood of the process of motion, was omitted.

The measuring process can be schematically represented somewhat like this:

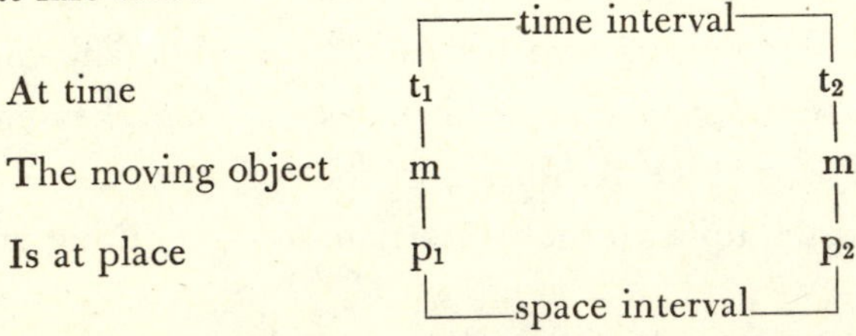

3. The problem of motion is discussed in his *Essai sur les données immédiates de la conscience, Matière et mémoire, Creative Evolution,* and *Durée et simultanéitée.*

This is still perfectly acceptable—or better, the difficulty has not yet appeared, for the very good reason that the time interval t_1–t_2 is large enough to leave room for a "between" between the corresponding p_1 and p_2. The picture changes, however, when we bring the shortest conceivable length of time into consideration. Now the schema looks like this:

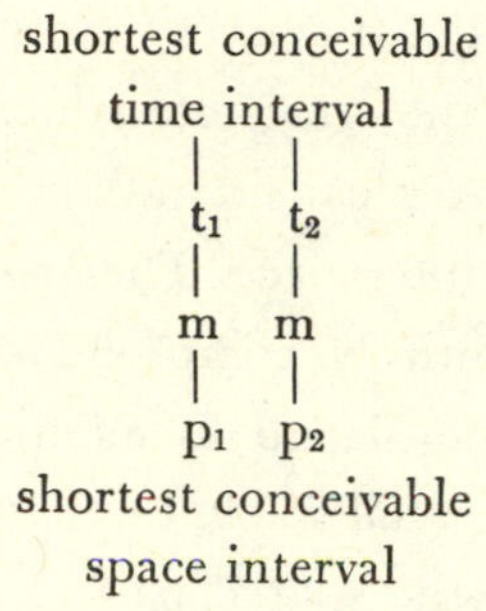

Another point cannot be inserted between p_1 and p_2; otherwise it would not be the shortest conceivable space interval, nor, consequently, would t_1–t_2 be the shortest conceivable time interval. The "between" has vanished. And without a "between" in which it can develop, no motion is possible.

These are not logical tricks, intended to confuse the mind. Things move in space. Space has no gaps. The course the moving thing follows is a line in space, a continuous series of places. Motion thus actually takes place through such shortest conceivable and, so to speak, "betweenless" distances. How are we to understand that motion can develop at all; that space does not nip it in the bud?

The "between" that finally disappears in this measuring process is a "between places," an interspace. But who is to tell us that the "between" from which motion lives is precisely that: an inter*space?* If "place | between | place" is the schema of the process of motion, then the between *cannot* be interspace. Space is a continuous chain of places, and every interspace is likewise to be thought of as continuously filled with places. Thus "place | between | place" would have to become "place | place | place | place | place"—the image of perpetual stasis, the negation of motion. However, from this it by no means necessarily follows that motion *is* impossible, must be mere illusion; but that it *would be* so if its "between" were nothing but "between places," interspace. Consequently, it *cannot be* inter*space.*

Thus we recognize the error into which Zeno and his successors fell. Without further consideration, they equated the "between" of motion with interspace. They assumed that the process of motion could be entirely comprehended in spatial data; in Bergson's language, they failed to maintain the distinction between motion and its spatial track, the *path* traveled. Now, everything that was true of the spatial path of motion had also to be true of motion itself; nothing might be true of motion that was not also true of its spatial path. The contradictions and paradoxes thus arrived at cannot, however, serve as proof of the intrinsically contradictory character of motion; on the contrary, they merely show that motion *cannot* be entirely comprehended in spatial-local data. It is precisely the essential element of motion which slips through the net of spatial relations—and the more surely, the tighter the net is drawn. If thought perpetually brings us back to a point where it appears that space, as an uninterrupted chain of places, inevitably robs motion of the breath of life, then we can only conclude that motion draws its life elsewhere than from the space of places. If things and places do not suffice to make us understand the process of motion, then this process must in some essential aspect extend beyond the realm of things and places. Rightly understood, what Zeno's paradoxes teach is that the stage on which motion is enacted cannot be—or cannot be only—the space of places. Motion must be something else than things changing place; it must also occur—and perhaps occur essentially—where no more things change their places.

Is all this mere empty playing with ideas? We shall let a psychologist answer the question for us.

PSYCHOLOGICAL CONSIDERATIONS

The problem of motion is presented to the psychologist in the form of the question, How is motion perceived? How do I see, how do I feel, a motion?

The older psychology sought to understand all psychological phenomena, including sensation and sense perception, after the pattern of physical phenomena, that is, mechanistically and atomistically. A phenomenon was supposed to be understood when, in thought, one had succeeded in reducing it to its elements and reconstructing it from its elements. The phenomenon of seeing a motion was schematically conceived more or less as follows:

To see means to react to light stimuli. The elements of seeing are the individual sensations that are aroused when light rays fall upon cells of the retina. A bundle of light rays stimulates a spot on the retina: I see a thing in a place. The same bundle of light rays successively stimulates adjacent spots on the retina: I see the same thing successively in adjacent places; I see the thing in motion. The same holds for the sense of touch: to feel motion means to feel the same tactile sensation first at one spot on the skin, then successively at adjacent spots on the skin. According to this, perception of motion would be a complex phenomenon, the elements that go to make it up being successive perceptions of the same thing at different places.

The similarity between this way of conceiving motion and the procedure for measuring velocity is obvious. Hence it is not surprising that, in both cases, the same problem arises. The older psychology explains how we see "thing now here," "thing now there"; but it does *not* explain how we see "thing *on the way* from here to there." The transition, the "between," the very core of the process, is again not accounted for in the explanation.

In opposition to the older mechanistic theories, William James maintained the primordiality and immediacy of perception of motion; he saw in it not the result of collocating various elementary data but *one* elementary datum, and indeed, in a certain sense, *the* elementary datum of perception. "We have the feeling of motion," he writes, "given us as a direct and single sensation . . . it [motion] is the most immediate of all our space sensations." [4] He denies that, in order to see or feel motion, we must see or feel a thing first in one place, then in another, and then somehow fill in the transition mentally. In support of his view he cites the following observation:

The skin's sensitivity for localizing a contact is different in different parts of the body. The distance between two contacts that are actually to be felt as contacts *at two different points* must be greater at some parts of the body than at others. If, for example, a fingertip is touched with the points of a pair of calipers set about one centimeter apart, the subject clearly feels two contacts. The same contact on the thigh produces only *one* sensation; the two stimuli flow together; they are too close to each other; the skin at this part of the body is not sensitive enough to separate them locally. This means that two places one centimeter apart here pass as *one* place. But if, on the same spot, the caliper points are moved even as little as one millimeter, motion is immediately and unmistakably perceived. So motion is still registered even when the sense organ is no longer capable of registering differences in place: the perception of motion does not result from the perception of a thing at different places.

---

4. William James, "The Perception of Space."

A still more radical departure from the mechanistic view has been achieved by Gestalt psychology. Its principal contribution to the discussion of motion is Max Wertheimer's "Experimentelle Studien über das Sehen von Bewegung." The results of this study are of the most immediate concern for our purpose, the understanding of tonal motion.

The concrete question with which Wertheimer's study deals may be simply formulated as follows: against a dark background, two narrow oblongs that meet at a right angle are alternately illuminated at different rates of speed. What is seen?

The answer is sought and found in a long series of experiments. First of all three "distinct phases" appear. When the rate of speed is slow, that is, when the two oblongs are illuminated at intervals of $\frac{1}{5}$ second and more, both are successively seen at rest, first ▯, then ▭. When the rate of speed is rapid—interval about $\frac{1}{30}$ second and less—both oblongs are simultaneously seen at rest, ▯▭. At an intermediate rate of speed—about $\frac{1}{15}$ second—one oblong is seen to *turn* from one position to the other, ▯↘. This is the case of the moving picture, illusory motion.

Now what happens if we gradually change the speed of the succession from one of these "phases" to another? What takes place in the transition from the middle phase, in which we see a thing in motion, to one of the two extremes, in which we see two things at rest, successively or simultaneously? Since the production of the illusion of motion in the middle phase depends upon the speed of the succession, we should suppose that a change in speed would impair the conditions for the illusion; that the result would be simply a more imperfect, vaguer impression of motion. But something entirely different happens.

If the speed of the succession is raised a little above the middle stage—the stage favorable to the production of the illusory motion—what appears is not a vague intermediate stage between one thing in motion and two things at rest; we see, with perfect precision, *two things and,* equally precisely, we see *motion,* . We see the same motion as before, and we see the oblong at the beginning and the oblong at the end as *two different things.* The impression of motion is preserved, but the identity of the moving thing, its remaining the same, ceases! We see motion that, paradoxically, is no longer motion of one and the same thing, motion that does not require that its conveyor remain the same. The thing that emerges from the motion is different from the thing that entered into it.

Let us continue and increase the tempo further. Again the impression of motion is not lessened; but the motion breaks apart in the middle; we get it in two sections, thus, 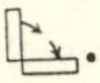 . If the tempo is further accelerated these sections become smaller and smaller until finally the two oblongs stand motionless together. If in this intermediate phase we concentrate on one of the two oblongs, we see it perform its section of the motion alone while the other remains at rest, . Often we see only one oblong perform its section of the motion; the other has vanished entirely, e.g., . In the face of these observations, what becomes of the doctrine that perception of motion is made up of several successive perceptions of a thing at different places; that seeing motion must somehow be understood as a filling of gaps in perception or sensation? In each separate case of these sectional motions, where would be the successive perceptions of the thing at different places; where would be the gaps between them? Each of these sectional motions is based on only *one single* perception of "thing at place"; the motion flows into it or runs out of it. Where the one motion stops, , where the other begins, , there is nothing in a place, nor is anything seen in a place. If we want to apply the basic schema "place | between | place" here, we should have to drop one or the other of the two cornerstones; what we see here could at best be characterized as "place | between," or "between | place." (If we reverse the procedure and, starting from the intermediate speed, slow down the tempo instead of accelerating it, analogous phenomena result.)

As for the manner in which motion itself appears, the event in the "between," these experiments have clearly shown that "moving is something different from being successively in successive places." [5] The seeing of motion is *not* a seeing of intermediate positions, of a traversal of intermediate places by the moving thing. Even in the case of the complete illusion, when the one oblong is clearly seen first in the starting position, then in the transition, finally in the end position, motion is never motion *of the oblong*. We see motion passing over the background; we do not see a moving thing passing over the background: "The oblong was seen in the first and the final position, motion in between, no intermediate positions, the oblong did not pass through the field, the background remained completely undisturbed, but the motion passes over. . . . I saw a strong motion, but had no impression of objects. . . . I see motion, not *something* passing by. . . . There was simply motion, not referable to an object. . . ." Such are the concurring testimonies of the observers. If the time of the flash that illuminates the oblongs is further shortened, the first and final positions are no longer clearly perceived, but the impression of motion remains unimpaired. The actual datum—oblong first in one position, then in another—is now practically not seen; but where there is no datum, in the empty field between the oblongs, something is seen: motion. Now the basic schema "place | between | place" has lost *both* its cornerstones; *only* "between" is seen, pure "between," pure passage. The motion that thus appears cannot be classified as a thing; freed from all connection with things, it bears the same

5. Wertheimer, "Experimentelle Studien."

relation to the so-called conveyor of motion as the electric current in the wire bears to the telephone pole.

Nothing would be simpler than to class all these phenomena offhand as optical illusions, than to say that since we see motion where, "in reality," nothing moves, it can only be a matter of our being deceived by our senses. One may adopt this standpoint —if one wants at all costs to block the road to understanding these things. Certainly one can say it is an illusion when a stick held under water looks bent at the surface; but to say this is only to say something about oneself, about our own narrow perspective, which, out of the whole universe, sees nothing, can see nothing, but the stick; which is unable to conceive that such an image might relate to something else, might contain a statement about something other than the stick. The stick is straight, so the image of it as bent must be an illusion. The image is dumb, it can only present itself; if we attribute false statements to it, something that it does not mean, and then accuse it of leading us astray, it can only persist and wait until we arrive at understanding. Today we know that the image did not refer to the stick but to light; did not want to make a statement about the stick but about the bending of light when it passes from air into water. How long did it not take for us to understand what the eye, in its wonderfully clear and simple way, had since time immemorial been presenting for our understanding! But what do we, with our incorrigible stick-mindedness, do? We boast of what our intellect has accomplished and go on calling the image an illusion.

What, writes Wertheimer, if study of the seeing of illusory motion should further our understanding of the seeing of motion in general—"if, in this way, essential elements could be experimentally isolated, perhaps *the* essential element that is the basis for real seeing of motion?" He carefully compares what takes place when we see illusory motion and when we see real motion.

The process is the same in either case: what is true for the seeing of illusory motion also holds true for the seeing of real motion. But this must not be read with a secretly derogatory emphasis on *seeing,* as if we were investigating how motion "merely appears," not what it "really is" (in the current terminology, the "subjective," not the "objective," side of the process). Wertheimer lays the strongest emphasis on the fact that the phenomena which he describes "are of an objective, not a subjective, nature; have the same kind of objective significance as the content of any given color or shape sensation." This means that seeing motion tells us exactly as much about motion as seeing colors does about colors, as seeing shapes does about shapes. If seeing motion is *not* a seeing of things in places, if the process that we see as motion is able to free itself from connection with things and places, appears as a progression neither *in* places nor *through* places, but over them, as a pure passing over, this means that motion *is* such. The definition "transfer of a thing from one place to another" does not embrace it; it is not entirely contained in its spatial track. It reaches beyond the realm of places, transcends it—our schema "place | between | place" does not do it justice; the differences in level would have to be represented, perhaps thus:
b e t w e e n
place | place. The flesh and blood of the phenomenon—to use Wertheimer's expression—would, then, have to be sought not on the level of place, of the many places, but on that of the one "between," of the one "passing over."

To see colors, to see shapes, to see motion, does not simply mean to have visual sensations; in all these cases one sees *something.* In the case of colors and shapes this something is always a material thing—it is the pigment on the canvas which is red, it is the crest of the mountain which is jagged—and where we see change, the thing that changes is always present; is the persisting, the static core of the phenomenon. What is the something that we see in these motions which are a pure "passing over," since it is not a material thing? Wertheimer calls it something *purely dynamic.* This is to say that a dynamism detached from everything static, change detached from a thing that changes, is not only conceivable but perceptible. "Why should there not be purely dynamic phenomena?" At first blush every seen motion may appear to be motion of a thing: Wertheimer's researches have revealed the core of pure dynamism, of dynamism transcending the material, that motion contains; they have disclosed that every seeing of motion is, essentially, a perceiving of purely dynamic phenomena that transcend the level of things and places.

MUSICAL CONSIDERATIONS

It is not fortuitously that Wertheimer ends his essay with a reference to music—to the "living interval"—as a terrain in which similar studies would lead to similar results. Parallels force themselves upon us at every step. Often we should have only to substitute "tone of a certain pitch" for "thing in place" and we should have a perfectly valid statement concerning heard instead of seen motion. Even more: many statements seem to apply much more naturally, much more easily, to the former than to the latter. Indeed, it seems that a great deal of intellectual effort and laborious experimentation are necessary to isolate from visible motion phenomena that music, heard motion, simply hands us, as it were, on a silver platter.

Let us recall what we said about the elementary experience of musical motion. A series of tones is heard as motion not because the successive tones are of different pitches but because they have different dynamic qualities. The dynamic quality of a tone, we said, is a statement of its incompleteness, its will to completion. To hear a tone as dynamic quality, as a direction, a pointing, means hearing at the same time beyond it, beyond it in the direction of its will, and going toward the expected next tone. Listening to music, then, we are not first *in* one tone, then in the next, and so forth. We are, rather, always *between* the tones, *on the way* from tone to tone; our hearing does not remain with the tone, it reaches through it and beyond it. The usual concept of melodic motion as motion from tone to tone and of the individual step from tone to tone as the bridging of the distance in pitch between two tones (schema "tone | between | tone") does not fit the facts at all. But neither would a schema like this

dynamic quality	b e t w e e n	dynamic quality
↑		↑
tone		tone

do them justice. Dynamic qualities are not stationary, of the nature of fixed pillars, with no bridge between them until one is provided by the connecting transition of the step, they are themselves completely of the nature of a step, of a transition; they are, in other words, dynamic, not static, they are themselves the going on beyond the tone—a passing over, a "between." The schema must be this:

b e t w e e n	
tone	tone

. It is a process on two levels, on one of which, the "lower," there is nothing but the pillars, tones of definite pitch; on the other, the "higher," nothing but the transition, the passing over. And the motion we hear is not at all the "tone | tone" of the lower level; it is the "between" of the upper level, pure betweenness, pure passing over.

But this is where Wertheimer arrives too; the investigation of seen motion and the investigation of heard motion coincide in their end result! Whereas elsewhere we found nothing but contradictions and paradoxes when we tried to understand heard motion after the pattern of seen motion, now suddenly there is helpful agreement. The only difference lies in the fact that, in the motion of things, the core of pure dynamism is well concealed and had to be isolated artificially, whereas in tonal motion hardly anything is perceived but the purely dynamic. The irreconcilability of the phenomenon of musical motion with the traditional concept of motion has its parallel in Wertheimer's investigation: the concept of motion to which he was led by his observations is in sharp opposition to the traditional concept. On the other hand, it corresponds beautifully with the facts of tonal motion. Wertheimer's concept of motion is simply the *musical concept of motion* —and the fact that it could be reached from the opposite pole, from seen instead of heard motion, from the motion of things, not the motion of tones, seems to indicate that *all* motion, seen as well as heard, motion of things as well as motion of tones, is, in the last analysis, "of one flesh and blood." Not unjustifiably may we say that musical motion is at the core of every motion; that every experience of motion is, finally, a musical experience.

The position from which we set out is now completely reversed. Instead of doubtfully asking if we had a right to speak of motion in music, since after all there is nothing in music that moves, and no places in which things are, we now say that it is precisely *because* there are no things and places in music, precisely *because* music has freed itself from all connection with things and places, that the passing over, the "between," the core of motion, can be manifested in absolute purity and immediacy. It is precisely *because* hearing music is a perception of purely dynamic phenomena that the core of the process of motion can be elementally experienced in music, and above all in music. Hearing music means hearing precisely and only the core of motion. Philosophers and aestheticians are wrong when they talk of "ideal" motion, of "abstract" motion, in music. There is nothing ideal or abstract in it. The elimination of thing and place takes away nothing of the reality of motion, of the concreteness of its experience; on the contrary, it reveals its inmost core. *Tonal motion is the most real motion.*

And the problem of continuity? A few pages back, it still seemed impossible to abide by the experience of motion in melody in the face of the fact that the tones from which a melody is constructed do not themselves move at all, that they present a picture of stases and gaps. But now this seems as little paradoxical as the fact that the telephone poles do not run along with the electric current, or that they are poles, with gaps between, not a continuous wall. Certainly, the tones are static, there are gaps between tone and tone; but the motion that we hear in music, the continuous occurrence, does not take place where there are tones and gaps, on the lower level, is not *motion of the tones,* is not "tone | tone," but is "between," is manifested on the upper level. Stasis of the tones and motion of the melody, gaps here and uninterruptedness there, continuity and discontinuity, do not enter into opposition because they concern phenomena on different levels that must be kept apart.

An example to make this clear. The step of a fourth, $\hat{5}$-$\hat{8}$: on the level of tones there are two events, two stases, and a gap; on the level of "between," of passing over, there is one step, one event, one single move. Here there is no question of duality, of gaps. The continuity of the step is not that of an unbroken transition from tone to tone, of a continuous passing through all the "points" between one tone and another; it is the unity and uninterruptedness of the single move, which transforms one dynamic state into another. This unity and uninterruptedness are completely unaffected by the greater or lesser distance of the tones from each other, by the greater or lesser number of intermediate degrees, of intermediate tones, which are "skipped" in the step. As motion, $\hat{5}$-$\hat{8}$ is as perfect, as uninterrupted, as continuous as $\hat{5}$-$\hat{6}$-$\hat{7}$-$\hat{8}$. Nor is the motion $\hat{5}$-$\hat{8}$ to be understood as the sum of the fractional motions $\hat{5}$-$\hat{6}$, $\hat{6}$-$\hat{7}$, $\hat{7}$-$\hat{8}$: a leap is not a sum of steps, and steps are not fractions of a leap. One can subdivide a difference in pitch and reconstruct it from its fractions, but one cannot divide and reconstruct a motion. If the continuity of tonal motion had anything to do with the "lower" level, with differences in pitch, with traversing these intervals, with touching upon intermediate tones, then $\hat{5}$-$\hat{6}$-$\hat{7}$-$\hat{8}$ would necessarily produce a better, more continuous impression of motion than $\hat{5}$-$\hat{8}$. But then, logically, the motion would appear still better, still more continuous, if the gaps between $\hat{5}$ and $\hat{6}$, $\hat{6}$ and $\hat{7}$, $\hat{7}$ and $\hat{8}$, were to be filled with more and more intermediate tones, until finally, when all intervals were completely filled, a perfect impression of motion would be achieved. The exact opposite is the case: the sirenlike glissade from tone to tone does not give the most perfect impression of motion but no impression of motion at all. Actual continuity on the lower level eliminates the possibility of motion; order becomes chaos, music a mere shriek.

With this shriek, tones show us in exemplary fashion how motion feels when its two-level structure is compressed onto one level, when the upper level is absorbed in the lower, when the "places" swallow up the "between": it is deprived of the breath of life. The siren shriek is the protest of tones against the error into which Zeno of Elea fell when he equated motion with the *path* of motion, "between" with inter*space,* until motion choked to death in his hands. In the realm of tone we hear what is concealed in the realm of things: in the final analysis motion and uninterrupted traversal of intermediate steps have nothing to do with each other; they can certainly not be equated. If motion of things in space actually and necessarily appears as an uninterrupted traversal of intermediate steps, then "uninterrupted traversal of intermediate steps" belongs among the necessary conditions for the existence of things in space, not for the existence of motion. Instead of "Motion is continuous transfer of a thing from one place to another in space," we ought to say: "Moving things in space continuously change their place." But then we shall look for the purer, more elemental phenomenon of motion in tones, not in things.

Bergson writes: "There are changes, but there are underneath the change no things which change: change has no need of a support. There are movements, but there is no inert or invariable object which moves: movement does not imply a mobile." To be sure, the eye shows us unaltered things that change their place. But the ear? Hearing a melody is "the clear perception of a movement which is not attached to a mobile, of a change without anything changing. This change is enough, it is the thing itself." We introduce spatial concepts, concepts of "thing in place," into melody if we view it as a succession of individual tones. If we eliminate this false spatialization, "pure change remains, sufficient unto itself, in no way divided, in no way attached to a 'thing' which changes. . . . Change is the most substantial and durable thing possible." The inmost being of things is the indivisible continuity of this change; all things are given us in the indivisible continuity of a melody. [6]

The attempt to understand tonal motion in the light of the motion of things has proved futile. Now it appears that the opposite course is the more promising: to understand motion in general, including motion of bodies, in the light of tonal motion. Should he who searches for the essence of motion perhaps look to music for an answer?

---

6. Quotations are from Bergson, "The Perception of Change," in *The Creative Mind*.

X. The "Third Stage"

ELSEWHERE in "The Perception of Change," Bergson writes: "Our personality is precisely that: the continuous melody of our inner life."

Here we pause; a question frames itself. If Bergson, in these thoughts, connects motion and music, music and human existence, what kind of motion has he in mind? Is it any longer the outer, perceptible phenomenon, a phenomenon of the external world, at all? Has not his attention shifted imperceptibly from outer to inner, from physical to psychological motion? Has the boundary between the two been maintained? Does Bergson, when he says "motion," perhaps originally have in mind the psychological, not the physical?

We do not pose this question here for its own sake, but for the sake of the reminder that it provides: it points to another question that should perhaps have been settled earlier.

When, at the beginning of this section, we cited a number of eloquent witnesses to the immediacy of the experience of motion in music, we pointed out the fact that, in their testimony, the concept of motion was used in very different senses—sometimes in the sense of a physical but also frequently in the sense of a psychological phenomenon, as, for example, in Hegel's characteristic statement that music "echoes the motions of the inmost self."[1] For our part, however, throughout this discussion we have always considered motion as an external phenomenon; have compared tonal motion only with such phenomena of motion as we encounter in perception of the external, physical world. Have we overlooked the fact that the one word "motion" embraces two worlds: physical motion and psychological motion? If not, why have we followed only one of the two roads—and perhaps the wrong one?

One thing we shall *not* adduce in justification: that the word "motion" strictly has only one meaning, refers directly only to phenomena of the external world, to bodies in space, and can only be used in reference to phenomena of the psyche by extension, metaphorically. When we speak of images *unrolling* in fantasy, of the *flow* of thought, of *reaching* a decision, we are not speaking in metaphors but directly expressing definite experiences. When William James coined the expression *stream of consciousness,* he was certainly not concerned with finding a striking metaphor but with precisely characterizing a specific fact. There is no doubt that the word "motion" is as native to the inner as to the outer world.

But then it must seem all the more incomprehensible that we did not do the obvious thing and conceive the experience of motion in music above all in the sense of inner, psychological motion—especially in view of the difficulties which we have encountered along our path. That music is incomparably closer to the world of the psyche than to the world of bodies, that it is a pure manifestation of the psychic, are almost commonplaces. And indeed, we should have had an easy time of it if we had looked at musical experiences from the point of view of the phenomena of the inner world instead of doing as we have done. We said that music is motion, and yet we find nothing of things and places in

1. Hegel, *Vorlesungen über die Aesthetik.*

it. But in the psyche too there are neither things nor places; yet it has motion. We said that music is motion, and yet in it there is no thing that moves. Is not the same true of inner motion, the motion of the psyche? The stream of consciousness is not a thing, "consciousness," which "streams," but a streaming in consciousness; feeling is no more motion of a something, the psyche, than is melody the motion of a something, tone. Finally, we said that music is motion, a continuous progression, and yet, objectively, nothing but stases and gaps are given in it, no transitions, no filling of gaps, no passing through intermediate steps. But this is the distinguishing characteristic of what occurs in the psyche. What could be more continuous than the stream of consciousness, and what more discontinuous than the actual data in consciousness, the various contents and states of consciousness that so often succeed one another with no transition, with a complete lack of intermediate stages? The mutual correspondence between the phenomena of the psyche and the phenomena of music could not be more perfect.

Certainly it would have been easier and simpler to follow the inward course rather than the outward, but it would not have been honest. For one basic fact must not be shirked: music is *not* a phenomenon of the inner world, nor is it something projected from the inner to the outer world; it is a phenomenon of the outer world. It is not felt, it is not imagined, it is not willed—it is perceived. It does not arise from our psyche; it comes to us from the world around us. It is not in our consciousness—or, better, it is there in the same way as, and neither more nor less than, are all other perceived phenomena. The motion we hear—not the passing by of the band but the $\hat{5}$-$\hat{8}$ of the march it is playing—and the motion we see belong, in this respect, on the same plane. Tones move where birds fly and meteors fall; and if the brief that music is motion is to be defended, we must argue it in the court that has proper jurisdiction.

But under what jurisdiction does music fall? It exhibits the general characteristics of psychological processes, but its stage is not the psyche. It comes from without, but it does not exhibit the general characteristics of what comes from without, body and place. It is distinguished from all psychological phenomena by the way in which it is given, by accuracy, reliability, one might almost say palpability; from all physical phenomena, on the other hand, it is distinguished by the characteristic of impalpability. Thus it rejects the claim which *either* world makes to it, the physical world *and* the world of the psyche; thus it extends beyond *both* of them in the same fashion. Music makes us aware, unmistakably and inescapably, that "beyond the world of things and places" is *not,* as common belief has it, identical with the world of the psyche; nor is "beyond the world of the psyche" identical with the world of things and places. A *third stage* must exist which is neither the world of the psyche nor the world of bodies nor yet a mixture of both, and which stands to the two others in the relation of the general to the particular, of the primary to the derivative. Motion that takes place entirely on this stage is "pure" in the twofold sense that it is bound neither to things and places nor to a stream of consciousness. Such is the motion of tones—motion that has not yet been wedded to a body or a psyche, the purest, most primal form of motion that we know. And if it is true that, in the last analysis, all motion is of one flesh and blood, that at the core of every motion, even the motion of bodies, music lies hidden, then every motion, including the motion of bodies, belongs to the "third stage" perforce of its inmost essence.

We recall that at the beginning of this section we asked what it meant to *hear* motion. To see motion, to touch motion, is understandable. But to hear motion? Now, on the contrary, we can ask, What is there in motion which can be seen and touched? Certainly not its core; for that lies beyond body and place, and what has neither body nor place can neither be seen nor touched. But this does not mean that it cannot be perceived at all; can at best be "felt." Instead—music tells us so—*it can be heard.* Compared with seeing and touching, hearing proves to be the faculty that gets at the essence; that pierces to the core of the phenomenon. Instead of asking how we can perceive motion with the ear *too,* we find that the core of the process of motion, what takes place on the "third stage," is *directly* perceptible *only* to the ear. Other senses, whose principal function is to serve orientation on the physical stage, can attain to the perception of the phenomenon of motion in its pure essentiality only under special conditions.

The statement that bodies and their motions in space are, in the last analysis, the only reality is as old as European philosophy. Born in the mind of Democritus, for two thousand years it led a sort of hermetically sealed existence. Then the seal bursts. The advance guard of a new scientific spirit takes up the thread—Hobbes, for example: "The things that really *are* in the world without are *motions* [of bodies]." This passes as materialism, and it is certainly meant as materialism. But in the light of the knowledge to which musical experiences bring us, such statements begin to sound peculiar: they suddenly seem to say exactly the opposite of what they intend to say. If the universe is real as moving bodies are real, if motion of a body is not wholly contained in the physico-spatial world, if the very core of the phenomenon of motion goes beyond the physico-spatial, this means not only that the reality of the universe is *not* exhausted in the physico-spatial, but that precisely its very essence reaches beyond that stage, is transcendent in respect to the visible and tangible—transcendent in the same sense in which a melody is transcendent in respect to tones as acoustical phenomena. It is, so to speak, an internal transcendence; it does not lead away from the phenomenon but into it, to its core. In the first section of this book we discussed the particular way in which dynamic qualities exist in tones and compared it, remotely, with the way in which the divine being is present in the religious symbol. It would seem, then, that, in the same sense, the entire universe would have the nature of a symbol, and that, among all experiences, musical experience might be distinguished by the fact that in it the symbolic nature of the external world would be revealed in direct perception. We *see* the rind, or, under special conditions, *through* the rind, but we *hear* the core of this world.

Those who believe that music provides a source of knowledge of the inner world are certainly not wrong. But the deeper teaching of music concerns the nature not of "psyche" but of "cosmos." The teachers of antiquity, who spoke of the music of the spheres, of the cosmos as a musical order, knew this. A celebrated English physician and scholar, who lived more than three centuries ago, has left us the beautiful statement that melody, *every* melody, is "an Hieroglyphical and shadowed lesson of the whole World and creatures of God." [2] Only a little more than a century ago, Schopenhauer could still write: "A correct, complete, and detailed explanation of music—that is, a full restatement, in terms of concepts, of what music expresses . . . would also be a sufficient restatement and explanation of the world in terms of concepts, or completely in harmony with such a

2. Sir Thomas Browne, *Religio Medici.*

restatement and explanation, and hence the true philosophy."[3] Today we consume music in greater quantities than any previous generation. But we no longer know how to read what stands written. We have forgotten the meaning of the characters.

---

3. Schopenhauer, *The World as Will and Idea.*

TIME

XI. Meter and Rhythm

We have come to know—music itself has taught us—that no objects and no object space are necessary to motion. For tonal motion begins precisely where all that—things and their space—comes to an end. But we can name one factor without which motion cannot be, that is, time. Motion in a realm from which things and space are absent is, thanks to music, a substantiated fact; motion in a realm from which time is absent is self-contradictory. All things, together with the space that appertains to them, may vanish—motion remains, for melodies remain. But should time vanish, all motion must instantly vanish too, tonal motion not excepted. A God enthroned beyond time in timeless eternity would have to renounce music. The visible world in the fullness of its beauty lies spread out before the spatial omnipresence of God; but temporal omnipresence would make the revelation of audible beauty impossible. It argues against God's timelessness. Are we to suppose that we mortals, in possessing such a wonder as music, are more privileged than God? Rather, to save music for Him, we shall hold, with the Greeks, that God cannot go behind time. Otherwise what would He be doing with all the choiring angels?

In the conventional division of the arts into spatial and temporal arts, music figures as the temporal art par excellence. The division and its underlying principle are, as we shall see, poorly founded; yet the systematists are right when they see "the universal element,"[1] "the primal form,"[2] of music in temporal succession. Schopenhauer writes: "Music is perceived solely in and through time, to the complete exclusion of space."[3] This statement too will require further qualification. But one thing is certain: to one who is hearing music, the physico-spatial existence of the world becomes indifferent precisely to the degree to which music reveals existence as the flow of time. The many eulogists who have paid music the doubtful compliment of saying that its voice is "not of this world" must have forgotten time. If our world is a temporal world, if temporality is one of its bases, and indeed—as recent thinkers increasingly agree—represents its inmost core, then music is anything but superterrestrial; it is peculiarly terrestrial, of this world. Indeed, there is hardly a phenomenon that can tell us more about time and temporality than can music.

Inevitably, then, anyone who speculates about music sooner or later finds himself facing the problem of time—first, simply the concrete question of what the function of the temporal element in music really is, and what particular musical effects are based upon the flow of time as such. And this question may well imply another: How are we to think of this entity "time" if we want to understand how it can produce such effects?

"How we are to think time"—what a tremendous subject has been touched upon here! For this most obvious, most self-explanatory of all things, time—yesterday-today-tomorrow, now, not yet, no longer—this most certain of all the data of our consciousness suddenly becomes insidious, questionable, delusive, glides away like a will-o'-the-wisp, when thought tries to

1. Hegel, *Vorlesungen über die Aesthetik.*
2. Schlegel, *Vorlesungen über dramatische Kunst und Literatur.*
3. Arthur Schopenhauer, *The World as Will and Idea.*

comprehend it, to master it. What is time? "If no one asks me, I know; but if someone asks me and I want to explain it, I do not know."[4] Thus St. Augustine, the first whose vision plumbed the whole depth of the problem and whose intellect was powerful enough to master the vertigo that abyss produced.

Time—presumably we first think of hours, minutes, seconds. What is an hour? One twenty-fourth of the period that elapses while the earth revolves once upon its axis. Minutes and seconds are correspondingly lesser fractions of this period, the minute $\frac{1}{1440}$ of it, the second $\frac{1}{86,400}$.

In these statements we have been concerned with quantity, with fractions, we have named specific figures; hence we are dealing with *magnitudes,* with definite magnitudes established once and for all and always remaining the same. We find a similar establishing of definite magnitudes in other realms: kilometer-meter-millimeter, ton-kilogram-gram. Such magnitudes have a perfectly definite function: they are measures. We *measure* the lapse of time by hours, minutes, seconds.

But saying this is saying that hours, minutes, and seconds are not what time *is*. Measure and thing measured are not one and the same. A kilogram weight is heavy, but it is not heaviness. The degrees of the thermometer scale by which we measure heat are not heat; we heat food on a stove, not by means of a thermometer. In the case of time, there even seems to be a contradiction, an opposition between measure and thing measured: the measure remains; time passes.

Is it possible at all to measure a thing in passage? Try to measure exactly one meter on a moving band of which we have only a very small section before us. In order for us to measure something, it must be given us as a whole all at once. But what time have we before us as a whole all at once?

4. St. Augustine, *Confessions,* Book XI.

Yet we not only measure time; we also compare time with time, present time with present time, past time with future time. The same hour that, for someone in a state of expectation, drags out interminably passes in a flash for one in a state of contentment. "The same hour"—what is it, then, that we are comparing, that we find the same? Nothing, certainly, but the paths that the hands of two clocks, the hands of all clocks, have traveled in the interval: paths of bodies, then—not time. Or we say that the time it took on August 6, 1225, for a shout to reach the ear of a listener 330 meters distant is the same that it will take a shout to reach an equally distant listener on July 2, 2552. In both cases the time measures one second; one second is the time that elapses while the earth performs $\frac{1}{86{,}400}$ of its revolution upon itself. Basically, then, we have said nothing except that in both cases, between the shout and the hearing of it, the earth will have traveled the same distance in its motion about itself. Certain mathematicians do not mince matters. Says Lobachewski: "The motion of one body, if it is taken as the measure of the motion of another body, is called time." [5] If, then, at a given moment, all the motions of the heavenly bodies, all physical, chemical, and biological processes, were to become twice as fast or twice as slow, we should have no possibility of determining the change. The assumption does not even make sense. Twice as fast, twice as slow, in relation to what? The earth would still revolve upon itself in twenty-four hours; hours, minutes, seconds would still be "the same length" before and after the event. Not only, then, are hours, minutes, seconds measures of time, not time itself; but it also appears that what we measure with them are not times but spaces, extents of space traversed by moving bodies.

Hours, minutes, seconds are not the only way to think "time";

5. N. I. Lobachewski's definition of time is quoted from J. Alexander Gunn, *The Problem of Time,* p. 24, n. 3.

there is also past, present, future. We were unable to discover time in that which makes all hours, all minutes, all seconds equal. Perhaps we shall discover it in what distinguishes past, present, and future from one another, or better, in what bridges the abysses between what is eternally divided. Certainly, this must be time: the future becoming the present, the present becoming the past. But what *is* time, if it is this? What is in the future is not yet, what is in the past is no more; what remains? The present—but in the present too the flux of time does not stand still; in the present too the future steadily and irresistibly becomes the past. The present, of which alone we can say that it *is* and that in it *we are,* shrinks to an immeasurably small instantaneous section of the everlasting process of change from what is not yet to what is no more, from one nonbeing to another nonbeing. "We cannot truly say that time *is,*" writes St. Augustine, "because its being is a tending-not-to-be." [6]

But what, then, becomes of us, who live in time and by the grace of time? What a precarious situation, balancing on the hairline of the present, which, itself evaporating into immeasurability, separates two oceans of nonbeing. The existence of man is inevitably drawn into the uncertainty which surrounds time; and so it is not surprising that the problem of time has long been one of the principal themes of theological and philosophical speculation.[7] One could even distinguish periods in the history of culture in accordance with the various attempts that have been made to master the problem of time. Medieval thought, for example, following Plato and Plotinus, seeks to solve the problem by regarding time as a subordinate form of eternity, as eternity that has relinquished its eternal repose and exchanged it for

6. *Confessions.*

7. For the history of the philosophy of time, see Gunn, besides Werner Gent, *Die Philosophie des Raumes und der Zeit.*

eternal motion. As motion in comparison with rest, so time in comparison with eternity represents the lower plane of existence; temporal existence is imperfect existence; the problematic character of time reflects the problematic character of the created world after its fall from the state of perfection. The scientific age, whose chief interest was in material-spatial phenomena and processes, saw the problem of time wholly in the light—or rather in the darkness—of the problem of space. The time concept was subordinated to the space concept. For Descartes, who gave this view of the universe its classical formulation which prevailed for centuries, space is the paramount reality of the physical world; time is merely the consequence of our inability to experience the all-embracing simultaneity of things in space except as a succession. For our limited consciousness, what, for a higher consciousness, would be a simultaneous datum unrolls in a temporal succession. Here too, then, time characterizes the imperfect. In our own day the picture has changed. To use the expression of a modern philosopher: now, as never before, time is taken seriously.[8] We even hear of a *discovery* of time, and this is held to be the essential mark of modern thought. The crucial arguments turn upon distinguishing the old and new concepts of time. Time is recognized as the foundation of all existence; even inanimate matter is shown to be, in its core, vibration—a temporal phenomenon. The concept of time has everywhere taken precedence over the concept of space. Subordinated to no higher concept, time itself, indeed, assumes absolute primacy. To renounce temporality is not to renounce imperfection but rather to renounce true being.

The parallel between what has here taken place in philosophy and what has taken place in the realm of artistic creation is rather obvious. In the arts too the purely temporal art, music, has taken

8. Samuel Alexander, *Spinoza and Time.*

precedence over the spatial arts. For the first time in history, it is temporal art, not spatial art, which distinguishes the period from others and characterizes it; the Phidiases, the Erwin von Steinbachs, the Michelangelos, the Rembrandts of our day are the great masters of music. We said earlier that music could tell us more about time than could any other phenomenon. May the new discovery of time through modern philosophy be in any way connected with the musical experience of modern man, with the musical revelation that has been accorded him? Do we perhaps take time more seriously and know more about it than other periods because we have heard Bach's organ fantasias, Beethoven's symphonies, whereas other periods have not?

So perhaps we are not without justification if we expect an investigation of music to cast some light upon the problem of time, one of the central problems of modern philosophy.

THE TEMPORAL COMPONENT OF MUSIC

We have first to deal with a concrete question. What is the role of the time element in music and what particular musical effects are based upon it?

The principal manifestation of time in music is *rhythm.* Tones do not simply follow one another in time; their temporal succession exhibits a definite organization, a definite order, which, in accordance with its structure and effect, we characterize as rhythmic.

With melody and harmony, rhythm constitutes the trinity of basic elements that are fused in the unity of the musical work of art. But whereas melody and harmony are essentially musical phenomena, native to the world of tone and not to be found elsewhere (the adjectives derived from these terms can be applied only metaphorically outside the realm of music), rhythm is a truly universal phenomenon. We perceive rhythm in a man's gait, in his handwriting, in the shape of a vase, in a verse as in a brush stroke, in the motions of a dancer as in a motionless statue, and in the colonnade of a Greek temple, the outline of Michelangelo's dome, no less than in the course of a melody. The processes of organic life, the processes within an atom, the structures of crystals, the imperceptible shifting of the continents on the earth's surface, the revolutions of the celestial bodies, the nebular formations in the depths of the universe—all these, and what not besides, have been called rhythmical. In the animate as in the inanimate, in the microscopic as in the macrocosm, nature has revealed dispositions to which no concept is better adapted than that of rhythm. Rightly has it been said that rhythm is one manifestation of the reign of law throughout the universe.

Now, in our music we have to deal with a very definite and special kind of rhythm, with rhythm that conforms to a *meter*. Two components must be clearly distinguished: on the one hand rhythm, on the other meter, or, in the restricted musical sense, "time." Waltz rhythm is not the same as three-four time; march rhythm is not the same as two-four time. "Play in time!" the teacher calls to his pupil; we disparage lack of rhythm, and we praise the pre-eminent rhythm in the interpretation of a mature virtuoso. Language, as ever sensitive to such distinctions, permits us to speak of metronomically *correct* and rhythmically *living* performances; the adjectives are not interchangeable.

We shall first consider a case in which rhythm does *not* conform to any "time." A poem is a rhythmic construction. Can one beat time to an intelligent recitation of a poem? Certainly not. To beat time is to indicate equal time intervals by the aid of a movement repeated over and over, to divide the uniform flux of time into equal fractions. We could beat time to a poem if the syllables in it were all of equal length or departed from a basic unit in accordance with simple numerical proportions—amounted, for example, to the basic unit multiplied or divided by two or by three. Of this there can of course be no question. "Time" and rhythm here appear even to exclude each other: rhythm resists regular time; "time" appears to suffocate rhythm.

Except for the special case of dance music, which is obliged to conform to the bodily movement it supports, musical rhythm in general is of the nature of poetic rhythm: free rhythm, in the sense that it is not constrained to keep time. There is one notable exception, Western music of the second millennium of our era—our music. It alone has imposed the shackles of time, of meter, upon itself, and indeed at the same moment when it was preparing to take the momentous step into polyphony. So long as only a single voice is involved, it is free to give each of its steps whatever duration it pleases. But if several voices, voices saying different things, are to proceed side by side and together, their motions must, for better or worse, be regulated by some time standard. Not that all steps are uniformly bound to be of the same duration; but the duration of each of them must be in an exact and simple proportion to a determined duration value, to a basic temporal unit. Our notation takes this situation into account. Whereas the old symbols for the duration value of individual tones expressed nothing definite, our symbols speak an unequivocal language. We have whole notes, half-, quarter-, eighth-, sixteenth-notes, and so on, 𝅝 𝅗𝅥 ♩ ♪ 𝅘𝅥𝅯 (and the corresponding symbols for rests, 𝄻 𝄼 𝄽 𝄾 𝄿); we have triplets and sextuplets, ♫♪ ♫♫♫; we have the dot, which increases the duration of a tone by exactly 50 per cent 𝅗𝅥., and the slur, which adds duration values together, 𝅗𝅥‿♪. The symbols express the subjection of the tones to a common measure of duration. No duration values are available to them other than those which can be represented as simple multiples and fractions of a definite temporal unit, the counting unit of the meter.

It might be supposed that such an inflexible prescription would have as destructive an effect upon musical performance as it does upon the recitation of a poem; and, at first, strict meter, compared with the wonderful freedom of the self-sufficient single voice of plainchant, may well have been felt to be a straitjacket. It developed, however, that confinement to the strict rule did not destroy rhythm but, in the course of time, led to the evolution of a completely new rhythm—rhythm bound to the law of meter, which finally proved to be nowise inferior in subtlety and power to the effect of free rhythm. And it is not rhythm despite meter, but, on the contrary, rhythm from meter, rhythm fed by the forces dammed up in meter. Antithesis has become synthesis. Voluntary subjection to a strict constraint has, in the course of evolution, led to a victorious advance into a new freedom.

MUSICAL METER

How is this synthesis of law and freedom to be understood? Is musical meter perhaps like the scaffolding that is necessary to the construction of a building but is removed when the building is completed; or like the geometrical figures that many painters use as the scaffolding for a composition, but that disappear behind the forms and figures of the completed picture? To put it concretely: do we *hear* only rhythm or do we *hear* the meter too? The conductor has to beat the meter, the time, in order to keep his men together; is the time that he beats also a part of the direct experience of hearing music?

At first sight the question appears naïve. How could we dance to a waltz, march to a march, if we did not *hear* the meter? After all, we do not have to *see* the conductor in order to move in time. And a glance at the notes of such a composition at once shows us why this is so. A whole constituent of the music—the so-called accompaniment—here seems especially designed to make the meter audible.

Chopin

The constant repetition of tones of equal length under the melody does for the ear just what the conductor's movements do for the eye: it marks the metrical units. Such music, so to speak, beats time with tones.

But things can look very different too—thus, for example:

Schubert

What has become of the tones that marked the meter for our ears? Now the question if we always hear the meter too does not seem so naïve and is no longer easy to answer.

To be sure, here too the tones in their temporal succession conform to a basic unit; but no tone makes us directly hear this basic unit itself. To be sure, the individual tones stand in a definite durational relation to one another: the second sound we hear, ♩, is exactly one and a half times as long as the first, ♪; the third, ♬, is half as long; the fourth, ♩., three times as long; yet there can be no question of our becoming directly conscious of these proportions as we listen, and of the ear, as it were, calculating the basic unit from them. And yet, there is no such thing as a piece of music to which, after we have listened to it for a little while, we cannot correctly beat time—in most cases we actually do so involuntarily. This shows that music imparts its meter to the listener, unfailingly, in every instance. We do not always hear the meter *directly* (as in our first example); we often hear only shorter and longer tones in temporal succession. But since the tones in their motions conform to a temporal measure, and we as listeners sympathetically participate in their motions, we are able to feel the measure to which they conform. Within the tones—if the expression be permitted—the beating of the pulse of the meter that regulates their flow becomes perceptible. Always our hearing of music is also an awareness of, and a sympathetic inner beating with, its meter.

But this does not exhaust the matter. Meter in music accomplishes more than merely subjecting the temporal succession of the tones to a fixed measure. A piece of music is not simply "in time"; it is in two-four time, in three-four time, in six-eight time, and so on. The metrical arrangement does not simply divide the temporal flux into many particles of equal length; in addition it collects the particles together into little groups, which we call *measures*. A measure in a piece of music—clearly separated from its predecessors and successors by bar lines—is a group of 2, 3, 4, 6 such temporal units. (For this reason, moreover, the conductor's beat is not simply the repetition of the same sign but of the same *group* of signs, thus, for example, 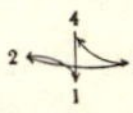 , or 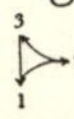 . And if we say that hearing music is also always an awareness of and a sympathetic beating with its time, we mean not only the constant emphasizing of the same basic unit but also the grouping process. Tones tell us not only the mensural basis which governs their motion but also how many such mensural units, how many *beats,* are in each case comprehended in a measure—to represent it graphically, not only this, ı ı ı ı ı ı, but this, for example, ı ı ı ı ı ı, or this, ı ı ı ı ı ı. In general this information which the tones give us leaves nothing to be desired on the score of clarity; it requires no musical education to distinguish the group pattern in the simpler sort of instance.

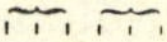

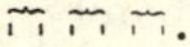

Now what is it that brings about this collecting of the temporal units into groups, of beats into measures? The unanimous answer that our textbooks give to this question is emphasis, accent—or, more accurately (since any demarcating of divisions in the time flux is in itself an emphasizing of the dividing points), it is the distinction between stronger and weaker accents. If in marking the time units we make each stronger accent be followed by a weaker accent, ı.ı., we get duple meter. If we make each stronger accent be followed by two weaker accents, ı..ı.., we get triple meter. If we emphasize as follows, ı.ı., strong-weak-semistrong-weak, the result is quadruple meter. The combination ı..ı.. gives sextuple meter, and so forth. This all sounds so self-evident, and is, furthermore, always advanced in such a matter-of-course way, that it never occurs to us to think it in any way doubtful. And yet, if we accept this explanation, if we remain satisfied with it, we have barred the way to understanding the rhythmical phenomena of our music. If meter were what this explanation professes it to be, its effect upon the rhythmic life of tones would be just as death-dealing as we found it to be in the case of the recitation of a poem. A synthesis of meter and rhythm would be impossible.

Beethoven's Violin Concerto begins with four soft kettledrum strokes,  . The thrilling effect of this opening depends entirely upon whether the player succeeds in producing absolutely equal tones—certainly no easy task. His entire attention must be directed to avoiding the least trace of a difference in accentuation between the tones. If he is unsuccessful, if he involuntarily falls into even the slightest emphasis in the direction of quadruple meter  , the effect immediately becomes silly or ridiculous; it sounds as if the leader of an amateur orchestra wanted to count out one full measure aloud to his uneasy troop before they began: one-two-three-four-*go!* But if the passage sounds as it was imagined, if the player succeeds in producing four really equal tones, our auditive experience still does not coincide with this acoustical datum. Even in the complete absence of any difference in accent, we do not hear one tone four times but *twice two* tones: groups, meter, measure.

If it were accent that produced the measure, the player or singer, in order to make the measure manifest, would always have to emphasize exactly as the metrical schema prescribes, to place and distribute the accents exactly as they occur in the metrical pattern—in triple time thus perhaps,  , in quadruple time thus,  . Now this style of performance is only too familiar: it infallibly characterizes the unhappy beginner or the hopeless case. It is the death of music, the strait-jacket, the poem recited in strict time. Tones talk music precisely to the extent to which they free themselves from the constraint of strictly metrical accentuation. This does not mean that the accents must never follow the metrical pattern; there is plenty of music that demands just that, a sharp emphasis in strict accordance with the metrical schema. But just as often the tones demand a different distribution of accents or even a suppression of all accentual differences. Freedom from the accentual schema of the measure means freedom to place the accents as musical declamation, not the metrical schema, demands—now one way, now another. Still, the measure, the group of two, three, four, six beats, *always* becomes manifest, no matter whether there is accentuation or not, no matter how the accents are placed—in conformity with the metrical pattern or without any relation to it or even in opposition to it. Music bears thousandfold witness to the fact that meter, beats-in-groups, does *not* require accent in order to emerge as a basic factor in musical experience. Otherwise, it would be impossible to understand the metrical organization of the following Bach theme, which, out of six strong beats, lets three fall by the wayside (the strong beats are 1 and 3):

Or take the opening melody of *Parsifal:*

Here tones sound on only 4 of the 11 strong beats and, of the total 21 beats, 13 are marked by silence. If emphasis really determined the metrical pattern, what sense would it make to write such a theme, or to think of it, in terms of 4-4 measures? What would be the meaning of so-called syncopation, the conscious, deliberate, and obstinate placing of all the strong accents precisely on the weaker beats, or even between the beats, ? The current explanation tells us that the meter of a piece of music to which we listen for a time takes possession of us, automatically pulses on within us, so that sudden accents *against* the meter, syncopations, jar with the continuing beat of the meter within us. Granted—but then what about pieces that *begin* with syncopations: Schumann's *Manfred* Overture, for example, or the Adagio from Beethoven's Quartet Opus 127? We shall go into these questions in detail later. Here we merely observe that meter and accentuation are processes on two different planes, which are free to go on together or to part company. Neither is dependent on the other—neither meter on accentuation nor accentuation on meter. Otherwise, the beginning of meter would have been the end of music.

What, then—if it is not accentuation—produces the grouping of beats into measures?

The answer to this question is given in the psychological laboratory.[9] A particular light, sound, or touch stimulus—a flash, a knock, a brief sharp contact—is repeated for a considerable time at regular intervals. The speed at which the stimuli succeed one another must be neither too high nor too low, so that the separate sensations shall neither coalesce nor be completely unrelated. Under these conditions we do not respond to the same unvarying stimulus simply by the repetition of the same unvarying sensation. Instead, a sort of process of crystallization occurs in the series of sensations; the sensations automatically unite into small groups of two, three, four. If the persons undergoing the experiment are told to count along with the successive sensations, in the great majority of cases the count is not 1-1-1-1-1-, or 1-2-3-4-5-, etc.—which would be the most obvious reaction—but, quite involuntarily, 1-2-1-2-, or 1-2-3-1-2-3-, or 1-2-3-4-1-2-3-4-; in other words, the count is not in units but in *groups*. The phenomenon has nothing to do with the nature of the stimulus; the result is the same whether light, sound, or touch stimuli are involved. Hence the factor responsible for the grouping must be the element that all these phenomena have in common: the division of the time flux into small portions of equal length. It is through their quality of marking off time that the stimuli produce the effect described. The constant demarcation of equal and unvarying time intervals sets up a sort of oscillation in us, a pulsation; the pulse lays hold of the individual sensations,

9. See, for example, Kurt Koffka, *Experimental-Untersuchungen zur Lehre vom Rhythmus.*

carries them with it, unites two, three, four, as the case may be, in a group, and thus organizes the series.

There is no doubt that we are here in the presence of the process that is responsible for the meter of our music, with its characteristic forming of groups. Directly or indirectly, we said, the tones always communicate to the listener the basic beat that regulates their motion: we hear in their succession the continuous demarcation of an identical time interval. A sympathetic oscillation, a pulsation, is set up in us, which, in turn, organizes the succession in the indicated manner—and so, counting with the tones, we shall not count 1-1-1-1-, or 1-2-3-4-5-, etc., but 1-2-1-2-1-, or 1-2-3-1-2-3-, or 1-2-3-4-1-2-3-4-, that is, in one of the familiar metric patterns. Hence musical meter can never be a mere dividing of the time flux into equal parts; inevitably, without any differences in accentuation, the parts will join into little groups and form measures. Which pattern—duple, triple, quadruple, or sextuple time—is given the preference in each case often depends—where accentuation does not preclude any choice—upon scarcely perceptible details of the melodic line. If the tones do nothing to influence our choice, we shall always involuntarily fall into duple or quadruple time, which thus shows itself to be the natural form of grouping; triple time is comparatively an art product.

Let us attempt to get a clearer view of what happens here. A piece of music is played; there is no accentuation. We count with the tones one-two-one- . . . Why did we say "one" here instead of "three"? What peculiarity in our perception of the third beat makes us count thus and not otherwise? If the new beat did nothing but bring us a further fraction forward in time, the phenomenon would be incomprehensible. If we involuntarily and unconsciously count "one" to beat number 3, this expresses the fact that it is not so much *further* as *back* that this beat carries us—and back to the starting point. To be able to come back, one must first have gone away; now we also understand why we count one-*two,* and not one-*one.* Here "two" does not mean simply "beat number 2," but also "away from." The entire process is therefore an "away from–back to," not a flux but a cycle,  , a constantly repeated cycle, for the "one" that closes one cycle simultaneously begins another.

A measure, then, is a whole made up, not of equal fractions of time, but of differently directed and mutually complementary cyclical phases. But since in time there can be no real going back, and hence, strictly speaking, no real cyclical motion either, since, therefore, every new beat does bring us to a new point in time, the process can be better understood and visualized as a wave, 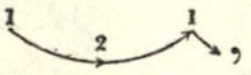 , which also best corresponds to our sensation of meter. Our sympathetic oscillation with the meter is a sympathetic oscillation with this wave. With every measure we go through the succession of phases characteristic of wave motion: subsidence from the wave crest, reversal of motion in the wave trough, ascent toward a new crest, attainment of the summit, which immediately turns into a new subsidence—a new wave has begun. In triple time the picture is different in as much as the two phases of the wave do not succeed each other immediately; there is an interval of hesitation and suspense between them: away-*and*-back, to-*and*-fro, 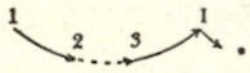 . Other kinds of time reveal corresponding variations in the organization of the phases; but the basic form of the wave remains the same.

Now we see the wrongness of the doctrine that musical time, that is, the grouping of beats into measures, springs from differentiation of accents. There is no need for externally derived accents in order to distinguish weak and strong beats from one another and thus establish the metrical pattern. It is the wave released by the regular succession of marks in the time flux that in each case emphasizes the beat which falls on "one"; brings all the beats between "one" and "one" into a group. The theory that the metrical pattern depends upon accentual differences confuses cause and effect. It is not a differentiation of accents which produces meter, it is meter which produces a differentiation of accents.

THE DYNAMIC QUALITY OF METER

In the course of this investigation our perspective has imperceptibly shifted. To begin with, we were interested in the demarcating beats. We called meter the division of the time flux into small portions of equal length; and so it was only natural to see the root of the phenomenon of meter in the beats that accomplished the division. But if we now describe the content of the musical experience of meter as a "to and fro," an "away and back," as a repeated cycle, as a wave, we no longer have the beats themselves in view: our little diagrams make it clear that our interest is not in the dividing points but in what goes on *between* them. We discover that it is not in the demarcating beats but where at first we did not look at all, where nothing happens, where *time simply passes*—it is in the apparent vacuum between the demarcating beats that musical meter is born. Only one thing may appear doubtful in this, namely, whether, if we are no longer speaking of what divides time but of what connects the divisions, we are still speaking of meter at all and have not rather already begun to speak of rhythm.

Ludwig Klages has said many profound and illuminating things concerning the relation between meter and rhythm in his essay *Vom Wesen des Rhythmus*. Meter, he points out, draws boundary lines, interrupts, and separates. Rhythm is the unbroken continuity of a flux, such a continuity as the wave most graphically represents. We cannot draw boundary lines on a wave; one wave passes into another without a break. The successive beats of a metrical series are all alike; no two waves are exactly alike. Meter is repetition of the identical; rhythm is return of the similar. The machine runs metrically; man walks rhythmically. Meter becomes the symbol of divisive, analyzing reason, rhythm the symbol of the creative and unifying force of life. The radical opposition between rhythm and meter is an expression of the basic conflict of two principles, one fostering life, the other inimical to it.

Such is Klages' interpretation of the phenomenon; no one will deny that there is something convincing about it. Actually, the mechanical, fixed division that is the law of meter and the indivisible flow that is the unity of rhythm appear as mutually exclusive as life and death. Strict time banishes rhythm from the poem; Prussian march time turns the living man into an automaton. And yet, music shows us that meter and rhythm can meet on other terms than those of enmity and opposition. To be sure, meter did stifle the free rhythm of earlier music—but not rhythm as such. What happened was the very opposite: out of the regular succession of measured beats rises the wave; the prototype of rhythm grows from the seed of meter.

Why, then, continue to speak of *two* factors, of *two* principles? Why not simply say that in our music meter is transformed into rhythm? There is no question anyway of mechanical accuracy in musical meter—who can play or sing musically to the beating of a metronome? If we look closely, we see that mechanical strictness is very far from being the rule here; the measure itself appears to be subject to constant slight alterations; it seems to be made of rubber not of steel. Does not this indicate that the wave has engulfed the measure and that meter has merged in rhythm?

Not at all; such an interpretation would not fit the facts. *Two* factors remain clearly distinguishable. In comparison with rhythmically free music, Gregorian chant for example, this is unmistakable. There we have longer and shorter tones in temporal succession, and this succession is itself already the entire rhythm. In our music too we have longer and shorter tones in temporal succession; but here the succession also gives rise to the metrical wave, whose uniform pulsation is perceptible through all the changes of the tonal surface. Both are always present simultaneously—the uniformity of the wave, the variegated pattern of durations, of long and short, in the actual succession of tones. Both together make up the rhythm of our music—not the succession of longer and shorter tones as such, but their succession supported, borne along by, the regular rise and fall of the continuing metric wave. An example is the beginning of Chopin's A-major Polonaise:

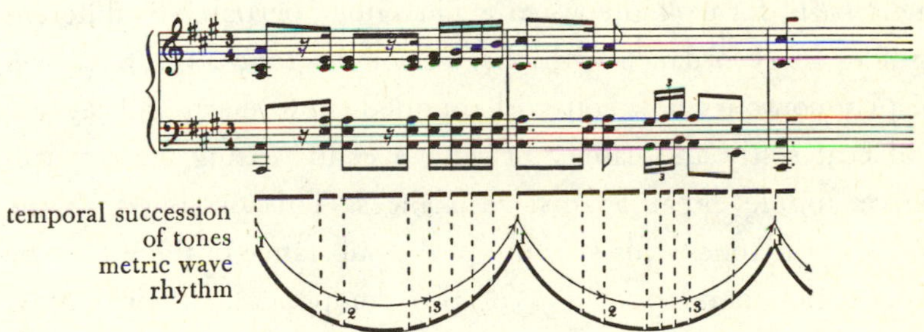

The tones fall upon the wave that they themselves have generated; the wave imparts its motion to the tones. Let us select one detail. The rhythmic quality of ♬♬ at the end of the first measure would be quite inadequately described as four tones of equal length in rapid succession, together filling up the last third of the triple measure. What we feel is, rather, four tones of equal length in rapid succession, *carried along by the ascending phase of the wave* to a goal, the wave crest. The rhythmic quality of the tone at the beginning of the second measure does not rest upon its comparatively longer duration, nor upon the accent it carries, but upon the fact that in it the wave attains its goal, the wave crest, and at the same time is carried beyond the goal, to a new cycle. And so on.

Such is the case in all metrical music. To put it metaphorically: the ground upon which the tones fall is itself in wave motion. The wave is the meter; rhythm arises from the different arrangements of the tones on the wave. The greatest possible latitude is accorded to the nature and manner of these arrangements. The tones may be distributed over the measure regularly or irregularly; may fill the measure in rapid succession or leave it empty for long stretches; at one place crowd close together, at another spread thin; may follow the pattern of the measure with their accents or run contrary to it. This freedom of distribution and arrangement makes it possible for the tones to give the constant basic form of the wave a changing, perpetually different profile. In accordance with the will of the tones, the wave will display contours now soft and rounded, now sharp and jagged; will beat softly and calmly or with ever-increasing impact; will heave, topple, break against resistances. This playing with the wave by the tones, this shaping of the substance of the wave; the conjunction and opposition of two components, their mutual tension and continuous adjustment to each other—this, in music, we experience as rhythm.

If from this point we go back to our original question—what the contribution of the time component to the musical work of art may be—we already see the inadequacy of the conventional finding that music unfolds in time. Certainly, tones follow one another in time, fill their accurately determined portions of time, and thus for our sensation (be it directly or indirectly) divide the time flux into equal fractions. But this is not all. We have seen that, in music, we never have to do with a mere sequence in time. The temporal succession here is revealed not simply as a progression but as a combination of progression and recurrence; it does not represent itself to us in the image of a straight line but in the image of a wave. The equal portions into which musical meter appears to divide time turn out, upon closer examination, to be variously directed phases of wave motion; the moment of time at which a tone enters is not a point on a straight line but on a wave; the interval of time that the tone fills in sounding is not a section of a straight line but a fractional phase of a wave. And as the tones fall on the different phases and fractional phases of the wave, the variously directed kinetic impulses of the different phases successively impart themselves to the tones. This is what we *hear* when we hear music whose structure is metrical: the various directions of the successive wave phases. When we identify the beat, the part of a measure upon which a particular tone falls, we do not do so because we had secretly counted along, or reckoned up in memory, but because the characteristic direction of the wave phase upon which the tone falls becomes directly perceptible in the tone, can be heard in and from the tone directly, just like any of its other qualities. Thus every part of the measure, according to its place in the cycle of the wave, is characterized by a particular *metrical quality,* which differs from every other solely by the direction of its kinetic impulse: the metrical order appears as a *dynamic* order, and the metrical qualities as *dynamic* qualities. From its side, the time component of music reveals an ordered working of forces, which, in the musical work of art, allies itself with the working of the tonal forces. And if we were able to define melody as motion in the dynamic field of the tones, rhythm now presents itself to us as *motion in the dynamic field of meter.*

POLARITY AND INTENSIFICATION

But the organization of the individual measure is far from exhausting the forces that develop in the time component of music. Their effect reaches beyond the limits of the individual measure in two important ways.

Music is always in demand when—for whatever reason—human beings are to be made to forget themselves. It is the tried and true resource when children are to be soothed or put to sleep, when masses are to be filled with enthusiasm for some cause and fired to extraordinary accomplishments, when dancers are to be put in a trance, when religious ecstasy is to be induced. The effect of music with which we are here dealing, and which could in a general way be called ecstatic, is based far less on tones as such, on melody or harmony, than on rhythm—and specifically on a rhythm especially designed to bring out the ceaselessly repeated beating of the metric wave. The listener is caught by the motion, drawn into it more and more, and finally carried irresistibly along with it. The phenomenon is not restricted to cases in which music serves as a means to an end; it is only exhibited most clearly and nakedly there. We always sense it, in various degrees of intensity, when we hear music whose structure is metrical; it is a basic element of our experience of music; it can become the medium of the most powerful artistic effects. What almost physically overwhelms the listener in certain compositions by Bach and Beethoven—the opening chorus of the *St. Matthew Passion,* for example, or the Gloria fugue in the *Missa Solemnis*—is the effect of the metric waves, which roll down upon us, broad and powerful, with ever-increasing impact, each new wave driven on by the concentrated force of all those which have preceded it, and in turn driving another before it, irresistibly and inexhaustibly, until finally it becomes impossible to conceive how this surging flood could ever be stilled, and we feel that we are seized and borne along by eternal motion itself.

The succession of equal metrical beats produced the wave; the repetition of the same metrical wave now produces *intensification.* Every new wave, in comparison with the similar wave that preceded it, is experienced as an increase (an increase in excitement or tranquillity, as the case may be). The two phenomena, the wave of the individual measure, the intensification of the successive waves, are closely connected. The sequence of measures is not a mere succession of equal portions of time. The individual measure does not merely traverse a definite and definitely divided interval of time; in every measure a cycle begins and closes, a road is traveled, a goal attained—in short, something is *accomplished.* Every measure is an accomplishment; with every new measure the same accomplishment is effected anew. The same accomplishment? If I raise a weight to a given height, once, twice, ten times, the accomplishment is not the same each time but *increased* each time. If the wave rises to its crest again and again, I feel an increase in accomplishment each time. The swing that makes the wave reach its crest at the same time carries it beyond its crest, toward a new cycle, a new crest. As the impulse that sets it in motion, the first wave lives on in the second, the first and second together in the third, the first three in the fourth, and so on and on. In this chain no link is lost; the earlier links are not obliterated but are preserved as active force in the successive present links. But for the same reason no link in the chain can ever be like another; each is characterized by the impulse it receives, increases by its own, and passes on: the links are not numbers in a numerical series but stages in an intensification series. As measure follows upon measure, wave upon wave, something grows, accumulates; it is a dynamic process through and through, only to be understood as the result of a constantly active force, which produces accomplishment after accomplishment. The graphic image of the process is ⁄‾‾ , a curve that first rises rapidly, then gradually flattens out, but without ever becoming horizontal.[10]

In the temporal component of music, then, we have to deal with a two-faced force, not to say a two-minded force. So far as it is responsible for the organization of the individual measure, it is perpetually intent upon closing a cycle, reaching a goal; it wills the finite. On the other hand, with its renewed, ever more insistent "On! Once again!" which hammers out measure after measure, it is a striving without end that accepts no limit, a willing of the infinite.

However, these two activities of the metric forces do not maintain a neat separation between their two realms, as if, for example, the one were responsible for what goes on inside the measure and the other for the connection of measure with measure. Rather, the force that closes, that forms cycles, peremptorily reaches out past the individual measure; asserts its claim beyond those borders too.

---

10. The effect of this force is familiar to musicians from a particular experience—the inevitable tendency to change tempo, especially in the direction of acceleration, when a piece of music repeats a distinct rhythmic formula for a considerable time. In musical circles some years ago there was much discussion of an argument between Maurice Ravel and Toscanini in regard to the question whether, in Ravel's *Bolero,* a composition based on the endless repetition of the same rhythmic formula, the tempo might be gradually accelerated or must be strictly maintained to the end. Wholly different effects are produced according to whether one does the former or the latter—lets oneself be carried along by the stream or meets its increasing force with increasing resistance. One could even divide artists into psychological types in accordance with how each decides the question.

Let us take a simple example, the beginning of the *Emperor Waltz:*

A naïve listener, asked to count along in time, will almost certainly count 1-2-3-4-1-, etc. If he is then told that this is a waltz, and that a waltz is notoriously in three-four time, not in four-four, he will be perplexed to explain his supposed mistake. Strictly speaking, however, he did not count wrong; he merely did not count with the basic beat, as the accompaniment gives it:

1 2 3 1 2 3 1 2 3 1 2 3 1

He counted with the melody: 1 2 3 4 1

His counting units are not the beats, of which three here make a whole measure, they are the whole measures themselves; the first two tones of the melody, each of which extends through a whole measure, led him to choose the whole measure as his counting unit. But here a remarkable phenomenon comes to light. The same thing happens with the whole measures as happened with the beats: they do not simply follow one another like the members of a continuous series; they join into groups. The phenomenon of the cycle, of the wave, which gave the individual measure its structure, is repeated on a higher plane, except that the individual phases of the cycle are now no longer beats but whole measures:

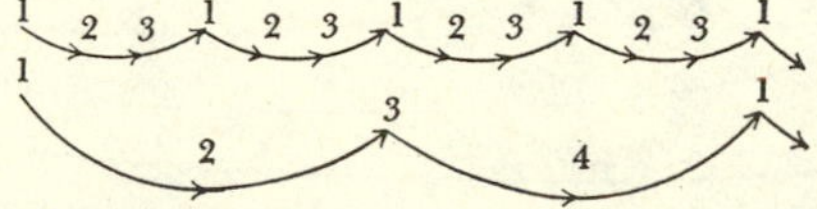

The phenomenon as it appears here is typical, an elementary expression of the activity of the metric forces—typical too in so far as the wave on the higher plane does not repeat the three-part structure of the individual measure but exhibits a four-part structure. We have mentioned that the natural form of the pulse is the two- or four-phase form, and that triple measure, so to speak, represents art going beyond nature. Now, on the next higher plane nature normally asserts herself, inasmuch as the groups that emerge are formed of *two* or *four* such triple measures. Occasionally the tones will force us to hear groups of three or even five or seven measures; this will always be meant as a sharp departure from the norm and will always be felt as such.

But even with this the activity of the group-forming component of the metrical forces has not reached its limit. Instead, as the closed cycle of the individual measure becomes a phase in the next higher cycle of the group of measures, so now again the closed group of measures becomes a phase in a still higher supergroup, and so on. An example is Mendelssohn's *Midsummer Night's Dream* Scherzo:

Wave superimposes itself upon wave, the closed cycle, the "to and fro" of the one is, from the point of view of the next higher plane, a mere "to," which demands the completing and consummating "fro." The same force that forms the wave of the individual measure expresses itself, in reaching beyond the measure, as a demand for ever more embracing *symmetries*. The whole of a group is always at the same time the half (a half either demanding symmetrical completion or fulfilling that demand) of the next higher group.

It goes without saying that we shall observe an analogous phenomenon if we look in the opposite direction, into the individual beat instead of beyond the individual measure. Even if the tones of the individual beat are divided into smaller and smaller time values, for example,

the temporal succession will not be experienced as a simple sequence; on these subordinate levels too the wave structure will unfailingly assert itself; we shall hear groups

. What, as a beat, is a mere phase of the cycle becomes a completed cycle from the point of view of the next lower level, and so on indefinitely. We can continue the subdivision to the limit of the perceptible, but we shall never come to a time value so small that time simply elapses in it, in which the flux is not also a pulse. The picture, then, is the same, whether we look beyond the measure or into the measure. Temporal flux in the sense of the wave-forming force is a multilayered texture of superordinate and subordinate waves, in which the wave of one stratum is in turn a phase of the next higher stratum, and, vice versa, the phase is in turn the wave of the next lower stratum.

Polarity and intensification—in these Goethe [11] believed that he had discovered the two principles governing all the phenomena of animate nature. Now we find them in the twofold activity of the forces that give all musical phenomena, in so far as they are temporal succession, their characteristic organization: in the tendency that closes, establishes symmetries, equalizes every weight by a counterweight; and in the tendency that drives on, accumulates, is responsible for constant augmentation. How the two tendencies work with each other and with the tones, or rather, let the tones work with them; how tonal forces and metric forces work together in general; how the tones bring out now the intensifying, driving-on tendency, now the closing, symmetry-establishing tendency, let the one gain the mastery here, the other there; produce all possible syntheses between the two; bring asymmetrical structures into equilibrium; how, finally, in its ever increasing outreaching, the twofold activity of the metrical forces in conjunction with the tonal forces brings into existence the *forms* of music, the ever astonishing, often overwhelming constructions of an architecture in time, serial structures and symmetrical structures of the smallest and largest dimensions, and structures in which the two principles interact in the most various ways—all these are questions that we must leave to musical theory to discuss in detail. The general problem of musical forms will later demand our attention.

CLASH WITH PHILOSOPHY

"Music is a temporal art." First this had only the naïve meaning that the tones and chords of music, unlike the forms and colors

11. *Naturwissenschaftliche Schriften* (particularly the remarks written upon the rediscovery of his earlier *Fragment on Nature*).

of a painting, are not all given us at once, but pass before our consciousness one after the other. According to this conception, time appeared as a vessel through which tones flow, or as the long, empty course down which tones can pass; time made it possible for music to exist—without time no music, as without space no visual art; but that was all. In respect to the musical context itself, time remained perfectly neutral, it had no voice in it; its relation to the world of tonal event was like that of the still empty strip of film to the pictures that are to be taken on it: it enables the pictures to appear, but itself—its chemical substance—has no influence whatever on the content and connection of the pictures.

We have now seen that, in fact, matters stand quite differently. From temporal succession as such, there arise elementary musical effects, the effects of meter and rhythm. It is not something coming from without, the different accentuation of beats, which creates musical meter; musical meter is not born in the beats at all, but in the empty intervals *between* the beats, in the places where "time merely elapses." The mere lapse of time here effects something; it is felt as an event, strictly speaking as a wave. In the macroscopic picture something else happens: to the wave, intensification is added. As wave and intensification the lapse of time sustains and nourishes the rhythmic life of music. The function of time here is, then, no longer that of the empty vessel, which contains the tones, or the bowling alley down which the tones roll; on the contrary, time intervenes, is directly active, in the musical context. It is time which makes differently directed cyclical phases out of beats of equal length, which transforms equal measures into different degrees of intensity. Music is temporal art not in the barren and empty sense that its tones succeed one another "in time"; it is temporal art in the concrete sense that it enlists the flux of time as a force to serve its ends.

With all this we have reached a position that could not be more diametrically opposed to a mode of thought that can summon a proud ancestry to substantiate its claims. The time flux as event, time an active force! "Of course no one will seriously assert," says the philosopher Bolzano, "that time and space can produce effects of any sort; to do so would be to confuse the forces of things *in* space and time with space and time themselves." [12] To be sure, by a sort of linguistic shortcut, as in the case of "action of force," we speak of "effects of time," the traces of time that we see in a face, in a work of art, in a geologic formation; but what we mean by this is not the effects of time as such but of the experiences and processes that have accrued *in the course of time.* For all this, time still gives merely the frame; by itself it does nothing, effects nothing, is not perceived. The great thinkers of the last three centuries, the men who have given our picture of the world its particular stamp—do they not all agree in seeing time as a mere *ordering* of phenomena, a mere *form* of experience, but not as phenomenon or experience in itself? What remains of time if we leave out all that fills it—experiences, phenomena, events, sensations? Berkeley admits: "For my own part, wherever I attempt to frame a single idea of *time* abstracted from the succession of ideas in my mind, I am lost and entangled in inextricable difficulties." [13] Hume says: " . . . nor is it possible for time alone ever to make its appearance or to be taken notice of by the mind." [14] Kant is here in agreement with him: "Time in itself cannot be perceived." [15] Schopenhauer says the same: "Time in itself is empty and without properties." [16] Ac-

---

12. Bernhard Bolzano, *Wissenschaftslehre.*
13. Berkeley, *A Treatise Concerning the Principles of Human Knowledge.*
14. Hume, *A Treatise of Human Nature.*
15. Kant, *Critique of Pure Reason.*
16. Schopenhauer, *The World as Will and Idea.*

cording to these views, one can no more ascribe effects to time than one can put the number six in the scales or inhabit the form of a house.

Modern science is in general agreement with these findings of philosophic speculation. Psychology teaches that there is neither a time consciousness nor a time perception. We perceive *change*—that is all. A being in whose ambient no perceptible change took place would know nothing of time. Psychologically speaking, it is not time which creates change but vice versa: change creates time. "There exists no reason to suppose," writes William James, "that empty time's own changes are sufficient for the awareness of change to be aroused." [17] We deceive ourselves if we think that we can overhear the flow of time in ourselves by emptying our consciousness of all the images, thoughts, and feelings that otherwise fill it. The residuum proves, on closer examination, to be still a dim sensation of our own body, confused organic feelings—a sensation, then, of something that takes place "in time," not a sensation of time itself. Time itself we never find.

For the physicists, finally, time has basically never been anything but a fourth dimension added to the three dimensions of space, a measurable extension. A body does not fall only through space but also through time; time is simply another kind of emptiness, which the body has before it (and leaves behind it), which it must have before it in order to continue falling into it, falling, in a manner precisely predetermined, past the markers of seconds, minutes, hours. In modern physics, to be sure, this somewhat primitive concept has been greatly refined; but the basic view has not changed. Today, as in the past, any talk of

---

17. William James, *Psychology: Briefer Course,* p. 282.

time as a force, of effects of time, has as little validity for the physicist as the statement that space moves bodies or that the barometer makes the weather.

Against this evidence from scientific research and thought, we now have the accumulated evidence of music. Basing ourselves upon it, we affirm—affirm in all seriousness, although, according to Bolzano's dictum, no one should seriously do so—that time can produce effects. Even if the philosopher or psychologist nowhere and never comes upon real, active time, the musician has to deal with it constantly, is always working with it. Nor in this—as Bolzano holds—do we confuse forces of things *in* time with time itself. Where, pray, are these things of which the phenomena of meter and rhythm are supposedly the effects? There are no such things; we shall not find them. There is nothing given but tones—and time. We can even dispense with differences in tone and leave nothing but the same tone sounding again and again for equal spans of time, _ _ _ _ _. Even here, and indeed here with particular distinctness, there is still the to-and-fro, the pendulum motion, the wave; never—as we have sufficiently shown—is there mere sequence. What produces the wave? What generates the distinction between to and fro? The tone is always the same; the interruption is always the same; the time interval is always the same. Only one thing is different: the instant at which the tones sound. Nothing happens from tone to tone save one thing: time elapses. The mere fact of the temporal succession of the tones, and nothing else, must produce the distinction between to and fro: the pendulum motion, the wave, must be the work of the mere lapse of time. The wave is not an event *in* time but an event *of* time. Time happens; time is an event.

Thus the musician, from his observations, is led to conclusions that are directly opposite to those of the philosophers and psychologists. Change does not create time; time literally creates change.

PROJECTIONISM

We are well aware of the gap in our chain of reasoning. When we just said, "Tone and time are given, and nothing else," we left something out. There is always another datum: a hearer. Does not this open a familiar way of escape? Can the state of innocence of "empty time" perhaps still be saved?

The familiar way of escape is projectionism.[18] A projectionist could argue more or less as follows: It is not surprising that we can find, in the tones or behind the tones, no thing or process of which we can say that meter and rhythm are the effect. We are simply looking in the wrong direction. The thing sought is ourselves, or, more accurately, our bodies. The processes sought are processes in our bodies. Tones automatically arouse certain sympathetic motions in the hearer; one cannot hear tones without moving with them more or less perceptibly. If the tones fit into a meter, our sympathetic motions do the same: they beat the time. Hence it is not in the tones that the metric wave beats, but in the hearer; it is not a motion of time that we perceive, but a motion of our own body. And these sensations of motion, arising from the tones and steadily accompanying them, are now projected back into the tones: just like melody and harmony, meter and rhythm are basically generated by the hearer; are the result of feeling subjective sensations *into* objectively given phenomena.

Projectionism appears to stand on firmer ground in tracing the experiences of meter and rhythm back to subjective sources than when it attempts to do the same for melody and harmony. It can appeal to a mass of concurrent testimony from experience,

---

18. On the projection theory of rhythm, cf. Ernst Meumann, *Untersuchung zur Psychologie und Aesthetik des Rhythmus.*

observation, and scientific research. Rhythm and bodily movement appear to be most closely and most fundamentally connected. The connection is not a learned one. The newborn infant often reacts to rhythmic stimuli with movements before it exhibits any other reactions.[19] The child of nine months who swings his foot back and forth in time when the sound of a piano comes from an apartment on a lower floor, who impatiently interrupts the motion and keeps his foot suspended when the player gets out of time, then at once greets the resumption of correct time by joyously resuming the motion, does all this without having taken a course in rhythmic gymnastics. The civilized listeners at a concert, to be sure, do not move their limbs, march and dance through the hall, in time to the music; but the many barely perceptible and for the most part unconscious movements with which they keep time reveal what they are suppressing. Even in a state of complete external repose, demonstrable changes in muscular tension, in breathing, in blood pressure, in the pulse, show how the hearer's whole body reacts to rhythm, is drawn into sympathy with it. So it does not appear to require any hair-splitting to seek the basis of the phenomena of meter and rhythm in internal bodily sensations of pressure and tension that accompany motion whether accomplished or suppressed or even merely intended.

Since the extremely simple and schematic examples of rhythmic experiences with which the psychologist in his laboratory commonly deals, and to which the considerations of the philosophers preponderantly refer, appear to be sufficiently explained by this interpretation, we commonly accept it without qualms. The musician, however, will think of a number of situations in the realm of meter and rhythm that are not only left out by such an explanation but directly contravene it.

---

19. Cf. Charles H. Sears, *Studies in Rhythm.*

We shall examine some of these situations more closely. It is not difficult to conceive how a metrically ordered succession of tones sets up a concurrent succession of kinetic impulses in the hearer and how the bodily sensations of these impulses fuse with the sound stimuli. But we have observed that the meter in a piece of music does not beat simply in a *single* wave but in a complex involving superordinate and subordinate waves, of which at least the two closest to the principal wave can be felt distinctly. That one and the same succession of tones should arouse in the hearer several differently articulated series of motions is less easy to conceive. Let us take the following simple example:

The beat indicated by the vertical lines is, from the point of view of the principal wave, "advance toward 'one' "; from the point of view of the subordinate wave, it is "departure from 'one' "; from the point of view of the superordinate wave, it is "advance toward 'two.' " All this together makes up the particular metric quality of this moment and is felt in it as such. It does not take much musical experience to be able to separate the complex sensation into its components; without much counting or reckoning, the hearer knows at what point in the cycle of each wave he finds himself. If this quality is nothing but the hearer's internal bodily kinetic sensation projected into the tones, it must be assumed that a corresponding complex of motions is gone through in the hearer's body. But projectionism fails to tell us what mysterious organization of our body makes us react to a succession of tones by a whole well-ordered system of differently articulated series of impulses.

Upbeat is the term for the beginning of a melody that does not coincide with the beginning of the measure but immediately precedes it—as, for example, in the following melody from Brahms's First Symphony:  . Such a beginning, such a first tone, has the character of a preparation, of an advance to the "real" beginning, the immediately succeeding "one"; we clearly feel that it falls on the ascending phase, on the last part of the ascending phase, of the metric wave. From the point of view of projectionism, we must ask, Upon what basis is it that we react to a first tone with a kinetic impulse of this particular kind? It will perhaps be answered that we are dealing with an illusion: the upbeat character of the tone becomes clear only retrospectively, after the following tone has somehow (perhaps through stronger stress) made us understand that it, and not the first tone, bears the principal accent of the measure. This explanation may apply to a poor performance; in such a case we often really do not know what such a beginning tone is supposed to be; only the stronger stress on the next tone reveals: "This is 'one'!"—so the preceding tone must have been an upbeat. With a masterly interpreter, to be sure, the case is different. One has but to hear Pablo Casals—the greatest rhythmic power among living musicians—play an upbeat: then we do not have to wait for a second tone in order to find out where we are with the first. The ascent and advance so characteristic of the last phase of the metric wave are so clearly perceptible in the tone itself that even if nothing else followed, if the player stopped after the first tone, we should still know that it was an upbeat. Certainly, it is the particular kind of tone production, scarcely apprehensible characteristics of the tone itself, which produces this effect and sets up in the hearer the kinetic sensation corresponding to the upbeat. But is not this as much as to say that the motion is in some way *in the tone itself;* that the tone in some way reproduces the motion? Now where do we stand with the projectionist interpretation? Are we to say that someone looking at a portrait projects the features of the sitter's face into the colors and forms of the picture?

(It may be objected here that it is not the observer but the artist who projects the features of the face portrayed into the colors and forms on the canvas, and does so out of his own mind—especially when he is not painting from a model. Why should not the performing musician likewise project into the tone a particular kinetic idea, which we then hear from the tone? It can be put in this way; but to do so only pushes the problem a step further back. We know what idea guides the painter's brush hand. We also know the reality of which his idea is a representation—in the case of our example, the human face. What idea guides the cellist's bow hand? The idea of a motion? What determines this particular idea; of what reality is it a representation? We shall soon undertake a more detailed discussion of the problem as it presents itself from the interpreter's side.)

We encounter similar difficulties in the case of *syncopation.* We have already referred to the phenomenon and to its usual explanation. If one deliberately and obstinately accents precisely the tones that fall on the more lightly accented beats, or even in the intervals between beats, the tonal accentuation clashes with the metric wave. Schematically represented:

An interpretation of this from the point of view of projectionism is conceivable only under two conditions: either both series, that of the meter and that of the syncopation, are simultaneously represented in the music itself and are able to arouse two countercurrent series of impulses in the hearer; or the composition has gone on in the same meter long enough for the metric wave to continue beating automatically in the hearer even if the tones temporarily move against it. The cases, already mentioned, in which a composition *begins* with a syncopation are completely inexplicable, and indeed meaningless, from the projectionist point of view. The last movement of Beethoven's Ninth Symphony begins, for all the instruments involved, with a heavily accented tone that enters on the last beat of a three-four measure and continues to sound through and beyond the "one" of the following measure:

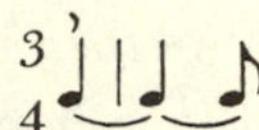

For the projectionist, this kind of writing is sheer nonsense, the foolishness of a musician who had been stone-deaf for years. The acoustical datum is a prolonged tone with a heavily accented beginning:

The tone arouses a kinetic impulse that, projected back, produces the beginning of the metric wave:

But what Beethoven intended should be played and heard is this:

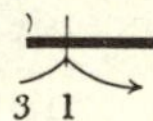

An impossibility! How should the held tone give the hearer's kinetic reaction this particular form, unless through a crescendo and decrescendo? But that is out of the question here. According to projectionism, the kinetic reaction, and hence the rhythmic quality, is exactly the same in the case of

and

But, for the musician, there is as much difference as between day and night. What is meaningless from the standpoint of projectionism is, for him, a conventional, everyday thing, which composers have used, interpreters communicated, and audiences correctly comprehended innumerable times. *What* it is, we shall not now ask; we merely assert that, whatever it is, it cannot be explained by projection.

But the greatest difficulty for projectionism is provided by another element of the language of music, the *rest.* When we were investigating melodic motion, we found that rests by no means always signify interruptions or sections in a melodic context; the distinction between rests that separate and rests that connect is a familiar one to the musician. If we now ask what is the role of the rest as a part of the *metrical* context, it is clear that normally it cannot be an interruption: the meter continues undisturbed whether each of its beats is actually occupied by tones or not. Whether we get

♩ ♩ ♩ | ♩ ♩ ♩ | ♩ or ♩ ♩ 𝄽 | ♩ ♩ 𝄽 | ♩

has very little effect on the meter; the "three" is always the same last phase of the cycle, going toward the beginning of a new measure, whether it is filled up or left empty. Those who wish to see the origin of meter in a kinetic reaction set up by a sound stimulus now face the question, How are we to understand it that the meter goes on even when the instigating stimulus ceases, when there is a rest in the place of a tone?

At first the difficulty seems slight. We have all heard of Pavlov's dog, which was regularly given food at the stroke of a bell until finally its saliva and digestive juices flowed when it merely heard the bell and no food was set before it. A reaction can become automatic through repetition and habituation, so that it appears even if the definitely expected event that originally aroused it does not occur. Perhaps we are simply Pavlovian dogs when we feel the meter beating on during rests. Normally, a composition goes on for a considerable time in the same meter;

our kinetic reactions become automatic, and continue even if the chain of tone is occasionally broken and the stimulus ceases. Then we simply project the kinetic sensation corresponding to the particular place into the rest instead of into the tone.

But there are musical situations that exclude the assumption of an automatic reaction on the listener's part. Let us take an extreme example, the theme of the last movement of Beethoven's *Eroica* Symphony. A short, stormy orchestral passage ends in a half chord, in which all metric motion ceases; then the theme enters:

Even the printed music shows that this tonal structure consists less of tones than of rests. In the actual hearing, the disproportion stands out even more strongly; since Beethoven prescribes pizzicato tones on the stringed instruments, we are actually given a minimum of tone, a maximum of vacancy. Now how about the necessary presuppositions of the projectionist interpretation? The acoustical stimulus is reduced to the utmost; there is no question of habituation to the meter on the basis of previous repetitions. The rests do not appear as occasional interruptions of the sequence of tones; on the contrary, the tones appear as occasional interruptions of the rests. The metric wave that should beat on even in this vacuum could no longer be interpreted as projection of the kinetic impulses by which we react to sound stimuli.

In fact the metric wave does beat here, and indeed as distinctly and regularly as if the measures were filled to the brim with tones. The rest that follows the sounding of the first tone corresponds in the hearer not simply to a consciousness of vacancy, nonhearing, eclipse of hearing—as if a light were switched on and off; instead, after the tone is heard, what fills the rest is *expectation* of the tone to come. We might say that we hear the tone, and listen through the rest for the next tone. As we know, it is the dynamic quality of the tone, its pointing beyond itself, its state of incompleteness, which expresses itself in this way. But there are yet other factors at work. For when the next tone sounds, terminates the rest, we do not feel merely "tone," expected event, but "two," the counterbeat of a pulse. The tonal event in time is likewise a metric event. In the next rest we do not merely wait for a new tone, but equally for a new "one." (We are counting here with the whole measures of the example as units, of which first two, then twice two, join into groups.) In general our expectation during the rests is as much directed to the next beat of a pulse as to the sounding of a tone. When, in the fifth measure of our theme, a note enters at a place that had previously always been empty, we do not feel "premature appearance of the expected event," but "counterbeat of the nearest subordinate pulse." In the tone that falls on the last beat of the sixth measure the drawing toward a new "one" becomes perceptible. Thus the tones, as they sound here and there, also disclose what is going on within the rests—the fact that there, in apparent vacancy, in nothingness, something *is* going on, namely, a pulse is beating. This does not seem particularly surprising to us. We have already found that it is not in the beats but in the intervals between them, where nothing happens, where time simply elapses, that meter is born. Since these intervals are usually for the greater part filled with tones, projectionism was able to propound the theory that the phenomenon of meter was a product of our reaction to sound stimuli. But now that it appears that the phenomenon of meter is exactly the same whether the intervals are entirely filled with tones or remain entirely empty of tones, projectionism has little left to stand on.

Let this not be misunderstood: there is no denying that we react to sound stimuli with kinetic impulses. What must be denied is that the metric wave has its origin in the sensations aroused by these impulses. The two phenomena belong to different contexts. One is the reaction of the hearer to the sound stimulus,

a reaction that has its peak at the beginning and fades quickly until the next stimulus starts a new reaction; the other is the process that connects the two tones across vacancy,

It is *this* process for which we must account. We cannot see in it anything like the dying away of the reaction to the preceding stimulus; its organization is not that of something that is running out but of something that is striving toward a goal. This we cannot attribute to kinetic reactions. Reactions to what? To the absence of tones? If instead of the continuous and well-ordered chain of external stimuli, supposed to produce as reaction a parallel chain of kinetic impulses, we have a vacancy interrupted by momentary stimuli, and if nevertheless the clarity, continuity, and order of the successive phases of the metric waves are not in the least impaired, then the phenomenon of meter cannot have its basis in reactions to external stimuli, cannot be something produced by the hearer. The metric waves that beat here were not set in motion by us. Our sensations are the consequences, not the causes, of the phenomenon.

Let us change our standpoint; let us pass from the position of the auditor to that of the performer. How do I keep time when I play or conduct? The textbooks tell us that keeping time depends upon the ability to let a particular succession of motions become automatic through repetition. We see the conductor going through the same series of motions—with slight variations—again and again. Once the motions have become automatic, they can of their own momentum—without his participation, so to speak—keep him in time. But it is not difficult to imagine less conventional ways of conducting. Constant repetition of the same motion is not required—time can be just as well indicated by a haphazard, heterogeneous succession of all imaginable bodily movements. Anyone with a modicum of metric sense will keep such a variegated series of motions in just as strict time as the repetition of the same motion. Metric sense—what is it? In this case, where no regulating kinetic automatism can develop, what guarantees the *uniformity* of the motions? What directs them so that each new motion comes exactly after the lapse of the same interval of time? What tells us each time *when* this fraction of time has elapsed? That metric sense is a sense of the length of a span of time, we may not say; for time, we have been taught, is not something that can be sensed. We here face the much discussed and still unsolved problem of the subjective estimation of time, man's ability correctly to gauge the duration of passing time—an ability that extends from simple manifestations of the metric sense to the completely incomprehensible feats achieved by persons under hypnosis. On the basis of what processes, on the basis of what sensations, can we arrive at knowing the equality of two spans of time? Many hold the view that our sense of the equality of intervals of time is basically a *rhythmic* sense, a sense not of the lengths of extents traversed but of the equilibrium between mutually complementary phases of cycles. Says Whitehead: "We have a primitive perception of equality [of durations] by our perception of rhythm." [20] But this, as we have seen, by no means solves the problem; it is now only correctly posed. The

20. Whitehead, *The Concept of Nature.*

physicist Eddington has gone so far as to suggest the hypothesis of a "brain-pulse" from whose unfailingly regular beat we would unconsciously read, as from an inner clock, the elapsing span of time.

Let us return to our conventional conductor. If we see him in the full swing of repeating the same succession of motions over and over, we shall be inclined to admit that here a kinetic sequence that has become automatic is keeping itself in time. But how did this automatism come into existence, what preceded it—how did the conductor *begin?* Certainly not with motions that roughly corresponded to his idea of the proper time for the piece to be played and that he gradually corrected until the correspondence became as close as possible, and then made automatic through repetition. That may be the case with the beginner on the podium, but not with the experienced conductor, who with his very first motion will unfailingly find the time unit that he has in mind. What guides his hand so that, from the flux of time, its motion cuts out exactly the span that corresponds to his idea of the correct time unit? It cannot be any idea of motions or kinetic impulses on the part of his own body, as projectionism would have to assume. No conductor about to begin has ever thought of his own body; if he did, he would, figuratively speaking, fall into the water just as much as the man who, in jumping a brook, thought about what his body was doing instead of about the opposite bank, looked within instead of without. The last thing the conductor has in mind when he begins is himself—instead, he is concentrating completely and exclusively upon *the tone* that is about to sound. Nor does he ever mentally anticipate the beginning; he always begins *with* the tones, not *before* them. And what guides his hand is not some idea of a motion by his own body, but an idea of the motion that *the tone* is to make, that, strictly speaking, the meter in the tone, *time* (why not?) in the tone, is to make. How is a conductor to begin Bruckner's Fourth Symphony?

Here the only thing that can impart the proper measure to his movements is his precise idea of the metric wave beating in the unmoving chord. But this idea cannot in turn itself be an idea of a movement of his own body; otherwise we should have to ask what provides the proper measure for this latter movement, and so on ad infinitum.

RHYTHM AS EXPERIENCE OF TIME

The evidence of music thus refutes the claim of projectionism to give an adequate explanation of the phenomena of meter and rhythm. Yet it is not only music which testifies in this direction; testimony of the same import comes from an entirely different side, and indeed from the source where projectionism otherwise finds its strongest support—from the side of experimental psychology.

In a series of tests Kurt Koffka, one of the founders of Gestalt psychology, has shown that rhythmic experience cannot be equated with internal bodily sensations.[21] A variety of rhythmically organized successions of lights, tones, noises, and motions were presented to a number of subjects, who were instructed to concentrate on the phenomena and report their reactions. Many had counted along involuntarily with the successive stimuli; others had reacted by constructing brief phrases, which they repeated over and over; yet others had moved with the phenomena. In the

21. Koffka, *Experimental-Untersuchungen zur Lehre vom Rhythmus.*

great majority of cases, the familiar group formation appeared, produced by a sort of sympathetic pulsation: "It is as if a pulse were beating in me." (The possibility of a confusion with the subject's own heartbeat was excluded.) *Three* elements in the process were clearly distinguished: first, the physical datum—lights, tones, motions in a definite temporal succession; second, the experience of rhythm instigated by these; and third, the accompanying sensations, images, and feelings, among which kinetic sensations predominated. The experiments unequivocally demonstrated that "the rhythmic experience cannot be identical with the sensations, images, and feelings which accompany it"—and this includes the kinetic sensations. Experience of rhythm and sensation of kinetic impulses could be kept clearly differentiated; were distinguishable as two things. Like sympathetic counting and sympathetic articulation, sympathetic motion (actual or merely intended) is an emanation of rhythm, not rhythm itself.

But rhythm is no more identical with the instigating phenomena than it is with the accompanying phenomena. Here too the tests unequivocally show that "rhythm does not coincide with any sensory content." To be sure, rhythm needs sensory material in order to become manifest, but "it is not identical with lights, tones, or motions; rather, it lies behind them." We perceive rhythm in the phenomena, but it is not what we see, hear, or otherwise receive through the senses: it is "something that lies behind the phenomenological, even though it is called forth by the phenomenological." Here the contradiction to projectionism becomes very clear: we feel the rhythm *out of* the phenomena, not *into* them. Instead of the two-element schema of projectionism—phenomenon (e.g., tone), reaction (e.g., sympathetic motion), rhythm the result of projecting the latter back into the former—we get the picture of a tripartite relationship:

the phenomenon (tone) contains the rhythm; the perception of the rhythm results in reactions (sympathetic motions).

How are we to perceive a rhythm that "coincides with no sensory content"; that can neither be seen nor heard nor otherwise sensed? Here too the experiments give much information. The experience of rhythm is consistently described as "a psychic function, in which the subject especially has the feeling of being active." But at the same time it is observed that the activity thus felt "does not necessarily depend on the will." One subject expresses it as follows: "Through the tones I get the rhythm, which is different from the tones; through my activity I experience the rhythm. But this activity is not spontaneous, it is occasioned by the datum." The experience of rhythm equated with the feeling of an activity occasioned by the datum, the tones? Is this not, after all, projectionism, an admission that rhythm is my—the subject's—addition to the exterior datum of the tones, is my creation? If one insists, one can express it in this way; only one must understand what the words really say. In this case there exists an intimate connection between the "subjective addition" and the "exterior datum"; the addition is suggested by the exterior datum, something that lies in the datum itself comes to expression in it—something is mirrored in it. My feeling of rhythm is a feeling of something, of some *thing*, a genuine experience, a cognizing if you like. If I call it an addition, then all experience is addition. It is the subject's creation in the same sense in which all cognition is creation.

What is it that I experience or cognize in rhythm? The preceding course of this investigation leaves the answer in no doubt. Music is temporal art, we said—first, in the banal sense that its tones are given in temporal succession. It appeared that, in this case, temporal succession is never given as simple sequence, as simple flux, but as a combination of flux and cycle, as wave.

The phenomena of meter and rhythm are productions of the forces active in the wave. The question arises, What is it that beats here as wave, what moves here? It is not the tones; it is not the hearer; what remains to be said except that it is time? The forces of the wave are forces of time—or better, are time as force. Hence the second formula runs: Music is temporal art in the more exact sense that, for its ends, it enlists time as force. If, accordingly, meter and rhythm are cleared of the suspicion of owing their existence to a mere illusion, if the feeling of rhythm must be granted the status of a genuine experience, perhaps even of a cognition, then what is experienced or cognized in rhythm can be only time itself. A third formula follows: Music is temporal art in the special sense that in it time reveals itself to experience.

XII. The Musical Concept of Time

WHAT DOES IT MEAN to understand a phenomenon, for example, the motion of a star? On the one hand, we have the observed facts; they are given, we cannot tamper with them. On the other hand, we have certain concepts, thought constructs, such as time, space, matter, body, force, energy, and so on. The task is so to construct, so to think, these concepts that the observed fact appears to follow from them with logical necessity. In the case of the star, given time, space, etc., as what according to my thought they are, the star *must* perform exactly the movement I observe. If this correspondence of fact and concept has been achieved, the phenomenon has been understood.

It is the same with musical phenomena. The observed facts are there; what must the concepts be if understanding is to result? Specifically, in regard to the present problem, what concept of time is required if the phenomena of meter and rhythm are to follow from it with logical necessity? How must I think time if I want to understand musical rhythm?

It appears that the concept of time that would achieve this correspondence of thought and musical fact—the *musical* concept of time—would have to have characteristics that the traditional or *physical* time concept denies to time, just as it would have to lack other characteristics that the traditional time concept attributes to time. The following schematic comparison results:

PHYSICAL TIME CONCEPT	MUSICAL TIME CONCEPT
Time is *order, form* of experience	Time is *content* of experience
Time *measures* events	Time *produces* events
Time is divisible into equal parts	Time knows no equality of parts
Time is perpetual transience	Time knows nothing of transience

EXPERIENCED TIME

On this point we can be brief; what is essential has been sufficiently stated. Generations of philosophers and psychologists have taught that although an awareness of time goes along with all our sensations, perceptions, feelings, with all possible states and contents of our consciousness, as the order or form of their appearance—namely, succession—in itself time can never be the object of any sensation, perception, or any other kind of experience. Anyone who thought that he could arrive at time by thinking away everything that is *in* time, the moving things, the sense perceptions that crowd upon us, our feelings, all the concrete content of our consciousness, and retaining "only the form," would be in for a rude awakening; with the things that are *in* time, time itself would have slipped through his fingers. What remains of a vessel if one thinks away all matter—hence not only the matter of its contents but also the matter of its body? Something that at best can be thought in pure abstraction. Time, says Leibniz, is idea, not reality.

To whatever else this doctrine may appeal for its support, it is *not* compatible with the facts of music. At first sight it might still seem that our observation concerning the nature of musical rhythm confirmed the thesis of time as pure form. Does not rhythm require tones, hence something material, in order to manifest itself? If the tones disappeared would not all rhythm disappear with them? Must we not, then, admit that here too the concrete content of the experience is not time itself but tone, something that occupies time—that here too time is nothing but the organization, the order, the form, for a content? Certainly time requires matter—in this case the matter of tone—in order to manifest itself; but does that necessarily make it mere form, an abstraction, deny it concrete reality? Light too requires matter to manifest itself; in a space emptied of all matter there would be no light. Yet no one thinks of denying the reality of light as a thing in itself. We clearly distinguish light and illuminated thing as two equally real entities, not as abstract form and concrete content. Certainly time requires the tones in and through which it becomes manifest as rhythm. But it is not true that here only the tones are concrete experiential content, with time an abstract, empty form, only to be apprehended in reflective thought. No—through tones, time becomes concrete experiential content; the experience of musical rhythm is an experience of time made possible through tones. In the unique phenomenon of the musical rest, we have as it were the crucial experiment for our thesis; the rest shows us, with a clarity that leaves nothing to be desired, what happens if tones are not just thought away but actually left out: what remains is not abstract, empty form but a highly concrete experience, the experience of rhythm. There would be no rhythm if time could not be experienced as such, in itself.

TIME PRODUCING EVENTS

The idea that effects of any kind could have their basis in time, in the flux of time as such, is, within the limits of the physical time concept, an absurdity. To be sure, snow melts with time, organisms age, the surface of the earth changes its configuration; but these effects appear not *because* time passes but because heat, chemical processes, erosion, and volcanism—forces of things *in* time—are at work. For the natural sciences, "time" is merely another word for the fact that natural processes are susceptible of a certain kind of measurement, measurement by clocks. The second hand of our watch moves 498.7 steps forward while a light ray passes through the space from the sun to the earth: that is all. Basically, natural science stands or falls with the concept of non-active time. What the law of nature accomplishes is precisely this: it enables me to know *now* what is *not yet;* it abolishes the dividing line between the now and the not-yet; strictly speaking, it destroys time as reality. If I say that in 5100 years this piece of matter will have given off half of its radioactive energy, what I mean is that the continuing activity of the forces now given in this object, *and nothing else,* will produce the prophesied effect after the lapse of the stated amount of time. The actual lapse of time of itself has nothing to do with the matter; it is—to use an expression of Eddington's—a mere formality.[1] Where natural laws hold, there can only be effects *in* time; there can be no effects *of* time.

But music has acquainted us with processes that cannot be comprehended except as effects of time, in the literal sense. This crucial point requires to be elucidated again in greater detail.

What takes place if I correctly answer the question on which beat of a measure a particular tone in a melody falls? Have I, perhaps, in expectation of the question, counted along in time and thus brought together the tone and the count that belong to it; or have I, surprised by the question, repeated the melody in memory, counted the beats afterward in memory? This may occasionally be the method; in difficulties one may fall back on such mechanical devices—for that is what they are. What actually takes place is, as we have seen, a very different process. Hearing music, we oscillate with its metric wave. Each tone falls on a particular phase of this wave; each phase of the wave imparts to the tone that falls on it—and, through the tone, to the auditor—

1. Quoted by Bergson in *Durée et simultanéité.*

its particular directional impulse. Not because I count "one" to a tone (or because the tone was emphasized by an accent—for often it is not) do I know that I am at the beginning of a measure, but because I feel that, with this tone, I have reached the wave crest and at the same time have been carried beyond it, into a new wave cycle. Because every tone (and every rest) is characterized for my perception by a particular quality, and because in these qualities the place of the tone (or of the rest) on the metric wave is expressed, I am able to hear directly from the tone—and from the rest—in what part of the entire measure I am at the given moment.

The remarkable fact, which we also encounter elsewhere in nature, that a part of a whole is, so to speak, aware of its being a part, of its relation to the whole and its place in the whole, and also imparts this knowledge to the observer—that, consequently, the whole is in some manner present in the part—to this fact our thinking seeks to do justice by the *field concept.* A field is the region in which a force is active—active, in accordance with a definite order, differently at every different point of the field. The iron filing feels the effect of the magnet differently according to whether it lies nearer to or farther from the magnet, to the right of it or to the left—in other words, in each instance according to the place it occupies in the magnetic field. What happens in the field depends, among other things, on *where* it happens. The event is marked by the characteristics of the situation obtaining at this point, and only at this point, in relation to the active force; and the observer who is able to read the language of these characteristics will be able from them to read the place of the point in the field. Between the field as a whole and the individual points as its parts, then, there is a relationship of the type described above—the whole being given with and active in the part and the part, as it were, being aware that it is a part and directly announcing its relation to the whole. And wherever we encounter a phenomenon that exhibits this peculiar relation between parts and whole, we may assume that a force, an ordered action of forces, is its basis.

Since the phenomena of meter and rhythm unequivocally exhibit this peculiar relation between parts and whole, we are justified in assuming as their basis an ordered action of forces, a dynamic field. The question remains: What sort of forces are active here?

The answer can only be that they are forces of time. In other cases where we observe an action of forces, we are usually in a position to point out certain things, states of things, processes in things, from which the effects proceed and which appear to us as the agents or sources of the forces in action. But in the case of the rhythmic effects of music, the world of things leaves us completely in the lurch. There simply are no things, no processes in things, as effects *of which* the processes of musical rhythm can be understood. It is not that we know none; it is that none are given. All that is given here is tones of definite durations and a listener. The tones are the element that instigates, provides the possibility; as agents or origin of the forces that produce the rhythm, they are as little in the picture as the listener, whose contribution to the rhythm lies in the fact that he experiences it, not that he produces it. So we are left with only one series of data in which we can seek the source of the phenomena of rhythm: the *durations* of the tones. The answer to the question, "Of *what* are meter and rhythm the effects," can, then, only be that they are effects of the mere passing of time in the tones, of their temporality. Because tones have duration, because time elapses in them, and for no other reason, we have the rhythm of our music. Only time can be the agent and source of the forces active in meter and rhythm.

When we speak of agents of activity and active forces, we generally think of two clearly separable data; we distinguish between them as between a substance and a function of the same substance, a thing and a quality of a thing. A nail is one thing; the ability of the nail to hold two boards together is another. When a stream carries tree trunks with it, heaves itself against bridge piles, sweeps soil away here, deposits it there, the forces of the flow that work in this way are bound to a flowing something, water, which, instead of flowing, could also stand still and yet remain water, which is able to do many other things too, for example, to nourish animals and plants. In these cases the agent of the action has its own existence, independently of the acting force—in contrast with which it appears as something comparatively stable, lasting, substantial. But it would be a grave error to understand the statement "time is the agent of acting forces" as if it said that first there is time, as a thing by itself, a sort of substance, and then the activity of the forces that manifest themselves in meter and rhythm, as a quality or function, perhaps among others, of this independent datum, the thing "time." Any such notion would go far beyond the result of our investigations. It is precisely the opposite which music has demonstrated for us: the impossibility of separating a thing "time" from the forces that produce rhythm; time was here nothing but the activity of these forces. What we were able to say about this activity was by the same token all that we were able to say about time; agent and acting force merge in each other; no reasonable distinction between them is possible. If we still use the two words, it is not because our observations confronted us with two data, but because *language* forces us to: we speak in sentences and every sentence must at least have a subject and a predicate—that of which something is stated and that which is stated—two terms. In so far as we accept the testimony of music as basic, the existence of time is the same as its activity. We observe an oscillation, an accumulation—and this oscillation, this accumulation, *is* time. That there is something else in addition, a something that oscillates and accumulates—however obvious such an assumption may seem to us, it has nothing to support it except habits of thought and speech. To express it in the simile of the stream: we see tree trunks moved, bridge piles subjected to pressure, soil carried away and deposited—but there is no water, the stream bed is empty.

TIME KNOWS NO EQUALITY OF PARTS

The meter of our music, we said, divides the regular flux of time into parts that are all equal. Now what about this equality of parts in time?

That in daily life we divide the flux of time, are able to delimit hours, minutes, seconds in it, and that all these hours, minutes, seconds are equal to each other, is taken as a matter of course, as much as that all centimeters are equally long, all kilograms equally heavy. These are measures, we are a measuring species, and we could not measure if the measures with which we operate changed size in our hands.

But this does not yet explain what it means that all hours are equal in length. We can only compare and find equal what is given simultaneously. Can two hours be given simultaneously? Here we obviously find ourselves in the situation of an imaginary one-dimensional creature whose living space is the line along which it moves and which wants to make statements concerning the equality or inequality of sections of this line. In order to measure and compare these sections, it would have to be able to step out of the line, to look at it from outside. But that is precisely what it cannot do. To step out of time, to look at it from outside—that we cannot. How, then, is it to be understood if we nevertheless maintain that all hours are equal in length?

Within the frame of the physical time concept, the question answers itself. If time as such cannot be perceived, can produce no effects, if there is never anything but phenomena *in* time, never time itself, the question whether we can compare two times with each other has little meaning. The strict scientific definition of time was: "The motion of one body, if it is taken as the measure of the motion of another body, is called time." [2] Hence to compare times means to compare motions of bodies. The equality of hours is the equality of the distances traveled by clock hands; it is in the last analysis an equality of spaces, not of times.

But then what is the meaning of the equality of measures and beats in our music, that equality upon which we so emphatically insist when we train musicians above all to keep good time? It certainly cannot be referred back to space, to the lengths of the paths of moving bodies; for in music we are beyond the realm of bodies and space. Is the equality of measures and beats, then, still a true equality of times, of parts of time?

The meter that arises from the rhythmically arranged succession of tones and conveys itself to the hearer is, as we have seen, experienced as an oscillation, as a wave. Beats are the differently directed wave phases that add up to a full cycle. What is equal here?

The duration of the individual beats, it will be answered—but this answer implies a distinction between what occurs and its duration; it regards the metric wave as a process that takes place *in* time. It tacitly assumes that we are confronted with two data: first, the thing that occurs, the wave; second, a neutral medium, "duration," which underlies the wave as the empty strip of film underlies the pictures that will be taken. Actually we have *not* two data, first the metric wave, or the forces active in the wave, and then a neutral medium "time" or "duration" *in* which the forces work, *in* which the wave pulses; on the con-

2. Cf. p. 154, n. 5.

trary, the pulsing of the wave is itself already time, is itself already duration. But with this it has become meaningless to talk of an equality of beats. Where is there place for equality on a wave? Observation has shown us that the elements of meter are not equal stretches of time but differently directed phases. It is not length which makes the beat, but the kinetic impulse. The condition that beat two of a duple meter has to fulfill is not that it must be equal in length to beat one, but that it shall close a cycle. To play in time musically does not mean to play tones that fill equal lengths of time, but tones that give rise to the metric wave.

Is equality perhaps to be found in the succession of measure to measure, of wave to wave? Is not the succession of impulses in each individual measure taken as a whole the faithful repetition of the succession of impulses in every other measure? Yes and no. We have observed how, in music, the succession of measure to measure is never a mere sequence; how, instead, either measure joins with measure to form measure groups in which the equal waves of the individual measures appear as differently directed phases of a wave of higher order. Or how, from measure after measure, from measure group after measure group, a continuous intensification series is built up, in which every measure differs from every other as "more" differs from "less." In neither case is there any room for equality. To talk of an equality of times, or of parts of time, has no reasonable meaning in the realm of meter.

What do we mean, then, when we demand that musicians play in time; demand, that is, that they preserve equality of measures and beats? The poor performer who takes all sorts of liberties with time is censured for the capricious inequality of his measures and beats. By what concept of equality do we measure this inequality? Certainly not by the concept of measurably equal lengths. We have pointed out what happens if the meter of an automaton is substituted for the meter of music: music ceases to exist. It is not the unequal length of the beats which disturbs us in a performance where the time is erratic, but the fact that *they do not give rise to the metric wave.* Variations from absolute mathematical equality do *not* disturb us, if they serve to give the metric wave the form that is musically right. There is no such thing as a musician whose performance does not depart from mathematical equality within certain limits; accurate experiments have given amazing proof of how great such departures can be without even being noticed by the listener (even listeners with a thorough musical training). What, on the other hand, everyone notices instantly, what disturbs everyone, is the departures that do not serve the metric wave but go counter to it. The commandment that is broken in a performance in poor time does not, then, refer to equality in length between intervals of time but to symmetry of mutually complementary wave phases. The so-called equality of time proves to be a rhythmic quality, rhythmic balance.

The picture has undergone a strange reversal. The physical time concept postulated equality of times as something self-evident, but closer examination has shown that this equality had been registered under a false name; it appeared rather as an equality of spaces. The musical time concept rejected equality of times; but, within it, that equality now experiences a sort of rebirth, although in an essentially altered form. The one-dimensional creature to which we referred by way of comparison before, is still unable to see outside of its path; cannot look from without on distances traversed and compare them by measuring them. But it now seems that, under certain circumstances—that is, when its course follows the line of a wave—we can ascribe to it a sort of rhythmic feeling that tells it when phases of its course balance each other. It is as though passing through—or let us rather say living through—a phase of its course had established a demand, had created an emptiness, to fill and ulfill which is the function of the following phase: if the emptiness is filled, the brim reached, equilibrium is restored. The two phases do not stand side by side, are not compared and found equal; the sensation is that of a mutual complementing, a mutual interpenetration, a mutual balancing. It is to this sensation, a rhythmic sensation, that our concept of an equality of times reduces itself. The statement already quoted from Alfred Whitehead comes to mind: "We have a primitive perception of equality [of durations] by our perception of rhythm." [3] The expression "equality of times" makes sense only in so far as we take equality to mean rhythmic equivalence. Our definition must be: We call two times *equal* if together they form the "one-two" of a metric wave. If we want information concerning equality of times, it is not from our clocks that we shall get it, but from our music.

DIGRESSION I: REPETITION IN MUSIC

Not until we have recognized that, in the ordinary, literal sense, there is no equality of times, that—to put it in another way—time never repeats itself, are we able to understand how it is that *repetition* plays such an overwhelming role in music.

There are various kinds of repetition in music: the patent, more or less literal repetitions of themes, motifs, melodies, whole complexes, comparatively large sections of a composition; others that, as it were, veil the pattern to be repeated in a just-transparent robe of tone; yet others, more secretive, that represent various degrees of the transformation or development of an original pattern; and finally the most mysterious of all, those which are unknown even to the creating artist himself, which are hidden in the inmost depths of the very tones, whose presence was first

3. Cf. p. 195.

pointed out by Heinrich Schenker,[4] and in which the miracles of the organic formation of great masterpieces are revealed. Whereas some of these concealed repetitions are heard only upon increased familiarity with the composition, while others are never heard as repetitions at all (not everything that is repetition is also meant to be heard as such), the patent repetitions are obvious to anyone who has ever listened to a piece of music. Only this kind of repetition, which is part of the immediate experience of music, shall concern us here.

We are so accustomed to repetition in music that we accept it as something self-evident; that we never become aware of what an extraordinary phenomenon it is. A theme, a melody, is a definite statement in tones—and apparently music can never have enough of saying over again what has already been said, not once or twice, but dozens of times; hardly does a section, which consists largely of repetitions, come to an end before the whole story is happily told over again. How is it that a procedure which, in any other form of expression, would produce sheer nonsense proves, in the language of music, to be thoroughly sensible—to such an extent that rehearing what has already been heard is one of the chief sources—for many, *the* chief source—of the pleasure given by music?

Looking for analogous phenomena elsewhere, our first thought is of carpets, tapestries, and other ornamental creations, in which a motif reappears countless times; or of architecture, with its series of like formal members and repetitions of entire extensive formal complexes. The analogy is, however, only superficial; here, in space, the effect does not depend upon the repetition of the individual element as such but upon the *simultaneous presence* of many like elements—in other words, upon the

4. Cf. p. 78, n. 6.

fact that all the repetitions are given us at once, as a whole. The question arises how much pleasure we should take in looking at a carpet if the repeated elements of its pattern were given us not together but successively, if each came before our eyes by itself. More apt is the comparison with the frequent repetitions of groups of words and whole sentences in many epic poems, the repetitions of single verses and entire stanzas in lyrics. But how small this is, how strictly limited, how exceptional and unusual, compared with the role that falls to repetition in the musical context! What should we say if a poet expected us to swallow this:

Say not the struggle, say not the struggle
Naught availeth, naught availeth,
The labor and the wounds are vain,
The labor and the wounds are vain.

The enemy faints not nor faileth,
And as things have been they remain,
The enemy faints not nor faileth,
And as things have been they remain.

If hopes were dupes, fears may be liars;
Your comrades chase e'en now the fliers.
Your comrades chase e'en now the fliers,
Your comrades chase e'en now the fliers.

Say not the struggle naught availeth,
The labor and the wounds are vain,
The labor and the wounds are vain,
The labor and the wounds are vain.

Its musical analogue would be a meaningful construction from beginning to end, and indeed one comparatively poor in repetitions.

Let us examine a few concrete examples of how repetitions actually function in music. First a simple and typical example, a melody by Mozart, the Adagio from the great Piano Fantasy in C minor. The strophe of this melody consists of ten lines of equal length, each of which is divided into two equal hemistichs. The procedure is as follows: the tonal statement of the first line is repeated by the second, except that the end of the second hemistich is differently put; the third line repeats the first note for note, the fourth does the same with the second; the fifth line is new, yet its second hemistich is a repetition of the first; the sixth line repeats the first, with a new variation of the line ending; the seventh is the exact repetition of the second, the eighth the exact repetition of the fifth; the ninth line exactly repeats the sixth; the tenth begins as a repetition of the first, but then loses itself, leading into a new section. We get the following schema:

Line		
1	a	b
2	a	b′
3	a	b
4	a	b′
5	c	c′
6	a	b″
7	a	b′
8	c	c′
9	a	b″
10	a	- - - - - -

If we knew nothing about the existence of music, we should not find it easy to imagine a language in which a reasonable statement is 80 per cent repetitions—repetitions of "words" and "sentences," not of "letters."

Let us examine another melody, the Huntsmen's Chorus from Weber's *Freischütz:*

Then we get the whole thing over again from the beginning, with a change only in the very last measure. The schema is as follows (each line of the melody extends over four measures):

Line						
1	a	a	b	b	b	b
2	a	a	b	b	b	b
3	c	c	d			
4	a	a	b	b	b	b
5	a	a	b	b	b	b
6	c	c	d′			

This is not the aberrant experiment of a composer who wants to see just how far he can carry the principle of repetition without falling into imbecility; it is a completely normal melody, simple as a folk tune and universally popular. It will perhaps be advanced—since we are dealing with a choral piece—that the words contribute the element of variety which is so lacking in the tones. But this is not the case; the melody, it happens, is sung without any text; its linguistic foundation is nothing but the syllable "la" repeated exactly one hundred times—scanty nourishment for our intense hunger for variety.

A really extreme case of repetition looks quite different. One occurs, for example, in a famous passage from the first movement of Beethoven's *Pastoral* Symphony. Schema:

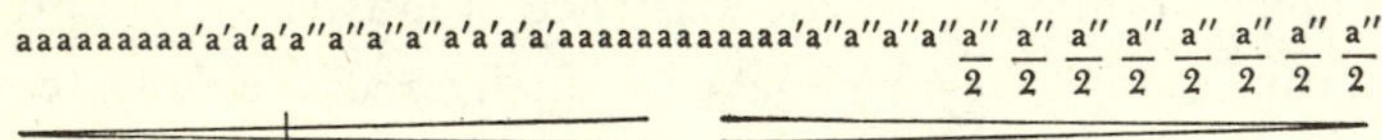

A brief tonal formula, comprising a mere five tones, in three variations—as if I should say: "I gave him apples, apples gave him I, I apples gave him"—repeated thirty-six times in all, followed by eight more repetitions of half the formula. (This $\frac{a''}{2}$, the last two tones of a″, is, in addition, identical with the first two tones of a.) And hardly have we got through it before it begins again, and the whole thing is repeated tone for tone! The sudden change in harmony after the twelfth repetition—indicated in the schema by the vertical line—though, to be sure, it changes what we might call the background against which the statement stands, does not change its content. The increase and decrease in tonal intensity (represented in the schema by the corresponding symbols) and the slight changes in tone color determined by the changing orchestration are equally powerless to detract from the overwhelming monotony of this endless series of repetitions. Regarded purely as the schema of a statement, it is sheer imbecility. How is it possible that, in music, such a thing becomes a meaningful and effective element in the whole of a masterpiece?

What is true of repetition on a small scale is equally true of repetition on a large scale. Innumerable compositions proceed according to a basic plan in accordance with which their often quite extensive first part is first repeated note for note, only to reappear again in a slightly altered version after an interlude that is often very short. Imagine a play of which the first scene should be played twice and which, after the second scene, should begin at the beginning again! But the situation is even more paradoxical. In many compositions this interlude follows the pattern of a process of gradual intensification leading to a climax; and what appears at the climax, the event for which we looked with such tension and which actually forms the culmination of the entire development, is nothing but the repetition of the story that we have already heard twice through. What would be sheer idiocy in a narrative, a drama, a poem—this beginning all over again—in music conveys the most powerful effects.

There must, then, be some peculiarity about repetition here. What is it?

The customary interpretation attempts to justify repetition by the *lack of objective content* in music. The other arts, it is held, find their objects ready in reality—the visual arts in the visible world, literature in life and thought in general; even architecture is given enough of objective reality in its material and in the practical function of its products. Music, on the other hand, must, like Münchhausen, hold itself in the air by its own pigtail, must give itself its own objective content. Themes, melodies, motifs—these are the "objects" of music; as a painting, for example, "repeats" some objective reality, so a piece of music repeats its particular "objects." The interpretation seems applicable only where repetition is at the same time alteration and transformation, for every artistic representation alters and transforms the objectively given; the representation is never an exact repetition, a duplicate of its reality. But the type of repetition with which we are here concerned, and especially the accumulation of exact repetitions, are not explained by the object theory. What sense would there be to "representing" a given "object" ten times, twenty times, eighty-seven times? Moreover, if we assume that the objective content of a piece of music is the theme destined to be repeated, we leave unanswered the question what the objective content of the theme itself may be. The theme, after all, is already a piece of music.

If the repetitions that we have observed in our examples were really nothing but repetitions, nothing but "the same thing over and over and over . . ." it would be incomprehensible how they could pre-empt so much space in statements intended to be meaningful. From the point of view of the tones, they are precisely this: the same thing again and again and again. . . . But music is not only tone; it is tone and time. Tones may repeat themselves; time cannot repeat itself. It is only because time does not repeat itself that so much repetition is possible here; or, vice versa, that so much repetition does not become meaningless is only to be understood if time does not repeat itself, if there is no equality of times. Measures, beats, groups of measures may be exactly alike so far as tonal content is concerned, but since they must occur at different times they can never be mere repetition; they are necessarily different, as the phases of a wave or the degrees of an intensification are different. The repetition of a tonal statement never simply says the same thing over again; it accomplishes its particular share in the metric process, whether as the fulfillment of a demand for symmetrical complementation or as a link in the chain of intensification. Indeed it would seem that this very equality of tonal contents brings out with especial clarity the inequality of successive measures and groups of measures. If the tones say the same thing again and again, they disappear as the object of attention; they become merely a medium through which the beating of the wave emerges ever more clearly and strongly. The peculiar effect of our example from the *Pastoral* Symphony depends upon this very fact. The more repetition there is, the more clearly and forcefully will time become manifest. We might almost say that if time had its way, tones would never say anything but the same thing; as time projects wave after wave, the tones are to do nothing but to reproduce wave after wave in their material. This is actually the situation which we find in primitive music, where often enough a composition consists of nothing but the endless repetition of one and the same brief tonal formula. Repetition is a sort of natural state of music—and it is not by chance that the extreme example of repetition which we have discussed occurs in a composition whose particular closeness to nature is expressed even in its title. Accordingly, the "exceptional case" would be not repetition but nonrepetition, something new. If the tones say something new, they have of themselves broken through the magic circle of enforced repetition. Every new tonal statement in the course of a composition is, in this sense, made *against* the will of an ever-present urge for repetition, an urge fed by time itself.

It might be asked why, if this is true of music, the same should not be true of all the other arts in which the time flux is an element, hence especially of poetry. After all, the verses of a poem are a temporal sequence and are just as much heard or read at successive times as the phrases of a melody. Why does the use of repetition in poetry reach its possible limits so soon? When a modern poet, Charles Péguy, tries this,

> Il allait commencer l'immense événement
> Il allait commencer l'immense avènement
> Il allait commencer le grand avènement
> Il allait commencer le grand gouvernement
> Il allait commencer le grand ébranlement
> Il allait commencer le grand revêtement
> Il allait commencer le grand embarquement
> Il allait commencer le grand rechargement
> Il allait commencer le nouveau réglement
> Il allait commencer le renouvellement . . .

his critic, André Gide, rightfully reproaches him with the illegitimacy of the procedure: it is, he says, repetition for the sake of the hypnotic effect of a litany, repetition as incantation, comparable to the flute playing of the Arab, who tirelessly begins the same melodic phrase over and over again.[5] Language fails in attempting to do what tone is privileged to do. The reason for this would appear to lie in the different capacity of word and tone to act as the medium of time perception. It is conceivable (we shall take up the question later) that tone, in and for itself, quite apart from rhythm, as a result of its basic independence from any relation to the world of objects, clears our sight for the perception of time as such, of time as event. The word has no such virtue. Hence repetition in verbal art is narrowly restricted, even with rhythm making its necessary and obvious contribution.

---

5. Péguy's lines and Gide's criticism are quoted from the latter's introduction to the *Anthologie de la poésie française*, pp. xliv, xlv.

And it occurs almost exclusively in lyrics and epics, the forms of poetry that were originally closely connected with music and still tend toward music. Much the same, furthermore, is true of the dance. The endless repetition of the same succession of motions is possible, meaningful, and enjoyable only because the motions are induced and carried by the rhythm of the accompanying music. Dance without music, dancers in silence, always make an impression that is somehow dreary and slightly silly.

In this connection, finally, yet another type of musical repetition appears in a new light: altered repetition—not what is expressed by the technical term "variation," that often far-reaching transformation and recasting of a given tonal entity, but the kind of repetition that leaves the original tonal entity untouched in essentials but here and there supplies alterations that decorate, enrich, and emphasize some of its individual characteristics. In the usual view, these alterations serve the need for variety: the composer has recourse to them if he fears that mere repetition would not be sufficiently interesting. But we have seen that there is no need for such external aids in order to keep interest alive even in the case of note-for-note repetition: time itself takes care of that, time as event, which holds our attention even when, and especially when, the tones of themselves have nothing new to say. Often enough, such slight alterations are mere ornamentation applied more or less externally; but in other cases—as when a master of this kind of repetition like Mozart or Schubert is at work—the effect of a barely perceptible change in the repetition goes far beyond satisfying the need for variety, points toward a source that lies deeper. If a tonal statement can vary within certain limits from its original form and yet remain the same—and that is what happens in this kind of repetition—the possibility is present of having the basic fact of *meter* reflect itself in the tones: the fact that the thing which is constantly repeated is always also something else, a new thing. The tones do not alter for the sake of variety, that is, in order to give the same thing an appearance of being different; on the contrary, because what is apparently the same is basically always different, the tones too do not want always to remain the same. What is expressed in these alterations is, then, in the last analysis, the action of time itself, in which there is no sameness. The will of time that on one occasion is bent upon note-for-note repetition, on another occasion motivates variation from exact repetition.

A possible objection must be briefly discussed here, because it urges itself with particular force in this connection. We go on talking, it may be said, as if music wrote itself. We say the tones do this, that, and the other because the meter does this, that, and the other; the tones repeat themselves, alter themselves, in reaction to the effect of time, and so on. What has become of the composer? After all it is the composer who repeats or alters the tones; does one thing or another with them. Are not the tones the material from which the mind of the creative artist forms the work? Behind this there lies an old, unfortunate, half-true concept of material, of *medium* in the arts. It is not that the mind of the creative artist expresses itself in tones, words, colors, and forms as its medium; on the contrary, *tone, word, color, form express themselves through the medium of the creative mind.* The finer that medium, the better tone, word, color, form can express themselves. The greater the genius, the less it speaks *itself,* the more it lends its voice to the tones, the words, the colors, the forms. In this sense, then, music *does* write itself—neither more nor less, by the way, than physics does. The law of falling bodies is no invention of the genius of Galileo. The work of the genius consists in bringing his mind, through years of practice, so into harmony with things that things can express their laws through him. (Many geniuses appear to have been born in harmony with things; in such cases not much practice is required.) This is true of the scientific as of the artistic genius. Every great musical thought is, in its way, rather a discovery than an invention. But these are questions the more thorough discussion of which must be reserved for another occasion.

TIME KNOWS NOTHING OF TRANSIENCE

This statement is meant in the sense in which we say: "A child knows nothing of guilt." Guilt is outside the circle of the child's being. Transience is outside the circle of the being of time.

Understood in this way, the statement contradicts not only the physical time concept but also the most elementary human feeling. "Time passes": this expresses a primeval experience, to which only the dullest of creatures can be blind. Whether we take it literally or as an abbreviated form of the fuller statement: "Things pass in time," the refrain is the same, "transience," and time appears as the decisive, the responsible factor. "Time: a perpetual perishing," writes Locke; and Schopenhauer: "Time is that by the power of which everything at every instant turns to nothing in our hands." [6] That we can grasp but not hold, that the same gesture gives and takes, and that we are never more powerless than when we say to the moment, "Stay, stay, thou art so fair!"—in this we recognize that we are prisoners of the order according to which the present—corporeal, tangibly close, and real as it may be—rises out of the future only to sink back instantly into a past from which, if at all, it can be conjured up only as a sadly incorporeal figment of memory. It is time which makes it possible for things to pass, and makes it impossible for

6. *Essay Concerning Human Understanding; The World as Will and Idea.*

them not to pass. To us, temporality and transience are words for the same thing, and only the timeless does not pass. It might be asked why, then, one aspect of this twofold process imposes itself on us so much more than the other; for the same time that turns the now into a no-longer has, after all, first made the not-yet a now. Yet we never talk about anything but time passing; no one says, "Time becomes." That time gives existence, and with every instant conquers it afresh from nonexistence, we take for granted; but that time takes away existence and with every instant consigns it to nonexistence we feel with the full pang of loss. The more occasion we have in individual cases to be conscious of time as a bestower—as when, after we have long looked joyfully forward to a particular moment, time causes it to be present—the more painfully do we feel that time has bestowed only to take away. Thus time as transience casts its dark shadow on time as becoming. And we mean to assert that time knows nothing of transience?

Music does not, as might be supposed, shift the accent from the transient side to the becoming side of the process. It questions the basic validity of the entire conceptual complex. The hourglass concept of time, it declares, is incompatible with the simple facts with which music confronts us.

We have encountered time in music in the form of meter. Meter is a creation of time; to experience meter is to experience time. Meter permits inferences concerning that from which it directly proceeds, that is, time.

Meter is experienced as wave. Let us think of the simplest, the two-phase wave. Its two phases follow each other, occur at different times; we have seen that their difference as phases is based upon nothing but their temporal succession. "Two," then, follows "one"—in other words, if "two" is present, "one" is past. Is this pastness equivalent to nonexistence? Could "two" be what it is if "one," because it was no longer, were really nonexistent? "Two" is not simply the beat that follows "one"; it is something quite different, namely, symmetrical complement, completion and fulfillment. The whole course of "two" is in direct correspondence with "one," it *is* this correspondence; in every instant of the existence of "two," "one" is also contained, as the partner in this relationship, the object of the symmetrical completion. If "one," once past, were lost in nonexistence, extinguished—as, according to the hourglass concept, past time is extinguished—"two" would be simply a second "one," and nothing more. And the new "one," which follows "two"—how could the *new* start, the "once again," which marks the beginning of the new cycle, be felt if the past start did not remain perceptible, as a sort of background, through the present start? No measure is a copy, each is original: the one-hundredth measure is not the one-hundredth copy of the first but the one and only measure, which adds itself to the ninety-ninth, and the ninety-ninth is the one and only measure, which adds itself to the ninety-eighth, and so on. "The one-hundredth measure *is* . . ." does not here mean "We can count it," but "Thus it gives itself to us, thus we experience it"; its entire past is preserved in its present and given directly with it.

Let us look in the other direction. "Two" follows "one"—this too means if "one" is present, "two" is future. Is this all we know about "two"—that it is not yet if "one" is? Yet "one" is something quite different from the beat upon which "two" will follow; it is the beat which *proceeds toward* "two," with which we ourselves move toward "two." From the first instant, it is not simply a stretch of passing time but a wave phase, the descending phase of a wave. The whole course of "one" relates to the not-yet-existent "two" just as the latter will later relate to the no-longer-existent "one." Through its entire course we experience "one" as something to be completed; its existence is a need for symmetrical completion. "One" could not be what it is if "two," because it was not yet, were really nonexistent, if the future "two" were not already part of the existence of the present "one." The present of "one" is a present directed toward the future, pregnant with future.

We must clarify the decisive point in this situation. At first it seems incomprehensible why we make so much of the fact that neither the pastness of "one" when "two" is present nor the futurity of "two" when "one" is present signifies nonexistence. After all, everyone knows that the past is not utterly extinguished; that the future is not absolutely dark. All higher intellectual activity, all thought, human speech itself, presuppose the ability to overcome confinement to the present instant and mentally to set past and present side by side. But once we have one section of the path of time, which runs from the present toward the past, in view, we can, in thought, extend it in the other direction, toward the future; we can anticipate the course of time. Why should we not interpret the phenomena of musical meter simply as accomplishments of our partly remembering, partly foreknowing or forefeeling, consciousness?

We need only observe the process itself closely to see that this interpretation fails to hit the target of the facts. Nothing of the sort takes place here—that is all; nothing is remembered and nothing foreknown or otherwise anticipated in consciousness. Let us first discuss remembering. Remembrance is making present something that is past: consciousness turns back toward the past thing, represents (re-presents) it to itself. But the way in which the past "one" is given in the present "two" is anything rather than a re-presenting. Do we *remember* "one" when we feel "two"? Does consciousness turn back toward the past moment? Not at all—instead, we are entirely concentrated upon "two," on what is directly present. We feel "two" as what it is, as symmetrical completion and fulfillment precisely in relation to something which *no longer* is, which is *not* present. If we tried, by remembering, to make "one" present simultaneously with "two," all perception of meter would instantly cease, to be replaced by something as meaningless as a photographic double exposure. The same is true of the relation of the present "one" to the following "two." We may be able to anticipate, in thought or feeling, the course of time, to make a future thing present in imagination. But the advance of "one" toward "two," which constitutes the nature of the first phase of the wave, is the exact opposite of such an anticipatory making present. Do we by any chance think ahead to "two," do we anticipatorily imagine "two," when we are feeling "one"? On the contrary, we are completely and exclusively concentrated upon the present "one"; with it we are directed toward a "two" as toward something that is *not yet,* that is in no way present, not even as a mere representation in our consciousness. Anyone who anticipatorily represents "two" to himself while "one" is the present can no longer feel "one." Anticipating the future arrests the phenomenon of meter just as calling back the past does. On the one hand remembering, on the other foreknowing, forefeeling—far from explaining the phenomenon of meter—are incompatible with it. Complete exclusion of any remembering and foreknowing is the necessary condition for experiencing meter.

The present of musical meter, then, contains within it a past that is not remembered and a future that is not foreknown—and not as something to be supplied by thought but as a thing directly given in experience itself. This is the fact of which we said that it overthrew the hourglass concept of time. What becomes of the point (or the saddle) "now" between the two abysses of "no more" and "not yet," in the face of a present in which "now," "not yet," and "no more" are given together, in the most intimate interpenetration and with equal immediacy? This is a present from which not *I*, thanks to my particular powers, look backward into the past and forward into the future, but which *itself* thus looks backward and forward. These particular powers of remembering and foreknowing, then, are not required in order that future things and past things shall *not be nothing*. The past is not extinguished, but not because a memory stores it; it is not extinguished because *time itself stores it*, or, better put, because the being of time is a storing of itself; the future is not an impenetrable wall, but not because a foreknowledge or forefeeling anticipates time; it is not impenetrable because time always anticipates itself, because the being of time is an anticipating itself. To a great extent the problems posed by the old concept of time arise from the fact that it distinguished three mutually exclusive elements, whereas only the picture of a constant interaction and intertwining of these elements is adequate to the actual process. In any case, the present of musical experience is not the dividing point that eternally separates past and future; it is the stage upon which, for every ear, the drama of the being of time is played—that ceaseless storing of itself and anticipating itself which is never repeated, which is every instant new.

Where, in the frame of this concept of time, is there a place for transience? It would seem that things pass, not because of, but in spite of, their temporality.

DIGRESSION II: TEMPORAL *GESTALT*

That we have not lost the firm ground of reality in these considerations is witnessed for us by the simple fact that melodies exist. Only upon the condition that time is thus constituted is the otherwise completely enigmatic process of the hearing of melodies to be comprehended.

A melody is a whole—and a temporal whole, a whole whose parts are given as a sequence, as temporal succession. Such a whole can, in general, be of two kinds. Either it is a sum of parts, which are successively added to one another, an *and-sum,* as it is termed, the result of simple addition; or it is "the whole which is more than the sum of its parts," a *Gestalt.*[7] If ten listeners each hear one tone, the totality of their sensations is an and-sum; if one listener hears ten tones, the totality of his sensations is a *Gestalt*—a melody.

The totalities that are called *Gestalten* are distinguished by the characteristic that in them the individual part does not acquire its meaning from itself (or not exclusively from itself) but receives it from the whole. We know that melodies exhibit this characteristic to an especially pronounced degree: taken by itself, the individual tone is meaningless, mere sound; it is only by entering into relation with other tones, and vice versa, that it acquires musical meaning, becomes a part of the totality "melody." Here there appears to be a contradiction. If the part can acquire its meaning only from the whole, then the whole must in some way be given *before* the parts or at least together with them. How is this to be reconciled with the characteristic feature of the temporal whole, which is always given piecemeal, part after part? The Gestalt psychologists have avoided this problem by applying themselves principally to the investigation of spatial *Gestalten.* In space—where the parts of a whole occur not successively but together, are all present at once—the difficulty did not appear. But once we

---

7. On *and-sum* and *Gestalt,* cf. Max Wertheimer, "Untersuchungen zur Lehre von der Gestalt"; Wolfgang Koehler, *Gestalt Psychology;* and Kurt Koffka, *Principles of Gestalt Psychology.*

are committed to dealing with music, we have no recourse but to pose the problem and ask *how a temporal Gestalt is possible.*

Once again, the most natural expedient is to fall back on the function of memory. An individual tone is not a melody; it takes a succession of tones to make a melody. When we hear the second tone of such a succession, the first has not vanished from our consciousness; memory has stored it up, and the tone now present stands beside the tone that, though past, is remembered; it can be related to the former tone, just as two things in space stand beside each other and can be related. The like is true of the third tone in relation to the first and second, and so forth. And even as elsewhere the line between past and present, which we survey retrospectively, is also prolonged toward the future, as coming events are anticipated, foreknown, or foretold, we can in the course of a melody reach beyond the present, actually sounding tone and relate it to tones that, though they do not yet exist, our consciousness anticipates. Temporal *Gestalten* appear possible because the past instant can be held in memory; the future instant can be anticipated in expectation. Although a temporal succession is always given us only part *after* part, in our consciousness part stands *beside* part, remembered part and expected part beside the part immediately given. Between immediate present, stored past, and anticipated future play the relations that make the individual tone a meaningful part of the tonal *Gestalt.*

Plausible as this interpretation sounds, it does not stand up. In the hearing of melodies, nothing is remembered and nothing anticipated. Let us first consider remembering. If it were the remembrance of the past tones which made us understand the present tones of a melody, understanding melodies would be contingent upon remembering them. We know what the situation is. Not one out of a hundred listeners will be capable of singing or playing from memory a melody that he has heard with pleasure—that is, with understanding. Or try breaking off a melody at random and asking listeners what tones, or even what tone, immediately preceded the one they last heard; the majority will be unable to answer. And then try the contrary experiment: let anyone who is capable of it call to mind the immediately preceding tone of a melody that he is hearing. *The instant he does so, he will have lost the thread of the melody.* The hearing of a melody is a hearing *with* the melody, that is, in closest connection with the tone sounding at the moment. It is even a condition of hearing melody that the tone present at the moment should fill consciousness *entirely,* that *nothing* should be remembered, nothing except it or beside it be present in consciousness. The essence of the musical tone, its dynamic quality, lies precisely in its relation to something that itself *is not there;* any turning back of consciousness for the purpose of making past tones present immediately annuls the possibility of musical hearing. Not only, then, is the individual tone in a melody understood in itself, without the slightest regard for whether anything is remembered; it *cannot* be understood *if* something is remembered.

The like holds for the anticipation of coming tones. It is certainly true that in hearing melodies we are always also reaching beyond the tone present at the moment; we are turned toward the coming tone, we listen toward it. This attitude is an expression of the pointing-beyond-itself, the state of incompleteness, of the individual tone—of its demand for completion. But this expectant tension of the present toward the future runs, so to speak, in a different groove from the anticipation of future events on the basis of foreknowledge or forefeeling. The normal process—that, in a state of expectation, one simultaneously imagines the future event which will satisfy the expectation—is foreign to the hearing of melodies and, indeed, is incompatible with it. If we go beyond the present tone in the sense that we imagine the coming tones, toward which we feel that the tension of the present tone is directed, we shall lose the thread of the melody just as we do by making consciousness revert to the preceding tone. Here too, then, it is evident that it cannot be its relation to other tones standing beside it in consciousness which gives the individual tone its meaning as part of the melodic whole. Indeed, the individual tone bears its meaning so exclusively in itself that it can only be understood at all if *no* past or future tone stands beside it in consciousness.

To convince ourselves that our ability to foreknow or forefeel future events has nothing to do with the peculiar relation between present and future that is revealed in music, we have only to think of the effect of surprise that characterizes certain tones in melodies. According to the usual explanation, this effect is based upon the fact that the tone heard is different from the tone expected, with a high degree of certainty, at that moment. Strangely enough, however, this effect is entirely independent of whether one is hearing such a melody for the first time or for the hundredth time; the questionable tone is poignantly heard as a surprise even when one *knows* for certain that it will enter. One may know the slow movement of Mozart's E-flat major Symphony by heart, play it by heart—the tone *d* in the seventh measure of the melody will always be the same startling event. We might almost say that in such a case familiarity, foreknowledge, even intensifies the element of surprise. Here, then, I am expecting, with a high degree of certainty, an event of which I know perfectly well that it will *not* occur; and I am to the highest degree surprised by an event of which I knew in advance that it *would* occur. The paradox reveals that we are here dealing with *two* levels, and that what occurs on the one does not affect the other.

One is the stream of events in time, the other the stream of time itself. Our foreknowledge is concerned with the stream of events; our hearing is concerned with the stream of time. So far as I know and represent to myself what is to come, I do not hear; and so far as I hear, I do not know and do not represent to myself what is to come. The expectation that I feel upon hearing a tone in a melody is not directed toward any *event,* toward something future that is to become present; it is directed toward futurity, toward what can never become present. It is not expectation *of something,* a feeling whose object is an event in time; it is pure expectation, which has time itself, the eventuation of time, as its object. I can anticipate events in thought or feeling and thus, as the phrase goes, leave the present behind me. But I cannot anticipate time—time already anticipates itself. But the self-anticipation of time can be the subject of an experience. This is precisely what happens when I hear music. Without leaving the present behind me, I experience futurity as that toward which the present is directed and always remains directed. I experience the present as a striving toward a future that it never does more than touch, and that forever draws back from it, a process continually producing tension, continually new. In this way we understand how it is possible in general to experience something foreknown as something new—in concrete terms, to hear familiar melodies again and again with the same enjoyment. Events that I can anticipate in thought are certainly not new when they appear. But time is always new; cannot possibly be anything but new. Heard as a succession of acoustical events, music will soon become boring; heard as the manifestation of time eventuating, it can never bore. The paradox appears at its most acute in the achievement of the performing musician, who attains the heights if he succeeds in performing a work with which he is thoroughly familiar, as if it were the creation of the present moment. In such cases critics commonly say that the familiar work sounded "as if new."

(The processes that we are here attempting to characterize are certainly not confined to music. They must be demonstrable in the other arts in which time appears as a factor. Otherwise, how would it be possible to read an exciting story over and over again with the same tension? If, for example, in rereading Dostoevski's *The Possessed,* I know perfectly well that at the end of the great scene in Varvara Petrovna's salon, Shatov, who until then has sat silent and unnoticed in a corner, will get up, walk slowly to where Stavrogin is sitting, and hit him in the face with his fist, my foreknowledge does not in the least impair the tension of the previous part of the scene, the part that leads up to the blow. Indeed, it has been said, with good reason, that it is only after the purely objective element of tension, the curiosity to know what is coming, has been disposed of that the other kind of tension and expectation can become manifest. Hence the heightened artistic pleasure one receives from rereading a great story. But what does this mean if not that foreknowledge of events does *not* dissolve the future; that the progress of time from present to future remains the same tense process, even if we know *what* is going to happen. If this were not so, foreknowledge of coming events would actually make the passing of time a "mere formality"; and the physicist, in so far as he wants only to foretell events, is quite justified in operating with just such a time concept. However, the simple fact that one can see a play twice with the same tension strikingly demonstrates that time *is* something other than a mere formality, a mere container for successive events.)

Let us summarize: melody is temporal *Gestalt;* temporal *Gestalt* presupposes that a temporal whole—a whole whose parts, with the exception of the one part present at the moment, either are no longer there or are not yet there—is given to us in an immediate experience. This is precisely what happens in hearing a melody. The existence of the individual tone in a melody is a being directed toward what no longer exists and what does not yet exist; thus past and future are given with and in the present and are experienced with and in the present; hearing a melody is hearing, having heard, and being about to hear, all at once. But the past is not a part of the future because it is remembered, nor is the future a part of the present because it is foreknown or forefelt. Anyone who thinks back to past tones or anticipates coming tones in imagination ceases to hear melody. The temporal whole with which we are here confronted is, then, certainly not the work of memory and foreknowledge or forefeeling. The simplest temporal *Gestalt,* the melody, shows the erroneousness of the view that the past can be given only as memory, the future only as foreknowledge. If this were so, if the past were, in the fullest sense, *no more,* were extinguished, and could only be summoned back to a chimerical existence by virtue of the gift of memory—if the future were, in the fullest sense, *not yet;* if it had existence only in so far as knowledge or feeling enable us to anticipate coming events in imagination—then there could be no melodies. Every melody declares to us that the past can be there without being remembered, the future without being foreknown—that the past is not stored in memory but in time, and that it is not our consciousness which anticipates time but that time anticipates itself. The possibility of music and of every temporal *Gestalt* rests entirely upon the premise of a time so constituted, of a time that stores itself and anticipates itself.

Only now are we in a position correctly to understand an essential element of the musical work of art, an element that we have not yet considered: its *form.*

When musicians speak of "form," using the word as a technical term, they refer to the arrangement of the larger sections of which most compositions are made up, as is a novel of chapters, a play of acts and scenes. In the course of the evolution of our musical language, and in the most intimate connection with the forces of tone and meter, certain schemas of arrangement have developed, which continually recur and in which, among other things, repetition plays an outstanding part. This circumstance has led to a widely disseminated misunderstanding of musical forms, and our first task must be to dispose of it. Since there is comparatively little difficulty in recognizing the repetition of a fairly long section as such, it has been thought that the study of forms provided the simplest and shortest approach to understanding musical works of art. That repetitions are not present here for their own sake, any more than they are elsewhere in music, has been overlooked; on the whole, forms have been regarded as stereotyped recipes for repetitions, as predetermined frames into which composers had to fit their ideas—if the repetitions were noted, the forms were understood. The usual "analyses" in the programs of our symphony concerts testify to this unfortunate state of affairs. What should be the acme of any real science of music—the study of the total form of a musical work of art, investigation of the processes that cause this form, in every instance, to manifest itself not as something predetermined from without but as an organic growth from within—has thus degenerated into the emptiest and most barren part of traditional musical theory.

What a melody is on a small scale, the total course of a musical work is on a large scale—a whole that unfolds in time and is so constituted that, though its individual members appear one after another, the whole, in order to be present, does not have to wait for member to be added to member, but is, so to speak, always already there, not factually, as with the spatial *Gestalt,* but as direction, as oriented tension. Let us think of the beginning of a movement from one of Bruckner's symphonies, one of those miracles of audible form. It is not simply "beginning," the start of something; from the first instant we hear in it *what* has begun, *toward what* it is a start: it is as if a great gate had opened upon an immeasurably wide and lofty space, through which we now move, not simply step by step, but step by step as one advances through a very wide and lofty space toward a very distant goal. And as the individual parts of this whole, the elements of the total form, unroll before us, that toward which we advance without seeing it becomes, bit by bit, tangible present, until, with the last step, the whole is not *past,* but is *built up*—built up not in our memory (how could a normal memory embrace such a span of event?) but in the perfectly definite dynamic quality of the last step, which is experienced as precisely what it is: the step that brings such a gigantic construction to completion. The incomprehensibility of melody upon any other premise except that of an anticipating and storing time which does not pass away is reproduced here, only at a far higher power. Audible forms are perfect temporal *Gestalten,* creatures of time, as spatial *Gestalten* are creatures of space.

Two structural principles can be distinguished in musical compositions regarded as wholes, together with two corresponding types of musical forms, circular forms and serial forms, or—to use Wölfflin's terms—closed and open forms. The architectonic principle of the one is symmetry, equilibrium, polarity; that of the other is "again and yet again and yet again . . ." ever-increasing intensification. The same twofold nature of time that became apparent in the formation of meter, the will to close every wave cycle and the will to inexhaustible production of wave after wave, manifests itself in the formation of the larger temporal *Gestalten.* We see that, in accordance with their nature, we must refer to the temporal *Gestalten* of music as *rhythmic Gestalten.*

The simple circular forms have a bipartite or tripartite structure. In the binary form, the two parts that balance each other succeed each other immediately:

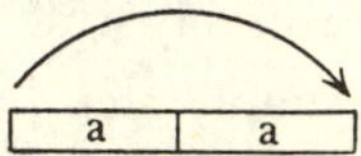

In the ternary form the dividing line that separates the two symmetrical halves has, so to speak, broadened into a dividing plane:

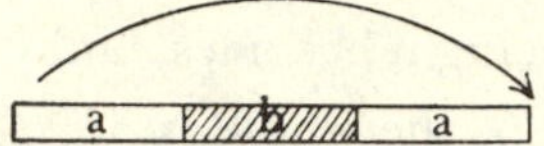

It has become an autonomous part, which now delays the fulfillment of the desire for symmetrical completion. The two parts of the binary form need not necessarily have the same tonal content. It is completely within the possibilities of tonal language to give the two parts, even though their content is different, a relation like that of question and answer, so that the meaning of the form, the symmetrical correspondence, is made apparent. In the ternary form, on the other hand, the third part must in essentials be a repetition of the first, because only thus can it be understood as its symmetrical counterpart across the separating middle part. (Here we see that the contribution of memory—awareness of the repetition—although it represents the necessary condition for understanding the form, is by no means equivalent to this understanding. The point is not that the first part is repeated at the end but that this repetition is a symmetrical fulfillment; establishes an equilibrium which was previously lacking. Memory cannot tell us this.)

We find simple binary and ternary forms in many songs, dances, small compositions of all sorts. With the increase in the dimensions of compositions, the forms extend, grow, as it were, through cell division. The result is the compound binary and ternary circular forms that are characteristic of many larger eighteenth- and nineteenth-century compositions:

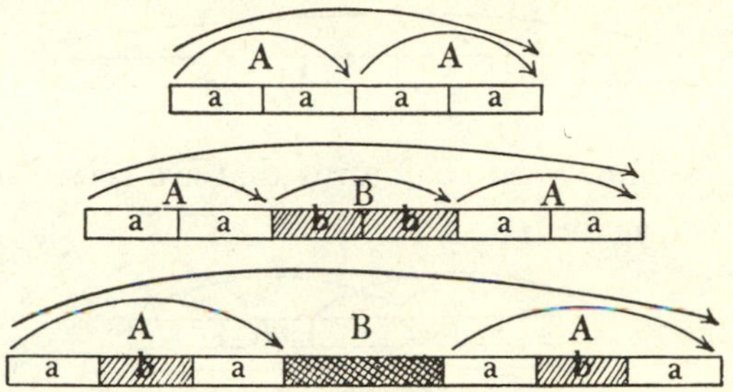

The schema of the serial form is

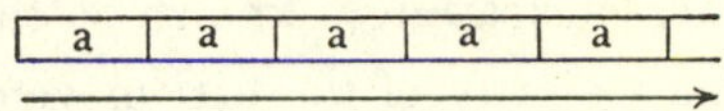

This in intention is an endless succession of form elements. Endless series, which are at the same time endless repetition, are to be found in much primitive music, or in folk ballads that repeat the same melody again and again to the countless stanzas of the poem. Yet this form too harbors powerful artistic possibilities: as repetition of the same tonal content in ever new transformations, as "theme and variations." Serial forms in which every form element has a new content are the natural recourse for many compositions to comparatively long texts, such as the early motets and madrigals. But we find this form in instrumental works too, for example, in many of Bach's clavier and organ fantasies. It appears, carried to the extreme, in an act of a Wagner opera. A great variety of combinations of repetitions with new material is possible in the serial form, as, for example, when, of every two successive sections, one is always the same and the other always new (rondo), or when one strand of the tonal texture keeps repeating the same thing, while another adds ever new things to it (chaconne, passacaglia).

Of particular interest are the forms in which the two structural principles, that of the circle and that of the series, compete with each other: series in which the circle principle finally asserts itself:

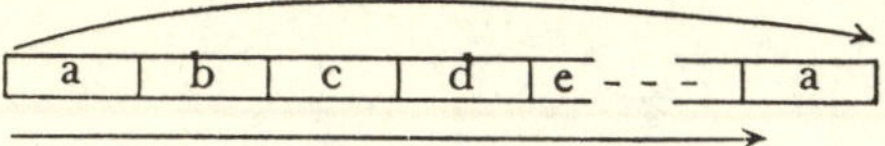

And ternary symmetrical structures that are seized upon by the stream of "yet again":

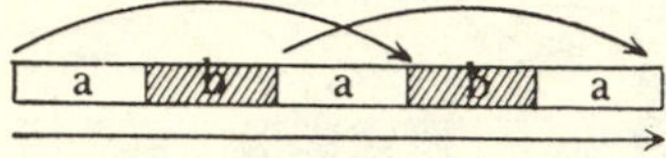

The two forces appear in most intimate interpenetration in the complex form rather misleadingly known as the "sonata form"; it is the form of the majority of the first movements of the great instrumental works of the classical and romantic periods. It was above all Beethoven who recognized the double nature of this form and the possibility it affords for a synthesis of polarity and intensification; his lifelong struggle for this synthesis, one of the chief motifs of his artistic activity, took place for the most part on the terrain of the sonata form.

That the great musical forms which we encounter in the works of Bach, Beethoven, Schubert, Bruckner, Wagner, that these gigantic superimposed and opposed blocks of tone, these tonal masses which balance one another or mutually support and intensify one another, have the character of works of architecture has often been remarked. The phrase, so much quoted, about architecture as frozen music seems to point to a real relation in essence between the two arts. To be sure, if the striking *aperçu* is taken too literally, it ends by misleading us. It conceals the problem instead of explaining it. Temporal architecture cannot be changed into spatial architecture simply by the process of freezing. Frozen time is not space, but nothing, an empty phrase, a round cube. Can we turn the phrase around and say that music is flowing architecture? A building that begins to flow—can it still be called a building? Does not to build mean to set up something firm, based, and enduring against the eternal flux? As builders, we try to rise above our fate of eternal motion and find a stay in the motionless, the enduring, the subsistent. But then must we not regard the art whose sustenance is time, the eternal flux—the art of music—as architecture's most inveterate antagonist? All fundamental opposition to music—an opposition that has become articulate in recent times, setting up its *cave musicam* [8] against the general enthusiasm for music—is rooted in the same concern: that music may hold the threat of chaos; that it may undermine the foundation upon which order rests. Music, so this school of thought maintains, does not build, it dissolves; it does not give us clearly outlined images; on the contrary, it dissipates all outlines and boundaries. Is not structure by its very nature linked with space; is not temporal structure, temporal *Gestalt,* a misleading metaphor? To surrender oneself to music is to give one's soul into the power of the principle that is contrary to all order; is to let oneself be seduced by the "fairest mask of universal chaos." [9]

Behind these and related interpretations lies a time-honored dogma—the dogma that order is possible only in the enduring, the immutably fixed, the substantial. Those who subscribe to this dogma must, to be sure, conclude, from the absence of any enduring and substantial elements in music, that it is irreconcilable with order. But what if music presents us with this very thing—the unprecedented spectacle of an order in what is wholly flux,

---

8. Nietzsche's warning, aimed particularly at Richard Wagner's music, in *Human, All Too Human,* Vol. II, foreword.

9. Erich Wolff and C. Petersen, *Das Schicksal der Musik von der Antike zur Gegenwart.*

of a building without matter? Music, which can even stamp order upon the flowing, which can even wrest great edifices from the immaterial, is anything but a power incompatible with order, a dissolvent power. Hearing music, we experience a time whose being is no longer a swift flare-up in the passage from one nonexistence to another nonexistence, which reveals itself rather as a self-storing and self-renewal than as a transience, a time whose flux does *not* exclude building. Even more: the miracle of nonspatial building, of a construction that no eye sees, no hand grasps, but that we nevertheless *behold,* descry, envision through hearing—where could it be manifested if not in the pure temporal *Gestalten* of music? Order, liberated from all relation to things, *pure order,* bodiless, detached, and free, not as a mere concept, not as a dream, but as a vision beheld—it is to music that we owe our awareness that such a thing can exist.

ARE THERE TWO TIMES?

Thus, step by step, we have been led to set up a time concept that disagrees in essential points with the one generally current and supported by science. Must we conclude that there are two times—one for music and musicians, the other for all the rest of the world, including science? Have musicians a time of their own? That would be a sad situation. In that case it would be permissible to dismiss musicians from the society of other mortals and set them up in a little world of their own, where interested observers could visit them occasionally, but where they would otherwise have no direct relations with the real world.

Fortunately things are not quite as bad as that. We pointed out at the beginning of this chapter that the traditional time concept—like the traditional motion concept—can by no means claim uncontested validity. The ambiguities and contradictions that it has always contained have been revealed with particular sharpness during the last decades, so that today, even in philosophy and science, the traditional time concept finds itself confronted by a revolutionary time concept against which it must assert itself. And now, startlingly, it appears that this new concept of time, gained from entirely different premises, agrees in essential points with the musical time concept.

For all the differences between individual thinkers, there is enough unity of direction for us to be able to speak, without oversimplification, of *the* new time concept. To characterize it briefly, our best recourse is to seek it at the source, in the pioneering work of Henri Bergson.[10] Here for the first time we encounter, as the result of analyses of psychological and biological processes, the concept of a time that cannot be divided and measured; that can only be lived and apprehended in immediate intuition. For Bergson, measurable time is *spatialized* time, time that has sacrificed its true nature. True time is not the succession of instants that rise out of the future and descend into the past; true time is a *duration* that, however, never stands still, survival of the no-longer-existent in the existent, growth of the existent by constant addition of the not-yet-existent, continuous process. Past is not lost, future is always the absolutely new, the unforeseeable—true time can no more be precalculated than it can be measured. Thus the concept of an active and conserving time stands in sharpest contrast to the traditional concept of an "empty" time that, with its points and stretches, provides the form or measure for processes "in" time. Bergson was well aware of the kinship between his time concept and the musical time concept. He did not pursue the parallel, yet—like Augustine a millennium and a half before him—he chose the image of music

10. For Bergson on time, cf. his *Matière et mémoire, Essai sur les données immédiates de la conscience, Creative Evolution,* and *Durée et simultanéité.*

when he sought to give his time concept a particularly vivid and unmistakable embodiment. A characteristic passage may be cited: "A melody to which we listen with our eyes closed and thinking of nothing else, is very close to coinciding with this time which is the very fluidity of our inner life; but it still has too many qualities, too much definition, and we should first have to obliterate the differences between the tones, then the distinctive characteristics of tone itself, retain of it only the continuation of that which precedes in that which follows, the uninterrupted transition, multiplicity without divisibility, and succession without separation, in order at last to find fundamental time. Such is duration immediately perceived, without which we should have no idea of time." [11] What Bergson here says must be done to find fundamental time we attempted to do when we undertook to search for the nature of time in the phenomena of meter and rhythm. It almost seems as if music furnishes experimental proof of the rightness of Bergson's basic idea. Indeed, in this context, it does something even more essential: it disposes of the weightiest objection to Bergson's time concept.

For the attempt has been made to reduce the opposition between the conflicting time concepts, and to re-establish harmony in our philosophic economy, by a sort of division of territories. Why should there not be two times? Have we not, after all, two worlds—the outer, objective world, bodies in space, tangible and measurable, and the inner world, the world of the psyche, the subjective world, states and contents of consciousness, flowing, intangible, finally losing themselves in the unconscious? Why should not these so different worlds have each its proper time concept: the objective world, objective time, the time our clocks mark; the subjective world, subjective time, which

11. Bergson, *Durée et simultanéité.*

we find in the flow of our consciousness, the time in which no points can be established and no divisions marked out, the conserving and creating time that can only be experienced, not measured? "Time which is the very fluidity of our inner life"—Bergson himself has made it clear again and again that the time of which he is in search is a process of the inner world, to be understood psychologically. To be sure, say his critics, he then failed to make the dividing line sufficiently clear; instead of distinguishing between *physical* and *psychological* time, and remaining aware that his investigations related only to the latter, he claimed to be discussing unqualified time, and indeed *true* time. As a consequence of this illegitimate crossing of boundaries, an imaginary conflict has arisen—which, however, may easily be disposed of by making a clear separation between the two realms of validity.

Whether this criticism of Bergson is justified or not need not concern us here. For, in either case, the attempt to restrict the new time concept by shutting it up in the inner world, by subjectivizing it, collapses in the face of the testimony of music. As we have seen, the musical time concept coincides with Bergson's time concept. Since Bergson reached his time concept through an intuition of processes in the psyche, through introspection, it is possible to question whether the validity of his concept can be extended beyond the frontier of the inner world. But in respect to the musical time concept, this discussion is meaningless, because the processes from which we have derived it were found not in ourselves but outside of ourselves. The time that is at work in music—whose work, indeed, music to an essential degree is—this time cannot be "in me," it is not "my" time. It is where music is; I find it where I find music—that is, in the same direction in which I find the sun, the moon, and the stars. Musical time exhibits all the characteristics of psychological time except one: it does not belong to a psyche. Thus the conflict between the two time concepts revives in full intensity. The physical time concept cannot safeguard itself simply by relegating the other time concept from the outer to the inner world; it must assert itself on the same terrain.

Here we will only add briefly that the rift has recently appeared even within natural science itself. Research is clearly bringing to light an increasing number of natural phenomena for which the physical time concept proves inadequate. Thus the study of an organic process, the cicatrization of wounds, has led the biologist Lecomte du Noüy to postulate a "second time"; the phenomena became comprehensible only when the investigator gave up applying the measure of our clock time to them: "There are two kinds of time. One corresponding to the classical notion, the sidereal, physical time, without beginning and without end, flowing in a continuous, uniform, rigid fashion. The other, the physiological time, the duration of our organisms. . . . It is a time which remembers . . . a living time." [12] Here, then, we have not objective versus subjective time; we have time versus time, on the same terrain of objectivity; only in the one case it is not a clock which determines the time but an organic process, the process of cicatrization. The organic process itself becomes a clock; we have clock versus clock, the organic clock versus the mechanical.

In this light, the attempt to set up a musical time concept, in opposition to the time concept that is generally prevalent and supported by science, ceases to be fantastic. In the great revolution of modern thought, which centers around the problem of time, music has something very definite and essential to contribute; we must make music yield this contribution. The physical

12. Lecomte du Noüy, *Biological Time.*

time concept does not need to be "refuted"; what needs to be refuted is only the assertion that the physical time concept exhausts objective time. Physics and music stand to each other as realms of the minimum and maximum activity of time. Physical events are less the work of time, musical events more the work of time, than events in any other realm. He who would inquire about the nature of time would do well to consider the testimony of music, where time represents an active force, not a "mere formality."

XIII. Tone as the Image of Time

A FURTHER QUESTION REMAINS: Do we encounter time in music *only* in the form of meter and rhythm?

A tone sounding on uninterruptedly is not yet melody and not yet rhythm. Strictly speaking, melody begins not with the first tone but with the first step from tone to tone. In the same way, rhythm is not born with the first sounding of a tone but with the first interruption and the sounding of a new tone (or the new sounding of the same tone). Before that, the tone simply lasts; but this duration is not yet a rhythmic, let alone a metric-rhythmic phenomenon. What is the situation with respect to time perception *before* the first interruption, *before* meter and rhythm have become manifest—what is the situation with respect to time perception in the first tone of a musical composition? If time attains to direct perception only in the form of meter and rhythm, then the first tone of a composition must, as time experience, be empty. Is this actually the case?

At first glance the question seems a little academic. In most compositions, the second tone comes so soon after the first that, before we even begin to think about it, we are deep in hearing melody and feeling rhythm. Yet there are compositions whose first tone lasts for a time that is comparatively very long, in any case long enough to make the question of what happens during this period a sensible one. It is not yet melody, it is not yet rhythm—what is it?

Here is the beginning of Beethoven's *Coriolanus* Overture:

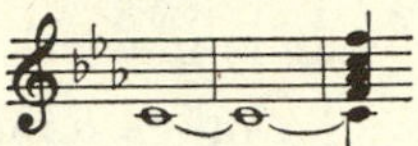

What do we hear? A tone, the tone c, held at the same intensity for about three seconds. Is that all? Such a description would fit a stationary phenomenon. But our hearing of the tone gives us not only the feeling of something stationary but, together with it, the feeling of a growth, of an inner swell, of a dynamic phenomenon—something like this:

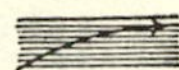

It is like a tugging and pulling in the tone, a rapidly increasing pressure, clamoring, as it were, for something to happen: to stand still and wait for the event to arrive is contrary to this state; one feels the steady sounding on of the tone almost as the result of a considerable counterforce, which keeps the tone in its place against its will. The effort cannot be long maintained; either the expected event occurs, and meter and rhythm have begun, or the tension breaks, the tone ceases to be a musical tone and becomes a mere acoustical sensation. The feeling for the critical limit beyond which a held tone or chord cannot be prolonged without simply becoming an irritating, ridiculous, or merely uninteresting aural stimulus distinguishes the experienced interpreter. (The inner swell in such a tone is certainly not to be traced back to an involuntary and unwitting increase in its intensity; the feeling is the same if the piece is played on the piano, where, as we know, once a tone has been struck it can thereafter only lose in intensity. If an increase in intensity parallels the holding of the tone, as at the beginning of the Overture to *Der Freischütz*, , we regard the inner dynamism of the tone not as the *result* of its growing louder but, vice versa, we regard its growing louder as a *radiation* of the inner dynamism into the outer dynamics.)

What force here tugs at the tone and transforms the stationary acoustical event into a dynamic musical event? It cannot be the force of another tone, for no other tone has yet sounded. The projectionist interpretations are excluded. If a tone held unchanged is heard as a dynamic event, as change, and the listener —that is, the listener's organic and psychic receiving apparatus— does not enter into consideration as cause of the phenomenon, the change can reasonably be connected only with the duration of the tone. We have met such a question once before. What turns the regular repetition of the same tone into the different phases of the metric wave; turns the mechanically uniform succession into a dynamic event? It is clear that here, in the phenomenon of the first tone, we have in germ the same process which, in the case of the repeated tone, led to the metric wave. The inner swell in the first tone is nothing but the germination of the first metric wave; is, as it were, the primary material out of which the succession of tones and rests will now model the specific metric wave of the composition: time become perceptible —one might almost say, become tangible, plastic. In the musical tone as such, then, even before any meter, even before any rhythm, time attains direct manifestation as a dynamic process.

The unique position of the tone among sensations here appears with complete clarity. No sensation besides tone is able to give us a direct perception of time. To be sure, there is no sensation that does *not* possess duration; but it would be useless to try to discover, in the duration of a color, of an odor, of a taste, of a noise, any traces of the dynamic phenomenon that distinguishes the duration of tone. What is our sensation when we look at a surface that is illuminated first with one color, then with another? The color is before our eyes, something enduring without change, comparable with the unchanging tone. But the other element, the inner swell, the intensifying drive that is given in the tone together with its duration, is not to be found. Christian Morgenstern's dream of a music of odors,

> Palmström builds himself an odor-organ
> And on it plays von Korff's pokeweed sonata.
> The thing begins with alpine-wildflower triplets,
> Continues with a pleasant locust air . . . [1]

is certainly not utterly nonsensical; but one thing would be definitely lacking in it: nothing in the alpine-wildflower odor of the beginning would impatiently demand the appearance of another odor.

We have already touched upon the question why, among the sensations, precisely tone should have this power of becoming the medium of the experience of time. It seemed that its immateriality predisposes it to this function. Every other sensation is that of a thing: I do not grasp simply hardness but a stone, I do not see simply red but a tile roof, do not hear a whistle but the whistle of a locomotive; and in a tone that I sense preponderantly as noise, I hear above all the piano or the violin. But when I hear music I hear *tones*, not sounding strings or vibrating air waves. All other sensations belong, as qualities or states, to some thing; the tone is self-sufficient. That these are not artificial distinctions, imposed on the phenomena, is confirmed by language, which has adjectival terms for all sensations except for tone. We say, smooth wood, blue glass, sour grapes, a shrill pipe—but there is no such thing as a C sharp-y violin. Tones simply are not qualities that can be predicated of things. At the same time language certainly does not lack possibilities of distinguishing between different tones as such, just as accurately as,

---

1. Christian Morgenstern, *Palmström.*

let us say, between different colors. Significantly enough, however, it does so not with words but with symbols—c, d, e, do, re, mi; and even the words that denominate the different intervals—second, third, fourth—are mere numerical terms. It is as if we were to name the colors according to their place in the rainbow and instead of saying red, orange, yellow, were to say first, second, third color. Our languages, which have been built up in closest connection with the world of objects, appear ill adapted to the conditions of the world of tone.

Not only is tone particularly suited, through its complete detachment from all bodily-spatial objects and hence from any connection with places in space, to become the medium of time perception. We can point out a further characteristic of the musical tone, which may help us to understand why we perceive time in tone *just as necessarily and immediately* as we perceive space in visible and tangible things: it is the *incompleteness* of the musical tone. We have shown that the quality which makes the tone a musical phenomenon is something dynamic, a pointing beyond itself, a demand for completion; and this demand for completion is not something we deduce *ex post facto* but hear directly from the tone. In general we take completion to be the filling in of what is missing: the datum lacks something, what is lacking is added. Such is the case, for example, with the restoration of a mutilated statue, of a partially destroyed painting. We see the need for completion, see too in what general direction it points; by supplying what has been missing, we make the incomplete complete. But this is not the case with the incompleteness of the musical tone. Its demand is not directed toward adding something to the datum, but toward *replacing* the datum—not only toward the appearance of something that is not yet, but at the same time toward the disappearance of what is now present. The state of incompleteness of the tone $\hat{2}$, for example, expresses itself as a demand that $\hat{1}$ shall appear. What is "lacking" here is the tone $\hat{1}$. But the demand of $\hat{2}$ would not be satisfied if $\hat{1}$ were simply added to it; on the contrary, this would make the situation even worse, even more unsatisfactory. Here, in order for what is incomplete to become complete, not only must $\hat{1}$ appear but at the same time $\hat{2}$ must disappear: what is lacking must appear *in place of* what is given. If, then, the visual-incomplete becomes complete by the fact that what is lacking appears *beside* the datum, the auditory-incomplete can become complete only by the fact that what is lacking *succeeds to* the datum. The auditory-incomplete requires time—as the visual-incomplete requires space—to become complete. The demand for completion on the part of a tone is a demand to cease being and to let something else, something that is not yet, appear. What we hear in such a demand is "now" striving toward "no more"; is "not yet" pressing to become "now." To *hear* incompleteness is to hear time.

In this sense, the hearing of a musical tone is always likewise a direct perceiving of time. The moment the tone sounds, it draws us into time, opens time to us as perceiving beings. We do not hear the tone and then add to it a perception of time from other sources; the hearing of the tone is itself already a perceiving of time. To be sure, every sensation possesses duration; the pressure of the weight in my hand lasts while I hold it; the green of the meadow lasts while I see it. But here the duration is nothing but the neutral base upon which the sensation rests; is not itself an element of the sensation: I do not see duration in the green; I do not touch duration in the heaviness. But I hear duration in the tone. "Time objects" is the term that Edmund Husserl applies to such objects as "in addition to their unity in time, also contain temporal extension in themselves" [2]—in other

2. Edmund Husserl, "Phänomenologie des inneren Zeitbewusstseins."

words, objects that not only possess duration but in which duration, temporal extension, has become an element of sensation itself. As examples of time objects, Husserl cites tone and melody. Visible and tangible things are not time objects; they are in time, to be sure, but time does not come to direct perception in them. What, on the other hand, does come to direct perception in them, just as temporal extension does in tone, is spatial extension: they are space objects. In general, we see not only color but always space as well; we do not touch simply hardness and contour but always space as well. In exactly the same way, in general we hear not simply tone but always time as well. Our hearing of time corresponds to our seeing and touching of space. Tones are time become audible matter, as corporeal things are space become visible and tangible matter. As space to the eye and the hand, time reveals itself to the ear.

We have quoted Bergson, who calls measurable time spatialized time. When we think of the instant as a point in time, of the present as a point in which past and future meet, of a duration as an interval that extends between two points and whose length can be measured, we use spatial representations. We comprehend time in the image of space.

It is proper that the eye and the hand should take the lead in building up the image of space; even with all the subtlety that science has given it, our image of space is the creation of seeing and touching beings. But if we see and think time in the image of space, this means that, in building up our image of time, we entrust ourselves to the guidance of eye and hand. Can this produce a true image? The knowledge of space that hand and eye possess is exactly matched by their ignorance of time. No eye has ever seen time; no hand has touched time. But ears have heard time. It is the ear, not the eye, not the hand, to which the lead is here rightly due. A true image of time must be an image for the ear, an audible image, an image made of tones.

An audible image, an image made of tones—is this not sheer nonsense? Is it not common knowledge that an image is something visible, hence something spatial? An eye must be able to see it; a hand must have formed it out of tangible material. The visual arts are space arts. To image something means to give it a definite form for the eye; the image stands in space, in front of me, my gaze can rest on it, it is something which persists, contemplation of which raises me out of the changing, the flowing. It is not as if only the spatial could be imaged; on the contrary, one of the chief functions of our creating of images is precisely that of retaining the nonspatial, the nonpersisting, in an image. This takes place through translation into spatial forms, into visibility and tangibility. All our allegories are such translations of the nonspatial, the ideal, into the spatial. Even of the transient itself, of time, we make spatial images—the straight line, the hourglass. From the earliest ages men have made for themselves images of supersensual powers, of gods. Even the images of poetry, which works with a nonspatial material, with words, everywhere strive toward spatiality, toward visibility: poetic speech conjures up forms that we behold in the mind; that appear as vividly to the inner eye as only material forms do to the outer eye. But an image of the nonspatial world that should *not* be a translation into the spatial, an image to be listened to, not looked at, an image of the flowing made of intangible material—such an image would necessarily overturn our ideas of images and their making.

Let us first consider that "image" is by no means an unequivocal word. We say, for example, that a writer's language is rich in images. Here "image" means metaphor. A metaphor is there for the purpose of bringing to light a previously concealed meaning in that to which it relates. Music is certainly not a metaphor of time; it is not there for the purpose of bringing to light a hidden meaning of time. One can listen to music all one's life with the deepest understanding, yet never once think of time.

Still less than a metaphorical image is music a representational image, a copy—in the sense in which works of the visual arts are copies. A copy in this sense is always an image of something, the image of a thing; and music knows nothing of things. But it is true beyond any doubt that a work of visual art is something else besides the image of a thing: it is always also a space image, space become image. Here the representational arts join ranks with architecture, which copies nothing. How does space become image? Space as such can be neither seen nor shaped; seeing requires color, shaping requires resistance, something solid. The colored and the solid are the materials from which the works of the representational arts and of architecture are shaped. The colored and the solid, the visible and the tangible: this is matter, and matter is space materialized. Artists cannot shape these materials without at the same time shaping space; an image composed of these materials is at the same time a space image, space become image. The remarkable thing is that the artist not only shapes space *in* these materials but also beyond them, where there is no material. An example will make this clear. Everyone knows the plaza before St. Peter's in Rome; the curving colonnades on either side, the two fountains in front of them, the façade of the church closing the vista. This enumeration includes all that the artist shaped from material in this case. (The central obelisk is a later addition.) But what, in so doing, he also shaped, and without setting a hand to it, is the *space* that is enclosed and organized by these material forms, the emptiness between them—an immaterial but none the less potent element in the total picture, as anyone can testify who, familiar with photographs of the plaza, sees it in reality for the first time. Yet here the material forms are so much in the foreground of interest that attention can easily be diverted from the immaterial form. This situation changes, however, when one has passed through the façade into the interior of the church. Now it is certainly not the sight of the shaped material, of the walls and the overarching dome, which, for a moment, takes our breath away; it is the sight of the space, of the immense extent of space, enclosed by the walls and the dome. The immense extent?—yet no one will say that the space has increased through the fact that we have left the outdoors and entered between walls and under a roof. What we here experience as immense extent is not a quality of the actual space but of the space *image* that the artist has created. The actual shaping of the material, the building of walls and dome, were merely means to the end of shaping space, emptiness. Now let us leave the church again, climb one of the surrounding hills, and look back on Michelangelo's dome. It has lost all materiality, all three-dimensionalism, has become a silhouette. But its outline—perhaps the most beautiful line ever drawn by a human hand—visibly stands in boundless space; it *makes* boundless space visible. One might almost say it creates space; if one screens the dome from sight, only emptiness remains; if the dome is there, it imparts, as it were, its rhythm to surrounding space—it reaches out beyond itself into boundlessness and draws boundless space into the image.

Even more impressive in this respect are certain masterpieces of Chinese painting that offer the eye nothing but a few lines, the barest outlines of some object or another, apparently placed quite arbitrarily somewhere in the emptiness of the paper. The lines, and the objects they outline, occupy a small fraction of the entire surface; elsewhere the sheet is untouched. Is it the image of a thing, a flowering branch, for example? Certainly; but that is not all. How does such an image come into existence? There lies the white sheet, still untouched, emptiness, nothing. The artist's hand draws a few lines on it—and immediately the white surface around begins to live; is transformed into a force-flooded medium that brings the lines into complex relations with one another and with the edges of the sheet. The lines have enlisted the emptiness; the result is a composition made up of a trace of the objective and a great deal of emptiness, and this emptiness, which just before was not yet anything, is now something: space. The artist's purpose from the beginning was not so much to copy a thing as to form a whole out of a minimum of "thing" and a maximum of emptiness, to shape space; the thing becomes his occasion for letting the surrounding space become manifest, for taking it in his hand, as it were—through the thing he shapes the space beyond the thing. What the beholder perceives is, then, not simply space, but a space formed and organized in a particular way, a space image.

Works of musical art are time images in the same sense in which works of the representational arts and architecture are space images. Tones are time become audible matter; to form in tones is to form in the stuff of time; an image composed of tones is always at the same time a time image—not an image *in* time but an image made *of* time. Tones summon time upon the scene as the Chinese master's lines do space. To be sure, time does not make its appearance from an emptiness around tones, as space does from the emptiness around things. "Around" refers to place, and in the purely temporal there are no places and no distinctions between places. Time and tone completely fill each other—there is literally no room for emptiness—unless we wish to think of the rest, that musical counterpart of visible emptiness. What the hearer perceives in the tones—and rests—of a musical work is not simply time but shaped and organized time. As shaped and organized time, as a time image, the tonal work stands before the auditor's perception, offers itself to his view. If it has nothing spatial about it, nothing material in the usual sense, nothing objective, nothing for the eye, this does not prove that it is not an image, but only that viewing, beholding, is not the sole privilege of the eye. So the conventional formula receives its final interpretation: music is a temporal art because, shaping the stuff of time, it creates an image of time.

Forming images and thinking are the two gifts that distinguish human existence from animal existence. The whole one-sidedness of our viewpoint is shown by the fact that we still essentially hold to the old definition of man as *animal rationale,* as a thinking animal. But it is in thinking *and* forming that man proves his freedom; concepts *and* images build up his mental world. At earlier stages it was, indeed, rather in the ability to form than in the ability to think that the break found expression; in degree of intellectual achievement primitive man and highly evolved animal are not so very different, but in no animal's lair shall we find frescoes. Animals may have religious feelings; they have no religious symbols. Images conquer strangeness; create the first intimacy between man and his surroundings, material and immaterial. Images support and orient; forming images and contemplating images, man reaches out beyond himself, broadens that self, enters into most intimate communication with the world, lays hold of the world, and gains power over it. It is images that create and preserve the tradition handed on from generation to generation; it is community of images more than community of thought that binds and delimits human societies. And this whole teeming world of images, the world of our symbols, to which myths and religions, art, science, philosophy have contributed and by which human life directs its course—this whole world is a world of *spatial* images. All our symbols are for the eye, the eye of the body or of the mind; we *look* at symbols, the eye looks at them. Even on to the "nonrepresentational" symbols of modern science, our whole symbol world is profoundly rooted in the visible, is born of space, is created by the eye, under the guidance of the eye, for the eye.

Now music comes and, for the first time since the beginning of human thought, the bond between image and eye, between image and space, is broken. It might be asked, Why only now? Has not music always been with us? Certainly, it has been; but in the music of earlier times, tones were not free; they were bound to words, as in song, or to actions that call for regular bodily movement, as in dance, work, ceremonial. Thus the world of things, the spatial world, forced itself into the tonal world, mingled with it, and was able to prevent an insight into the very essence of music. It was not until tones freed themselves from these ties, and, dependent entirely upon themselves, became a language out of their own content, that music wholly found itself; became the art that overturned our concepts of forming and constructing, of *Gestalt* and symbol, because it gave us images in which there is nothing to be seen, spaceless *Gestalten,* constructions in which everything flows. And if now, from this newly won level, tones again seek to be linked with words, with actions—in the song, in the music drama—they do not thereby lose any of their new freedom; on the contrary, they, in their turn, now free word and action from exclusive connection with the world of things, bring a new dimension to view in them. The new dimension by which music enriches our image world—a phenomenon that is comparable to the acquisition of a new sense—is not what the Romanticists saw (and see) in it: something supersensual, of the beyond, of dream; it is *time,* and everything for which the word stands: flowing, becoming, change, motion.

With music, time broke into our image world; in music our formative powers took possession of time. Thanks to music, we are able to *behold* time. Hearing receives its credentials as an image-creating and image-visioning function.

In the broadest sense symbols are man's attempts mentally to master the world, to make it his own. Our apprehension of the world reaches as far as our symbols. The spatial symbol, the symbol that we see with our bodily or mental eyes, is at rest; it persists; it is removed from change, motion, alteration. What is at rest enters naturally into a spatial symbol; the spatial symbol is suited to the state of rest. But what is in motion can be caught in a spatial image only if we freeze the motion at some chosen moment. For all eternity the advancing horse in the equestrian statue of Colleoni will not set down its raised foot. It is as in fairy tales: at a gesture from the wizard, all motion stops; the hand outstretched to strike remains suspended in air, the mouth opened to shout cannot close, the body crouched to spring freezes in its bent posture. The instant is fixed; time comes to a stop. Such is the action of every spatial image, of every space symbol; it brings time to a stop. But if all our symbols are space symbols, the result is that, though we have words for motion, for time, for becoming, for change, we have no images for them, and hence only blind words. Is it possible that the old preference of philosophers for what is at rest, for what is removed beyond change, is based upon this orientation of our image world? Would they have held that only the changeless *is,* and that only being is the truly real—while all becoming, all that is in motion, in process of transformation, was considered a reality of the second order, if not a deception and a dream—were it not that rest, persistence, being, could be put into symbols and contemplated in symbols, but not motion, change, becoming? However this may be, in forming images we are like the wizard in the fairy tale: in our image world motion is paralyzed, the instant fixed, time brought to a stop.

Music breaks this spell; it frees the image from bondage to the fixed instant. Since music is able to make time an image without a detour through space, it finds the symbolic language in which we can apprehend, can view, can grasp becoming, flux, change. The old prejudice in favor of being, rest, changelessness, which had the whole weight of our symbols on its side, is discredited: a completely new symbol world opens, in which we discover genuine, immediate symbols of becoming, of motion, of change. Since the Greeks, no more far-reaching revolution in our symbol world has taken place. In music we have, on another plane, repeated the achievement of the Greeks; what they did for space, we have done for time. Greek art gave the world a new space image; our music has given it the first genuine time image. Now at last image is whole, embraces the world as space and the world as time. This is all still so new, so unfamiliar, we are so committed to space and the eye in the matter of images and symbols, that many can see nothing in music except a last desperate attack against the old image world, the undermining of the last vestige of spiritual order. In the sense of the old image world, to be sure, music is an end; but, taken in its own sense, it is beginning and promise.

Modern man, such as he has become, such as tradition has shaped him, is incomparably more at home in space than in time. How could it be otherwise? Not only are the images with which we are brought up space images; the materials in which we create, with which we work, are almost exclusively space materials. We always, so to speak, have space in our hands—and nothing makes one more familiar with a material than to work in it. So it comes about that we are far more familiar with the spatial component of our existence than with its temporal component; know so much more about space than we do about time. To what degree our thinking itself is spatial, guided by spatial concepts and adjusted to the conditions of space—which very fact makes it such a powerful tool in the mastery of space—the leading thinkers of our time have made us see. That they have been able to do so bears witness to the revolution that has taken place: thought is throwing off the tutelage of space. And to the extent to which it frees itself from that tutelage, time opens to it. Can anyone doubt that this change in ways of thought is connected with the change in imagery? Time images have become a part of our environment; we work in time-stuff, we are constantly dealing with it; so we have become more familiar with time than any earlier period could be. Three centuries of great music have not passed by us without leaving a mark. We have begun to think temporally, in the image of time. We have begun to think musically. It is not just a beautiful phrase, a poetic ornament, when Bergson speaks of "the continuous melody of our inner life"; it is the precise formulation of a scientific cognition and expresses the fact that we must search in music for the symbols that permit us to comprehend the connection of psychic phenomena, as mathematical symbols permit us to comprehend the connection of physical phenomena. When a biologist like Uexküll discovers the action of "melodic laws" in the genesis of organisms —"the genetic melody which forms the fish . . . the genetic melody of the mammals, which in its first measures repeats that of the fish . . ." [3]—it becomes even clearer that here organic phenomena are not being simply *likened* to musical phenomena; instead, musical phenomena give us the decisive indication that leads us to an understanding of organic phenomena. Because there is music, we can comprehend the genesis of an organism. When, finally, a mathematical philosopher like Whitehead, in his

3. Jakob von Uexküll, *Theoretische Biologie.*

analysis of our experiential world, is led to call a piece of iron a "melodic continuity" [4]—and thus refers the unity of the piece of iron back to the same principle to which Bergson refers back the unity of consciousness and Uexküll the unity of the organism—when, then, music becomes the *key* that leads to a new understanding of the world of the psyche, of organisms, even of inorganic matter, what is taking place here if not a comprehensive *musicalization* of thought, a change of orientation under the aegis of new images, of time images, a change that seems to be opening new roads to our understanding and, indeed, to our logic?

4. Whitehead, quoted in Jean Wahl, *Vers le concret,* ch. 2, "La Philosophie speculative de Whitehead"; also in Bergson, *The Creative Mind.*

SPACE

XIV. The "Nonspatial" Art

WHAT IS A SECTION on space doing in a work on music, the non-spatial art, the time art par excellence?

That the dynamic qualities of tone—the qualities that make music possible at all—are transcendent in respect to the world of space and bodies; that tonal motion cannot be understood as change of place in a tonal space; that time in music can only become an image because tones have freed themselves from every connection with things and the spatial—this, in brief summary, has been what we have so far found in our investigation of the relation between music and space. It is an altogether negative finding. Music seems to have shaken the last grain of the dust of spatiality from its shoes.

Let us try the opposite tack. Let tone and time be given: can we then build up music? Difficulties appear at once. Music puts us in the presence of a series of simple phenomena that seem to presuppose something other than tone and time, in which a third factor, a third component, must participate. And it appears that we cannot even talk about these phenomena except with words that, whether latently or patently, have a *spatial* meaning. Throughout this study we have found ourselves under the necessity of occasionally using spatial language—thus laying ourselves open to the reproach of first gallantly bowing space out of music and then secretly letting it in again through the back door. We shall now cite the most important instances in which we have been guilty of this loose procedure.

Music, we have repeatedly insisted, occurs where the sun rises and sets, where birds fly past, where a shout sounds: outside, outside of myself, not in me. Music that I hear does not arise in me; it encounters me, it comes to me—from where? What is the meaning of terms like "outside," "from outside," what is the difference between "within" and "without," if I am not allowed to think of space?

If music were only tone and time—then, if time were thought away, only tone would remain. But something else remains: the chord, the connection of several tones sounding simultaneously. *Where* does this connection occur? If simultaneously sounding tones coalesced into a mixed tone as colors simultaneously projected upon a surface coalesce into a mixed color, then the chord would simply be another tone, as blue-green is another color, and the question would be superfluous. But the tones that make up a chord do not disappear in it; each remains in existence as a separate component of the chord and, in simple cases, can easily be heard in the chord even by untrained ears. What keeps apart simultaneously sounding tones, so that they can jointly form a chord? Simultaneously appearing colors, as we said, coalesce into a mixed color—unless, that is, they appear in different places, unless *space* keeps them apart. It appears as if the fact of the simultaneity of different tones would in some way bring space, as its indispensable prerequisite, into music.

As the chord arises from the connection of simultaneously sounding tones, the texture of polyphonic music arises from the connection of several voices, or parts, proceeding side by side. Side by side? Pure temporal succession knows nothing of this nature, knows only a "one after the other"; only space makes us aware that there is a "side by side." And how am I to keep apart the individual voices of this polyphony, each of them a separate course of motion, if I am not allowed to conceive that one is "here," another "there"— how am I to keep apart motions that no space keeps apart? Let us assume that a ballerina is dancing in a circle on a vertically rising platform: in general, we shall clearly distinguish two motions, the vertical rise, the circular motion. But suppose that the thing takes place in darkness, with only a spotlight on the dancer's hand. Now we shall no longer see two motions, the vertical, ↑, and the circular, ⬭, but only one, ⟳, the ascending spiral; the two motions have coalesced. Can I speak of polyphony as the connection of several simultaneously occurring tonal motions—in the sense in which two lines become not *one* line but a combination of lines—without making any provision for the "space" in which such a phenomenon can take place?

In Bach's *St. Matthew Passion* there is a passage that makes a particularly powerful impression on any listener: it is the moment —the only one of its kind in the work—when the choral mass fuses together into a single voice, sings as with one voice:

Are they all really singing the same thing? Yes, because the tone is the same, and they all sing it at the same time. No, because the men sing an octave lower than the women. The tone is the same; the time is the same; whence the difference? What is the meaning of "an octave *lower,* an octave *higher,*" when the result is still the same tone? To be sure, we distinguish and say that the men sing *e*, the women sing *e′;* but what does the symbol ′ represent here? An answer involving frequencies is inadmissible; we do not hear vibrating air, we do not hear frequencies, we hear tones. What is it which makes what is the same appear different, what is different appear the same? It would be all very well if we could say that it is as in space, that it is the same object seen in different places, from different distances; or, better yet, as in a hall of mirrors, the many different reflections of the same object. But we cannot say this if music is to be the nonspatial art, the purely temporal art.

The problem, then, must be stated as follows: on the one hand music appears as the art that—in Schopenhauer's words—"is perceived solely in and through time, to the complete exclusion of space"; on the other hand, it is full of phenomena that seem to presuppose a spatial order and that in any case are wholly incomprehensible if space is "completely excluded."

We shall anticipate the result of the following investigation: Schopenhauer is wrong; the world of music is not the nonspatial world it is commonly represented to be; the experience of music is also an experience of space, and indeed a particular experience of space. Tones are not transcendent in respect to space as such but to *the* space in which bodies or objects have locations. Since space is commonly equated with this space—the space of bodies, the totality of all places—the spatiality of music *must* be denied. But then a full understanding of music as well as a full understanding of space have been precluded.

XV. Is Space Audible?

LET US ATTEMPT to settle the first dilemma. We assert that music takes place where the sun rises and sets. How is this assertion to be reconciled with the transcendence of music in respect to everything corporeal, to the motion of bodies, to the space of bodies, a transcendence that we have so painstakingly established? The sun is a body; its rising and setting betoken the motion of a body. How can music take place *where* bodies move, and at the same time be transcendent in respect to the space in which bodies move?

We have stated the same fact in words that perhaps express it better: music encounters us from where the rising and setting of the sun also encounter us. At least this seems somewhat to soften the contradiction. Much that has nothing to do with bodies and space comes to me from where bodies also move. I meet a man, who immediately impresses me by his abysmal stupidity. This stupidity is not in me; I encounter it; it comes to me from outside. Yet it is certainly nothing spatial or corporeal.

Heidegger defines space as *that whence something encounters me.* Tones that encounter me presuppose space; otherwise there would be nothing whence they could encounter me and they could not encounter me. But that is a long way from their necessarily being spatial themselves. What encounters me from space is marked, so to speak, to very different degrees by that whence it encounters me. Much is completely saturated with space, carries with it, and to me, so much of that whence it encounters me, that I always encounter space in it too. Such is the case with almost everything that encounters my eye or my hand. I do not see simply color but space; I do not grasp simply hardness or smoothness but space. Yet other things, though they come to me from without, though they come to me through space, are, as it were, immune to space, so that no spatiality clings to them. I open a book and read: "There is an enthusiastic reflection that is of the greatest value if one does not allow oneself to be carried away by it." [1] This is certainly an encounter. The fine thought does not come out of me; I find it outside myself; it comes to me from without. Nevertheless it remains unspatial. The black characters on the white paper, the letters that meet my eye, are spatial, to be sure. But the thought that emerges from the characters and comes to meet me leaves the characters, and with them everything spatial, behind. Are tones, which encounter me from outside, more of the nature of color and hardness or of thought?

When we say that color, hardness, thought encounter *me,* the "me" by no means always has the same meaning. Only thought encounters simply "me"; in the case of color and hardness, a more precise statement is necessary. Color encounters not me but my eye, hardness my hand. Here the sense organ is the conveyor and the stage of the encounter; whereas in my encounter with thought the reading eye, for example, merely performs a subordinate, ancillary service. In this context, there seems to be no doubt as to where tone is to be placed. Tone encounters my ear as color my eye, hardness my hand; it belongs here, in the category of sensations, not in the category of thought. But on the other hand we must not forget the peculiar nature of tone: it is the only sensation that encounters us not as the property of a

1. Goethe, *Maximen und Reflexionen.*

particular bodily-spatial thing. We see blue flower; we touch smooth wall; but we hear tone—not sounding string. The color we see, the hardness we touch, normally leads us directly to the thing, the bodily-spatial thing, of which it is a property—hence leads us directly to space. Tone, on the contrary, does not lead us to the thing, to the cause, to which it owes its existence; it has detached itself from that; it is not a property but an entity. So it might well be that, though tone presupposes space as that whence it encounters me, its connection with spatiality is limited to the *source* of the tone, to the necessity for the presence of the bodily-spatial thing which produces it but from which it immediately detaches itself as radically as thought does from the spatial characters, the letters, which are the means of the encounter. Thus, though tone would reach us through the sense organ, we should not necessarily encounter space in it. And this again makes it appear more closely related to thought than to other sensations.

We have already faced the question whether an element of spatiality clings to tones; when we investigated the meaning of "higher" and "lower," "up" and "down," in melodic motion, it appeared that these distinctions are not spatial but dynamic in nature, refer not to different positions in space but to different dynamic qualities. To this question we shall not here return. What we have to decide now is this: Is an element of spatiality to be attributed to tone itself, entirely apart from "high" and "low"? When tone encounters us, does it carry traces of that whence it encounters us? Is the experience "tone" a completely unspatial experience, or do we experience space in tone? Do we *hear* space, as we see and touch space—or as we hear time?

Compared with the other sensations, as we have seen, tone appears to be like thought. But compared with thought? Both tone and thought have, when they encounter us, completely detached themselves from the bodily-spatial thing that was the occasion for their appearance. Thus far they are comparable; but now their ways part. A simple question will make the distinction clear. *Where* is the thought, *where* is the tone—within or without? In reference to the thought, the question is meaningless; one could just as well ask if a molecule is cold or hot, if justice is fluid or gaseous. The distinction "within-without" is not applicable to thought. It is the same thought that first encounters me in the lines of a book and that I later call back from memory to consciousness; from within, from without—it makes no difference here. But in the case of tone it makes a tremendous difference. Only what encounters me from without is veritably tone; what I call from memory to consciousness is mere representation of tone. Here, then, the question "within or without?" is meaningful; and the answer is given: *tones are without.* To the tone when it encounters us, there must still cling something of that whence it encounters us, something of space; otherwise we could not definitely feel it as happening "without—not within." So only thoughts are really immune to space; tones are not. Hearing a tone includes a sensation of "without"; it is not a wholly nonspatial experience. The listener is aware of space.

Psychology has concerned itself rather intensively with the problem of auditory space. In contrast to older doctrines, which saw the experience of space as the joint work of sensory and intellectual functions and, among the senses, allowed only sight, touch, and the kinetic sense a part in it, modern psychology believes that it can establish an admixture of spatiality in sensation as such, and in *every* sensation, without the participation of the intellect. Whatever is sensed is felt as *extended;* and this feeling of extension is our original space experience. In tones, this feeling is particularly pronounced. We speak of *volume* as an essential characteristic of all tones—the expression signifies not simply something that *is* in space but something that *occupies* space. "Sounds," writes William James, "seem to occupy all the room between us and their source; and in the case of certain ones to have no definite starting point." [2] Géza Révész, to whom we owe the most comprehensive and thorough study of auditory space, concludes from his observations that "with the appearance of the sound, the subject enters into perceptual contact with the surrounding space." [3] With the *surrounding* space: this means with something that, viewed from the standpoint of the hearer, is "without, not within." That the place where the tone occurs "is situated outside of our self" Révész regards as "evident"; "musical tone is always localized in outside space."

Psychology, then, supports our finding: the listener must be aware of space. *What* does this awareness tell him of space? Is the "outside space" with which tone brings us into contact the same space that eye and hand have revealed to us? Does the space that we hear have the same characteristics as the space that we see and touch? William James has recourse to a simile to characterize the space sensation of hearing: it is, he writes, like "the empty blue sky when we lie on our backs." He speaks of a "simple total vastness," in which there are no parts and no subdivisions. The fact that a simile from the space of the seeing eye is here used to describe the space of the hearing ear does not yet mean that visual space and auditory space are the same or even closely related. It is only exceptionally that we lie on our backs and gaze into the blue sky; normally, as seeing and touching beings, we encounter space as something in which *things* are located in different *places*. The eye, and even more clearly the hand, encounters a thing; here a boundary is drawn in space, a part of space is demarcated from another part of space or from all

2. "The Perception of Space."
3. "Gibt es einen Hörraum?"

the rest of space, a "somewhere" is distinguished from an "elsewhere." But to the ear, to the tone-hearing ear, such experiences are foreign. The ear does not encounter a thing (this is precisely the point, that we do not hear a sounding thing but tone); nowhere in space does it encounter a boundary. Tones are not, like things, "there" or "elsewhere"; each tone is everywhere. A being that only heard, that heard only tones, would know what we mean when we say "space" and "without"; but he would not understand the difference between "there" and "elsewhere." We appear to be dealing with two space experiences that differ in essential points. The space experience of eye and hand is basically an experience of places and distinctions between places; and the space we see and touch, in which we also move, and which, finally, serves our science of space, our geometry, as starting point, has been defined as the *aggregate of all places.* The ear, on the other hand, knows space only as an undivided whole; of places and distinctions between places it knows nothing. The space we hear is a space without places.

Nor is this all. Let us again consider and compare tone sensation with color sensation. The color I see is the property of a thing; it is with the thing, out there, and it remains with the thing. But the tone I hear is not with the thing that produces it and does not remain with it, it has detached itself from it; to encounter the tone is, so to speak, something in a different style from encountering the color. Erwin Straus writes: "Of color we must say that it always appears confronting us, confined to a locality, organizing and delimiting space into parts; of tone, on the contrary, we must say that it comes toward us, reaches us and seizes us, passes by, occupies and integrates space." [4] I encounter the color in space; the tone encounters me out of space. To put it

4. Erwin Straus, *Vom Sinn der Sinne.*

more accurately: I encounter the color as something that *is without,* the tone as something that *comes from without.* Let there be no misunderstanding: it is not one and the same space, one and the same "without," *in* which the color is, *from* which the tone comes; "without" itself has a different bearing and content in either case; for the eye, it is "being," for the ear it is "coming from . . ." As a creature who sees, I know space as something that is without and remains without, that confronts me—here I am, there it is, two worlds rigidly and permanently separated; as hearer, hearer of tone, who has no conception of a "*being* without," I know space as something *coming from* without, as something that is always directed toward me, that is always in motion toward me. According to this, the step from visual to auditory space would be like a transition from a static to a fluid medium. Révész writes: "If, with eyes closed and in a state of repose, we are exposed to a tone or a tonal complex, it seems to us as if the space around us were suddenly filled with life. It is as if the space in which we find ourselves emerged from its indefiniteness [the result of our closed eyes and our motionlessness], from its potentiality, and, through the sound, received a definite directionality and a certain extension. It is obvious that the space that has become alive as a result of the sound is outside of us. . . ." [5] Space that has become alive as a result of sound! Hence not sound that has become alive in space. It almost seems as if we should here be forced to conclusions similar to those which we found necessary in the case of the time concept. Not tone that occurs in space, but space that becomes an occurrence through tone. In any case, the difference between visual and auditory space thus reaches a maximum. We see—and touch—a space in which things move; the statement that space itself moves is, for the eye and the

5. Révész, "Gibt es einen Hörraum?"

hand, meaningless. But not for the ear. We hear a space that itself is in a sort of motion; we hear—to try another formulation—"*flowing space.*"[6]

Does all this establish the existence of auditory space? One would think so. The more startling, then, becomes the fact that only a very few psychologists have drawn the affirmative conclusion from their observations. Most are doubtful and incline toward a negative answer. Should we suppose that the same man whose vivid and striking description of the spatiality of the auditory experience we have just quoted *denies* the existence of auditory space?

The reason for this apparently contradictory attitude is not hard to find. Most investigators approach these phenomena from a rigid position; *they already know for certain what space is.* As seeing, touching, moving beings who, furthermore, practice measurement and geometry, they have formed a definite conception of space; and when they inquire into the spatiality of tone sensation, this means for them not simply whether tones are spatial or not, but whether they are spatial *in the sense of this concept.* From this point of view, a spatiality that does not fulfill the conditions of visible, tangible, measurable space cannot be a genuine spatiality. If, by way of exception, an investigator breaks ranks and makes some such admission as "There is an auditory space, but in this space quadrangles and cubes are impossible,"[7] he is immediately called to order by science. He has failed, the accusation runs, to ask himself "if the supposed auditory space corresponds to those criteria which we are justified in demanding on the basis of our criteria for optical space and haptic space."[8] Here, then, it is not so much a matter of discovering *what* tone

6. Melchior Palágyi, *Neue Theorie des Raumes und der Zeit.*
7. Erich M. von Hornbostel, "Die Einheit der Sinne."
8. Révész, "Gibt es einen Hörraum?"

tells us about the "without" from which it encounters us; the crucial question is whether or not it tells us *the same* as the eye, the hand, and geometry tell us. "It must be determined whether the fixed relations between phenomenal and metric space are also to be found in auditory space." [9] If they are not, auditory space must be denied. At best it would have to be regarded as a sort of rudimentary spatiality, as something out of which genuine space may one day develop—if, that is, eye and hand lend their aid.

We find a confirmation of this attitude in the discussion of the *localization of sound.* The action of the organ of hearing to which this term is applied is, in the last analysis, a sort of seeing with the ear. In as much as the ear proves capable of determining, with comparative accuracy, the location in space from which a sound reaches it, it proves itself a useful ancillary and substitute organ for the eye; especially since it functions under conditions where the eye fails: ears see in the dark, see around corners, see through walls. It is not this ability—remarkable enough in itself—which interests us here, but the role it plays in the scientific investigation of auditory sensations—more precisely, the assurance with which the ability of the ear to localize is frequently evaluated as one testimony in favor of the existence of *auditory* space. In the first place, objection should have been raised to the term "localization of sound"; it ought to be localization of the *source* of sound. The ability concerns, not the "where" of the sound, but the "where" of the thing in space that causes the sound. But above all it is here necessary to draw the boundary between noise and tone. Localization is an essential characteristic in the case of noises, an unessential appendage in the case of tones. What is of prime interest in a noise is its cause. We might say that it is the meaning of the noise to draw our attention to the particular locality in space where it is generated; whereas it is part of the

9. Ibid.

meaning of tone to divert us from any distinguishing of localities in space. Noise, like color, hardness, odor, belongs among the properties or accompanying phenomena of things; I hear the automobile that overtakes me from behind, as I see the automobile that approaches me from in front. The line of demarcation, then, does not run between auditory sensations and all other sensations, but right through the sensations of the sense of hearing. Noises belong with all other sensations; only tones remain on the other side of the line. The hearing of noises, including the localization of their sources, is the faculty of the ear in which it comes closest to the other senses, especially the eye. But it is tones in which, as we said, hearing comes to itself; and what hearing come to itself creates is music. The question whether and how the ear is able to orient us in *visual* space has nothing to do with the problem of *auditory* space in its proper sense. The ability of the ear to localize no more speaks *for* the existence of a genuine auditory space than the placelessness of the space experienced in tones speaks *against* it. Assuming, that is, that musical experience is also a space experience, then the space that reveals itself to us in this experience will certainly not be the same space as that in which—whether by sight, touch, or hearing—we distinguish places.

Summarizing the results of investigations into the existence of auditory space, Révész writes: "The space that becomes alive through sound entirely lacks the essential spatial characteristics of optical space, such as three-dimensionality, spatial order, multiplicity of directions, form, and above all occupancy by objects; it has no direct relation to the world of bodies, is related to neither of the two sensory spaces which we are given [visual space and tactile space], either in its structure or in its phenomenal elaboration; it knows no geometric relations, and possesses no spatial finiteness." [10] In the opinion of its author, this list of the characteristics in which auditory space diverges from visual space and tactile space amounts to a refutation of the existence of auditory space. It does, of course—once it has been decreed that an experience which does not conform to the conditions of visual and tactile space and to the propositions of geometry cannot qualify as spatial. The dogmatism of the attitude becomes even clearer when, from the admission that "'spatial' in the realm of tone must mean something entirely different from what it does in the realm of visual and tactile perceptions," the conclusion is drawn that *hence* there *cannot be* space in the realm of tone. The reasonable conclusion would seem to be that there might be other primary sources of information concerning spatiality besides sight and touch; and if it is divergent information that they disclose, this can only be one more reason for subjecting it to a close scrutiny and using it for all it is worth.

10. Ibid.

XVI.

The Placeless, Flowing Space of Tones

WHAT WOULD BE our idea, our concept of space, if our communication with the outer world were restricted to hearing tones?

Let us return to William James's comparison. I lie on my back and gaze up into the blue sky. What do I see? The naïve answer would be, nothing. The space that we hear, then, is like the space that we see when there is nothing to see. "Nothing" here means no object. Compared with the strict nothing that we see when our eyes are closed, or in total darkness, the nothing of the empty sky is still a something. It has color, the color blue. Even more: in this case the seeing of blue is not so much the seeing of a color as of a boundless extension, a seeing of space, of empty space. It seems as if the removal of all objects, all hindrances, freed our vision, which is now able to apprehend a space picture that is otherwise concealed by objects. At the same time the sharp distinction "I here—space out there" vanishes; *this* space is not that implacable opposite, the without, which forever excludes me; it is space in which I lose myself.

Here we have a description of a space experience of the eye, which shares an essential characteristic with the space experience of the ear—undivided totality. Yet even here one thing will give us pause. Why does he who sees call this space *empty?* Does he wish to suggest that the space he here perceives is a mere vessel, intended to be filled with a content that for the moment is still lacking? Is that why he says he sees *nothing* when he sees only one color? To him who hears, at any rate, "empty" would seem to be the last word he would use in the analogous case. The space that reveals itself to him when he hears one tone appears to him anything but empty; seems to him, on the contrary, filled to the utmost, "become alive." It would never occur to him to say that he hears *nothing* when he hears only one tone.

But let the smallest cloud take shape in the open blue sky. Now the space will no longer be called empty. A second color has appeared. It has appeared at a particular place. It has set that place off from the rest of space. The undivided totality has been broken, a boundary has been drawn in the boundless, a place determined in the placeless. Where the new color is the old color is no longer; a "there" has been divided from an "elsewhere." A part has been cut out of the whole; the part is small in relation to the whole; as the cloud spreads, the part becomes larger, includes an increasingly greater part of space, finally the sky is a third overcast. He who hears would long since have ceased to understand us. He has no idea of what we are talking about. What does "boundary" in space mean; what are "places"? He understands "place" because the question *where* the tones are, whether within or without, makes sense to him; and "place" is that to which the question "where" refers. The place of tones is without—but "places," plural? A multitude of places, distinguished in the without? What does it mean that the new color is in a location where the other no longer is? What is the meaning of the distinction between "there" and "elsewhere"? A new tone added to one already sounding draws no boundaries in space, occupies no location that belongs to it alone, does not drive the first tone away from anywhere, is not in a different place from the first; they are both in the same place, namely, "without." What does it mean that the new color cuts a part out of the whole; what does "part" mean in relation to the whole that is space? Were the terms "whole" and "totality" perhaps overhastily chosen for auditory space? Now it seems as if these words have meaning only in relation to parts that can be delimited and distinguished in a whole, a totality. In that case "unity," "oneness," would be a better characterization of auditory space, which can never be given us save as *one,* in which there are no parts. And "smaller part," "larger part," smaller and larger in general—what distinction is being made here? As if one tone could take up more or less space than another; should leave more or less space unoccupied! To be sure, every tone has extension, but all tones are equally extended, namely, throughout the whole of space. And, finally, the sky "a third" overcast! Here not only are divisions made, but the divisions are treated as *magnitudes,* are measured and their measurements compared. To be sure, he who hears will also—for example, in the case of the simultaneous sounding of the three tones of a triad—speak of one of the tones as a part of the triad, even as a third of it. But it would never occur to him that these words—three, part, third—could mean anything but a mere distinguishing and enumerating of elements. It would never occur to him that they could signify magnitudes. If white and blue are the two elements of a picture, then each color has a part of space to itself, extends from "there" to "elsewhere" and no farther; this "from there to elsewhere" is in each case measurable, the measurements give figures, the figures signify magnitudes, which we can compare with one another: we say one of the colors takes up twice, three times, ten times as much space as the other. That each of several tones sounding together had a part of space to itself, extended from "there" to "elsewhere" and no farther, that this "from there to elsewhere" was measurable, amounted to so much for one tone, so much for another, so that one could reach some such conclusion as "a triad takes up three times as much space as each of its individual tones"—to think in this fashion would be unmitigated nonsense. To be sure, tones fill space; but this spatiality of theirs is not something that can be measured and expressed in figures. The spatiality of tones is in no sense magnitude.

Now we can better understand the difficulty our thought has with the concept of placeless auditory space. Is it not precisely their spatial extension which makes things susceptible of measurement and division, of quantitative determination? To us, space is the accepted foundation of all quantitative determination; what partakes of space thereby becomes a quantity, a "how much," a *magnitude.* What does not partake of space—time, for example—must be translated into the language of space if it is to be quantitatively determined, measured. Under these circumstances, what on earth are we to do with a spatial extension that is not divisible and measurable, with something that evidently partakes of space and yet is *not magnitude?* Musical tone: genuine perception, yet not of a body; not bodily, yet having spatial extension; having spatial extension, yet not divisible and measurable, not magnitude—after all, does not such an entity represent, to use an expression of Kierkegaard's, a veritable scandal for our thinking?

What is the situation with respect to the problem of the *dimensions* of auditory space? We have heard that auditory space "entirely lacks the three-dimensionality of optical space." [1] Then does it make sense to talk about dimensions here at all? More precisely, what is the situation with respect to the *depth* of auditory space?

1. Géza Révész, "Gibt es einen Hörraum?"

No one will maintain that the ear is insensible to the perception of spatial depth in general; after all, we are able to distinguish positionally between a nearer and a more distant source of sound, even when the nearer sound is not characterized by greater loudness, when it is a matter of comparing a weak nearby sound with a strong distant sound. This is part of the ear's power to localize sounds. But the perception of differences in the sense of the third dimension, the depth of visual space, is not here under discussion. We are inquiring into the depth of a space that "entirely lacks three-dimensionality," a space for which the distinction "nearer" and "farther" has no more meaning than any other local distinction. Perhaps a brief reference to an auditory anomaly will help us to see the problem more clearly. A functional disturbance has been observed in which the ear, with its faculties otherwise unimpaired, loses that of localization. The person affected by this disturbance hears everything that the normal person hears; but he does not hear from where sound comes, whether from in front or behind, from right or left, from above or below; he hears every sound from everywhere. Auditorily, he is unable to distinguish places in space. Yet he hears space because he hears the sound as coming from without. Our question, then, can be framed as follows: Does the auditory space of such a person possess depth? From all that has so far been said, it is clear that each of us, in a particular situation, functions to all intents and purposes as this person does: namely, when we hear music. In the case of the musical tone, the spatial position of its source is of no importance; compositions that prescribe a particular spatial arrangement for the instruments (at a distance, in the four corners of the hall) by that very fact introduce an element of the theatrical into music—and *theater* comes from a root meaning "to see." This is not said derogatorily; only the hopeless pedant would hold that I should lose nothing if the effect of the distant trumpet in Beethoven's *Leonore* Overture escaped me. Apart from such exceptional cases, however, this anomaly puts one at no disadvantage as far as the hearing of music is concerned; the ability to perceive musical tones correctly is entirely unaffected by the ability or inability of the ear to localize sources of sound in visual space. Hence we ask: Does the "without" from which tones encounter us, does the space which we hear in music and which is like the space of the person incapable of localizing sounds—a space in which there is no "there" and "elsewhere," no "nearer" and "farther"—does this space nevertheless have depth?

Let us imagine a spherical creature that drifts back and forth, up and down, in the water, incapable of any motion of its own, and whose only sense organ is its skin. Let this skin be so organized that, although it reacts to a contact by a sensation, it is incapable of localizing this sensation: in other words, the creature is aware that a contact has taken place but is not aware at what place it has been touched. Such an assumption is not fantastic. In an earlier context, reference was made to the variations in the ability of our own skin to localize contacts. If two pencil points 1 centimeter apart touch the fingertip, we feel two contacts; the same stimulus, applied to the back of the hand, we feel as only *one* contact; we cannot tell whether both points, or only one, are actually touching the skin. Simultaneous contacts less than 1 centimeter apart, then, here produce only *one* contact sensation; places less than 1 centimeter apart pass as *one* place. Let us assume that the circumference of our spherical creature is less than 2 centimeters and the localization sensitivity of its skin is the same as that of the back of the human hand. What will such a creature know of space? Generally speaking, it will know space —just as we do—as the without from which things (which, in the case of our creature, means whatever produces contacts, gives rise to tactile sensations) encounter it. But since no two places on its skin are farther than 1 centimeter apart, and since its skin feels places 1 centimeter or less apart as *one* place—and since, furthermore, it has no other sense to fall back on—it will experience all contacts as occurring at the same place; will experience the "without" as an undifferentiated unity, as *one* place. The notions of places in space, of distinctions between places, of distances, would be foreign to it; its space will be a placeless space, comparable in this respect to auditory space.

Has the space of this creature depth? One need only bring to mind the nature of tactile sensations in order to answer this question in the negative. Tactile sensations have no depth; they make no statement concerning the without except in so far as it is in direct contact with the skin. No matter how refined my sense of touch may be, it cannot tell me anything about the length of the pencil whose point my hand touches, or about the thickness of the wall into which I bump. The space of our hypothetical spherical creature will, then, be perfectly flat. Its experience of space cannot extend beyond its skin; for it, "space," the "without," is like another skin, belonging to another being, and closely and completely surrounding its own. But now let us endow our creature with hearing; let it hear its first tone. Instantly, the most violent revolution will occur in its space. The other skin has burst; the creature's without spreads explosively all around it. The new without, from which the tone encounters it, is no longer the flatness, the enclosure, of the tactile without; in the tone, it encounters the space that the tone fills. Thus for the first time, through a sensation, it reaches beyond its own skin, into a depth; for the first time it feels space, in the full sense, around it.

The step from an unlocalized tactile sensation to an equally unlocalized auditory sensation makes it clear that a placeless space, a space in which there is no distinction between "there" and "elsewhere," between "nearer" and "farther," can nevertheless have depth. Whereas we *feel* the thing in contact with us simply as "there," we *hear* tone as "coming from . . ."—not from any one location *in* space, nor yet from all locations *in* space, as if space were the inactive vessel through which tone approaches us. No, in tone, space itself—as we put it earlier—is in a unique way directed toward the hearer; is experienced as in motion toward him. In this sensation—"directed from . . . toward . . ."—spatial depth is revealed to the hearer. Depth in auditory space, then, refers not to the distance between my ear and the location in space where a tone is produced, does not refer at all to the space *in* which I encounter tones; it refers to the space I encounter in tones, to the "from . . ." element of the encounter. Depth in auditory space is only another expression for this "coming from . . ." that we sense in every tone. It is as if a swimmer in a river felt, in the pressure of the water against his skin, the whole depth of the extent through which its waters are in motion toward him from its source. One and the same sensation makes us experience auditory space as possessing depth and as flowing.

The term "flowing space" comes from Melchior Palágyi's notable paper, written about the turn of the century, *Neue Theorie des Raumes und der Zeit.* In it he attempts to show that such a concept of space is a logical necessity. The logical inconsistencies in the classical separation and opposition of static space and flowing time are pointed out. Space without time, he argues, is as unreal as it is unthinkable; time and space do not bear to each other the relation of flux and stasis; to the continuous series of moments in time there does not correspond one space, one static datum, but an equally continuous *series* of spaces, whose totality must be designated as flowing space. Whatever may be argued against these considerations, it is impossible to deny that they point in the same direction in which recent thought on the subject of space has been moving. More and more, modern science is getting us out of the habit of seeing space as the eternally unchanging datum, the inactive vessel in which bodies move and produce and undergo effects. More and more, in the concepts of physicists, space appears as itself entangled in physical event. Space that is less and less distinguishable from the dynamic field that fills it; space that curves; space that expands—to such a space, in any event, the adjective "flowing" is not essentially foreign.

The space of tones, then, is a placeless depth surrounding the hearer or, more properly, directed toward him, moving toward him, from all about. The depth of this space is not the depth that, together with height and width, makes up the three dimensions of visual space. Height, width, depth—there are no such distinctions in auditory space. Here there is only the one "from . . ."—which, if we like, we may call the one dimension of auditory space. Here "from . . ." does not mean "from there or from elsewhere" but "out of depth from all sides"; and "out of depth" is not a direction in space but a (nay, *the*) direction *of* space. A space that, as a whole, has the direction "out of depth from all sides" *must have a center,* namely, the position toward which it can be thus directed. To be sure, he who sees likewise finds himself, if no objects interfere with vision, in the center of the space he views; but this is a fortuitous situation, and for this reason the space of geometry, derived as it is from visual space, knows nothing of a center. But a being that only heard, that heard only tones, could simply have no idea of a space without a center; such a being can think away its own person, can think of space without a perceiving being, but not of space without a center. The space that, as a whole, has the distinguishing characteristic "directed from . . . toward . . ." must have a center as necessarily as a circle or a sphere must have a center. And, because of its nature, experience of this space must always be experience out from a center. For him who hears, to perceive space means to be at the point toward which space as a whole is directed, toward which it flows together from all sides. The space experience of him who hears is an experience of space streaming in toward him from all sides.

Only now does the difference between seeing depth and hearing depth become clear. To see depth means to read degrees of nearness and distance from the naturally flat retinal image. The depth that I see is distance, is there where I am not; the eye pushes the without away from me; the step from plane to space, to spatial depth, here has the meaning "away from me." The eye discloses space to me in that it excludes me from it. The ear, on the other hand, discloses space to me in that it lets me participate in it. The depth that I hear is not a being-at-a-distance; it is a coming-from-a-distance. To be sure, in thought and dream I can transport myself out into the distance that I see or that lies beyond my sight; but the distance that I hear comes, as it were, of its own volition toward me, streams into me. Where the eye draws the strict boundary line that divides without from within, world from self, the ear creates a bridge. "Seeing and hearing are distinguished not only by the difference in the physical stimulus, in the functioning organs and their objects, but also, and even more, by the mode of the specific connection between the self and the world." [2] For seeing, there are two poles; for hearing, there is one stream. The space experience of the eye is a disjunctive experience; the space experience of the ear is a participative experience.

Looking back from this point, we recognize the inaccuracy and superficiality of the common classification of music as a purely

2. Erwin Straus, *Vom Sinn der Sinne.*

temporal art. Space speaks from the tones of music; the musical experience is also a space experience, and indeed a very remarkable and special one. The seeming contradiction between this statement and the space transcendence of music, which we so emphatically maintained and so circumstantially demonstrated earlier, is resolved in the fact that tones are transcendent not in relation to space as such but only in relation to the space that the eye sees, that the hand grasps, that geometry thinks and measures. But this means that the space of our practical life and our scientific thinking is not *all* of space. Even where there is nothing to be seen, nothing to be touched, nothing to be measured, where bodies do not move from place to place, there is still space. And it is not empty space; it is space filled to the brim, space "become alive," the space that tones disclose to us. Far from being unable to testify in matters of space, music makes us understand that we do not learn all that is to be said about space from eye and hand, from geometry, geography, astronomy, physics. The full concept of space must include the experience of the ear, the testimony of music.

XVII. The Order of Auditory Space

"IN POSTULATING a sound space, it must be made clear that . . . it would be a space in which structure and form are unknown concepts. It is evident that the space which has become alive through sound is outside of us, but it is no less evident that this space . . . wholly lacks spatial order." [1]

Coming from an investigator so familiar with music as Révész, these statements seem surprising. The visible is spatial as such; in the visible, order (that is, relation of parts to one another and to a whole) is spatial order. The audible is, in its particular way, no less spatial. In the face of music, one of the most amazing, perfect, and powerful manifestations of order, the opinion that there is no order in the "space which has become alive through sound" seems absurd. Who, in the face of a Greek temple, would seek to deny the order of visual space?

To be sure, if there were no music, if the audible were limited to noises and sounds, the situation would be different. Noises and sounds exhibit no order in themselves. They can, to be sure, be ordered: noises are localized, sounds form languages—verbal languages, sign languages. But these orders do not have their basis in the audible as such; they are, as it were, imposed on the audible from without; the audible is simply fitted into them or

1. Géza Révész, "Gibt es einen Hörraum?"

used as the means of representing them. They do not imply an order of *auditory* space; if we disregard the testimony of music, nothing obliges us to assume such an order. Hence a psychology of the senses that in general pays scant attention to music and regards tones as acoustical rather than musical phenomena is only logical if it sees auditory space—so far as auditory space comes into question at all—as a space which is not, or is not yet, ordered, to which the senses of sight and touch and the kinetic sense alone can bring order, their own order.

But there is also music. Every music is based upon a tonal system, an order which is not applied to the tones from without, into which the tones are not simply fitted, but which, on the contrary, proceeds from the tones themselves, is the joint achievement of ear and tone, to the exclusion of everything else; an order, then, of the audible as such—that is (since the audible is also spatial), order in auditory space. The spatial nature of this order may remain veiled so long as music does not advance to polyphony, so long as tones are given only in succession—for space discloses itself in simultaneity of data. But in the polyphonic music of the West this very thing, order in the simultaneously audible, auditory-spatial order, is most magnificently revealed. Every canon, every triad, presupposes the possibility of order in auditory space; sets that order before us as simple fact.

But this observation does not dispose of the problem; on the contrary, it intensifies it. For the insights we have so far gained into the spatiality of music and the nature of auditory space would seem on the whole to indicate the impossibility of order in auditory space. A placeless and flowing space in which a boundary can nowhere be drawn, in which nothing can be segregated, which is never given to us except as an undivided and indivisible unit—in such a space, how should order be possible? Is not this precisely William James's "simple total vastness in which no order of parts, or subdivisions, reigns"? [2] Must not the flow first of all be brought to a stop, a "there" and an "elsewhere" be distinguished in the placeless, if spatial order is to appear? Is it true, after all, that we cannot order the space which we hear unless we also see it and touch it?

The problem may be posed as follows: (1) there is order in auditory space; (2) spatial order is relation of spatial parts to one another and to a spatial whole; (3) in auditory space the distinction between parts and whole is meaningless. We see that these three statements cannot all be true together. If 1 and 2 are true, 3 cannot be true; if 1 and 3 are true, 2 cannot be true; if 2 and 3 are true, 1 cannot be true. Our question, then, is not *if* there is order in auditory space (music answers that question every instant that it sounds), but *how* such an order is possible, or, more accurately, how we are to understand the possibility of such an order.

The solution is foreshadowed in this formulation of the problem. In respect to what they are based on, the three statements are in different categories. Numbers 1 and 3 are abstract statements of facts in conceptual language: 1 is equivalent to saying "polyphonic music exists"; 3 is equivalent to saying "no tone is anywhere where every other tone is not also." Number 2 is a definition—certainly not a definition pulled out of the air, but rather one that is a necessary logical deduction from a particular concept of space, the space concept of classical science. We are, then, left with no other choice: if we decide to take the testimony of music really seriously, we must re-examine a concept that is one of the cornerstones of our understanding of the external world.

TRIAD

In the following sections the phenomena of the triad, of the scale, of the octave, and of polyphony will be introduced as ex-

2. William James, "The Perception of Space."

amples of a spatial order that differs basically from the order represented by the classical concept of space. The purpose of this procedure is to free us from the compulsion to equate absence of order in the sense of visual space or of geometrical space with absence of spatial order as such. At the same time this procedure should make it clear that auditory space must not be thought of as a rudimentary stage of visual space or be in any other way subordinated to it. Equally justified, equal in value, equally perfect, on the one side auditory space, on the other side visual space, tactile space, geometrical space, confront one another—two possibilities of spatial order, two modes of the existence of spatiality.

Since we are concerned with basic principles, we can, for all the differences between them, regard visual space, tactile space, and geometrical space as one space; for they have one basic principle of order in common: their order is an order of *juxtaposition.*

The relation that we call "juxtaposition" is a local relation. It presupposes a space in which places are distinguished. To be in juxtaposition means the same as to be at different places in space at the same time. ("At the same time" here signifies only that the time element is of no account.) What is to be in juxtaposition must above all have the capacity of being spatially separated. Conversely, the relation of "juxtaposition" always, in the last analysis, exists between different places in space. Thus the most general principle of order in visual space, tactile space, and geometrical space is connected with the most general space concept of seeing, touching, and geometrizing beings, the concept of a space of places. Basically the two are one.

We state these commonplaces only in order to make clear the basis of the resistance that everyone inevitably feels when he is asked to consider the possibility of some other principle of spatial order than juxtaposition. In our instinctive rejection of the assertion that spatial order and juxtaposition are not one and the same, that there can be spatial order without juxtaposition, that the idea of such an order is not arrant nonsense, the dogmatic role that the traditional space concept plays in our thinking is clearly expressed.

Three tones sound. In each of them space encounters us and we encounter space. None of them is in a place; or better, they are all in the same place, namely, everywhere. Different places, juxtaposition, are out of the question. Yet there is order here, unmistakable and undeniable: a triad. Order of simultaneous sensations involving space, order that we hear, not merely think: spatial order without difference of places, without juxtaposition. This is the problem. In the incisive light of Ernst Mach's formulation: "Why do three tones form a triad and not a triangle?"

How can different things of the same kind be in space simultaneously without being at different places, without being in "juxtaposition"? Smoothness and bluish whiteness, or smoothness and coolness, can be at the same place simultaneously—at the place, for example, where I touch a piece of marble; but not smoothness and roughness, coolness and warmth, or bluish and yellowish whiteness; these can only exist simultaneously if they are at different places, if space separates them.

The example of the sense of sight is highly informative. The idea of "juxtaposition," of a distinction of places, may have its original basis in the ability of the eye to localize color sensations. Only because colors appear at definite locations in space and are bound to their locations can we see different colors at the same time, that is, colors at different places, colors in juxtaposition. From seeing different colors at the same time, the way leads to the space that separates them: the eye reveals space as the aggregate of places, and juxtaposition as the principle of its organization.

Let us assume that the eye lacked the ability to localize color sensations. Then each color, as soon as it appeared, would immediately spread over all space, fill all space—as tones do. A simultaneous seeing of different colors would no longer be possible; for all colors would be at the same place (namely, everywhere), and colors that are not locally separated immediately run together into a mixed color. The little white cloud in the blue sky, for example, originally a second color set off from the first, would be nothing but a gradual lightening of the blue, a lightening that the naked eye could not at first register but that, as the cloud grew larger, would slowly become visible. A being who saw in this fashion would know nothing of places, of distinctions between places, of juxtaposition (assuming that sight was his only, or most important, source of information). In his visual space no boundaries could be drawn, no parts distinguished, everything would always run together; it would really be the "simple total vastness, in which no order of parts, or subdivisions, reigns," in which "form and structure are unknown concepts." Is this the picture of auditory space? Is auditory space like a visual space of unlocalized color sensations?

Certainly not, because—and this is the crucial factor—simultaneously sounding tones do not run together into a mixed tone. No difference of places keeps them apart; yet they remair audible as different tones. Blue and yellow in the same place produce green, a new color, in which—so far as the eye is concerned—the two others are merged without leaving a trace. But the result of the simultaneous sounding of different tones is not a mixed tone—for example, a tone lying midway between the tones involved—is not a *tone* at all, but a *chord:* something of a new and peculiar kind, characterized precisely by the fact that the elements whose coming together make it up do not vanish in the new unity without leaving a trace, but preserve, audibly preserve, their identity. For example, in this figure □ four lines of equal length are not merged into one line four times as long but form a figure that is a whole made up of visually distinguishable parts. Different tones, then, can be present simultaneously without being in different places, without being in juxtaposition. We repeat our former question: *How* are different tones present simultaneously if they are not "in juxtaposition"?

For an example, we again choose the triad, which, as a key to discovering the order of musical space, can perform the same sort of service as the triangle in geometrical space. Let us build up a triad step by step. The first tone, as it sounds, spreads through all space. Joining the first, the second tone, however much it might wish to, could find no room to take a place beside it: all available space is already occupied by the first. The second tone has to spread out in the same space in which the first has previously spread. Nevertheless, it is not covered by the first: the first turns out to be, as it were, transparent for it. The second tone is and remains audible *through the first.* The same is true of the third tone: the tones connected in the triad sound *through one another.* Or let us say that they interpenetrate one another; the *interpenetration* of tones in auditory space corresponds to the *juxtaposition* of colors in visual space. (Here it becomes clear that the space in which chords occur is a different space from that in which we localize tones. The chord remains completely unaffected, whether the simultaneously sounding tones have a common tonal source—a phonograph needle, for example—or whether the tonal sources of the individual tones are audibly distributed among different locations in space.)

As the road leads from simultaneous seeing of different colors to the juxtaposition and the order of visual space, so the road leads from simultaneous hearing of different tones to the interpenetration and the order of auditory space. A being whose only connection with the external world was hearing would be aware not only of space in general but also of order in space, of an ordered coexistence of what is encountered in space. In a space that was nothing but an unorganized and unorganizable without, no triad could occur. The fact that the sounding together of different tones becomes such a chord is as irreconcilable with the idea of an auditory space without order as the idea of a visual space without order, which we constructed on page 298, is irreconcilable with the existence of visible forms. Hence the dictum, "No spatial order without juxtaposition," cannot be extended from visual space and geometrical space to spatial order in general. Wherever triads occur, form and structure cannot be unknown concepts. But the ordering principle has a different name.

From the fact that different tones can sound together, as different colors can appear together, Ernst Mach has drawn the conclusion that the realm of tone has an order *analogous to that of space:* it is space, the order of space, which keeps simultaneously appearing colors separate; if simultaneously sounding tones do not run together, the reason can be sought only in an analogous ordering principle. But the consideration is not conclusive as such; though the condition that supports it—simultaneity of sensations—is necessary, it is not sufficient. To be sure, the idea of a spatial order cannot even be conceived without a simultaneity of different sensations of the same kind; our hypothetical visual space of unlocalized color sensations, in which only one datum can be present at a time, is, on these grounds, without order. But the contrary does not hold; it is not true that a simultaneity of sensory data of the same kind must always necessarily lead us to the assumption of an underlying spatial order. There are many cases of a simultaneous existence of sensations of the same kind which are not in juxtaposition and hence not organized according to the principle of visual space, not locally separated, but which at the same time do not permit us to draw the conclusion of a different spatial principle of order. We need only think of many noises—the roar of wind, the rustle of rain, the rolling of thunder fill space simultaneously, are simultaneously in the same place, namely, everywhere; we separate them only auditorily. Yet no one will maintain that the simultaneous existence of these noises reveals an *order* of auditory space. The same is true of odors. I enter a room and sniff: lilac, fish. Vases and plates have been removed; the two odors have spread uniformly through the room—different sensations of the same kind in the same place. Yet no one would think of drawing the conclusion of a spatial or quasi-spatial order in the realm of odor from the fact of these odors being simultaneously present.

It is not, then, the simultaneous existence of different tones as such which leads us to the recognition of an order of auditory space; it is the particular nature of their simultaneous existence, their ordered connection, the chord. Odors do not make chords. Odors are simply present simultaneously; their simultaneous existence gives rise to no new *form*. For the present, at any rate, a music of odors, chords of odors, are sheer fantasy. Hence we must ask, Why do tones form chords, why does a chord proceed from the coexistence of tones, whereas noises, odors, remain sterile in this respect?

The answer is obvious: because tones relate to one another. The chord is the fruit not of the simultaneous existence of tones but of their mutual relation. Noises, odors, do not relate to one another. They are connected only in my consciousness, not among themselves; they simply encounter me. Tones, on the contrary, encounter not only me but one another. Thus it comes about that the space which we hear in noises, smell in odors, remains vaporous, embryonic, a "without" lacking further differentiation; whereas in tones, in music, we experience space as order. For space—we now enlarge our earlier definition—is not only that whence something encounters me; space is also that in which what encounters me is mutually related; space is the whence of the encounter and the where of the relation. In the encounter, space reveals itself as "without"; in the mutual relations of what is encountered, space reveals itself as order.

We have described what we hear in a chord as an interpenetration of different tones; we now add: of different and mutually related tones. But in what respect are tones at once different and mutually related? Again we need only think of the triad: what both distinguishes and connects the three tones that come together in the triad—what both keeps them apart and relates them to one another, and thus is the necessary condition upon which the chord as such arises, upon which order becomes audible—is the dynamic qualities of the tones. The "different tones" of this interpenetration are tones in different dynamic states, not tones merely different in pitch. Among tones merely different in pitch an "interpenetration" could not, strictly speaking, take place; the "inter-" element, the mutual relation, would be lacking. Tones of different pitch are simply present simultaneously, just like noises. To be sure, such tones can be ordered, arranged by pitch, but noises too can be ordered—for example, the different kinds of water noises, of wind noises, sensations of heat and cold, of roughness and smoothness, can be ordered, or different mixtures of two taste sensations; yet in none of these cases will the different elements of the order perceptibly relate to one another, will a form arise from their connection. Only through the quality that also distinguishes the musical from the acoustical phenomenon, through their dynamic quality, do tones become capable of constituting an order that expresses itself in forms, in chords—an audibly spatial order.

Differences in tonal dynamic quality are, generally speaking, differences in state. On this basis we can attempt to answer Ernst Mach's question. Three tones form a triad and not a triangle because they designate not three particular places in space but three particular states in space (or, shall we say, of space?). The concept of placeless, flowing auditory space has already familiarized us with the idea that space is of the nature of a state rather than of a place; so it should not cause a shock if we now think of audibly spatial differences as differences in state. Thus place differences in visual space would be matched by differences in dynamic state in auditory space. "State" is here taken in the particular sense in which equilibrium or disturbed equilibrium are states: a condition that wants itself perpetuated or wants to get away from itself, that points toward itself or points beyond itself, tendency, directed tension. But "direction" here must not again be misunderstood in the sense of visual space, must not in any way be interpreted locally, as "from somewhere to somewhere"; it is direction from one state to another state, from an "everywhere" to another "everywhere": direction, then, in a purely dynamic sense. Thus visual space and auditory space are clearly set off from one another: multiplicity of places and multiplicity of states, juxtaposition and interpenetration, local relation and directional relation, dynamic relation; order by places and positions that we see and touch, order of directed states of tension, dynamic order, that we hear: triangles and triads, geometry and music.

In consequence of the peculiar properties, the unique mode of existence, of tones, we are obliged, in dealing with them, to renounce one of the chief aids to comprehension—comparison. Parallels to musical phenomena are rare in other realms. If, by way of exception, a parallel turns up, it is sure to be something that, in its own realm, lies in the penumbra of attention and interest. Wolfgang Koehler points out several aspects of the field concept in physics that are given scant attention or wholly ignored by many physicists. In this connection he mentions a thought of Faraday's that surprisingly bridges the gap between the modes of existence of tones and of bodies. For Faraday, the dynamic field that emanates from a body belongs to the body itself in the same sense as do its mass, its shape, its hardness, its color; the dynamic field of a magnet *is* the thing "magnet" no less than is the horseshoe-shaped piece of metal at the center of it.[3] The sharp distinction that we are accustomed to draw, in respect to existence, between the mechanical tangibility and visibility of a thing, its corporeality in the usual sense and its more distant effects, is abolished: a body *is* where it *acts*. The current criterion, according to which a body is where I see it or touch it, directly or by the aid of instruments, thus becomes untenable; a body is also where I neither see it nor touch it nor can in any other way find it physically present. Its existence, its presence, does not stop where its visibility and tangibility stops; its limits do not coincide with the limits of its material form. With its dynamic field it extends into space, its limits are those of its field; that is—since a dynamic field is theoretically limitless—it has no definite limits at all. But with this the usual idea of a body being situated in a particular place loses its meaning. The body is not in a place but in all places, everywhere. And this is not true only of one body but of all bodies. All bodies are in all places, everywhere; all bodies are simultaneously in the same place.

With some effort we can imagine a consciousness whose direct experience of bodies would roughly correspond to Faraday's views. Let us think of a creature that should possess none of our

3. Wolfgang Koehler, *Die physischen Gestalten in Ruhe und in stationärem Zustand.* Faraday's thought (cited also by Bergson in *Matière et mémoire*) is from his "A Speculation Touching Electric Conduction."

senses but instead should be endowed with a sensitivity to magnetic influences, and let us suppose that this sensitivity was equally distributed over the creature's entire body, not definitely localized—a sensitivity comparable perhaps to the dull sensations of the sense of orientation or to the sensations that plants may experience when they turn toward the light: in short, a piece of iron endowed with consciousness. Let this magnetic sense be a telesthetic sense—that is, one in whose sensations the creature would be given not only a consciousness of its own body but also of something coming from without, from a distance. Such a creature, then, would have an experience of "without," a space experience, and this space would never be completely dark, empty; as a result of the magnetism of the earth, there would always be "something" present; or better, it, space, would always be a something, a perceptible tension. What idea does such a creature have of a magnet that suddenly approaches it? It does not see it, it does not touch it, it can only have—to borrow from Koehler's *Die physischen Gestalten*—"dynamic knowledge" of it. The horseshoe-shaped (or otherwise shaped) piece of matter does not exist for it; nothing exists except the sudden change in the dynamic state of the "without." For this creature, a magnet *is* not a body in a place, not an object in space, but a state of space. Let us surround our animated piece of iron by a ring of magnets, and let us assume that its magnetic sense has the same ability as our ear to distinguish the individual components in a combination of simultaneous influences. Our creature will experience these magnets not as bodies in different places but as superimposed, mutually interpenetrating dynamic states, all in the same place, "without," everywhere. Let the magnets revolve in a circle around the piece of iron; the result will be identified not as "bodies changing place" but as "dynamic states changing direction and tension." Or let some part of terrestrial nature, the sea, for example, be invested with personality. Let us assume that the sea has "dynamic knowledge" of gravity, knows nothing but gravity. Let the seat of this consciousness lie in its deeper strata, to which the superficial disturbances of the waves do not reach. What knowledge would this being have of sun, moon, and earth? It would be aware of them, without any doubt; for its behavior shows that it is sensitive to the influence of their gravity. For it, earth *is* the influence because of which it forever revolves in a circle; sun *is* the influence because of which it forever traces an ellipse; moon *is* the influence to which it responds by a constant rise and fall. Sun, moon, and earth—not three bodies, different in place and position, but three gravities; dynamic states, different in direction and tension, each separately (and all together) extending through all space; present simultaneously, but not in the mode of juxtaposition: simultaneously in the same place, an interpenetration, a chord of gravity—simultaneous existence that is more like a triad than a triangle. For such a being, we see, "music of the spheres" would not be so fantastic after all. And motion, motion of the moon, for example, would not be manifested to it as a body changing place in the sky but as a change of state in the "without," a purely dynamic event, whose stage is all space. All this is not intended as a playing with ideas, but as an attempt to co-ordinate a reality with Faraday's speculations; to show that perhaps they are abstract speculation only in respect to particular modes of sensation, such as seeing and touching, but not in relation to sensation as such. In this case, there would be no logical basis for regarding the spatial mode of being of tones as exceptional rather than as one of the modes of being of reality. If atomic physics has recently reached the point of attributing an ambivalent mode of being to the most minute elements of the corporeal, of understanding them now as thing, now as state, according to circumstances—as particles situated in a place, or as waves spreading out in space—we cannot entirely escape the thought that the inmost core of the visible-tangible participates in the mode of being of the audible. At the basis of the materially real, we have—if the expression be permitted—come up against a grain of musical reality.

This is the occasion for a brief discussion of a phenomenon that will be familiar to every sensitive hearer of music: the different degree of the spatial impact in chords and in single tones. Compared with the individual tone, the chord seems to give us a greater sense of the presence of space, as if the chord occupied more space than the individual tone. In extreme cases, such as one of those chords of Bruckner's which builds itself up step by step into a gigantic complex, the impression of gradually increasing volume and spatial power is inescapable—as if a sound that at first took up little space should spread more and more until finally space was filled to capacity, filled to bursting, with tones. We know that it would be wrong to interpret the phenomenon in this manner; sounds do not occupy more or less space, and auditory space is not first empty, then filled. Auditory space is always "full," even when only one tone sounds. A chord does not occupy more space than a single tone; *every* tone occupies *all* available space; the whole of space is affected by the individual tone as by the chord. If, then, we are to maintain that more spatial impact is felt by the listener in one case and less in the other, it must be in a different sense. Perhaps it can be put in this way: in the single tone, space is already present as a whole but is, as it were, still *closed;* without a plurality of tones sounding simultaneously it does not reveal its order. But in the chord space *opens.* It opens in that, instead of the previous unbroken uniformity, it now exhibits diversity and structure; where previously *one* dynamic quality extended through all space, there is now a multiplicity of dynamic qualities, superimposed and interpenetrating. In this sense, then, in the sense of an interpenetration of dynamic qualities, of an enrichment of itself, we may say that space is "fuller" when a chord sounds than at the sounding of a single tone. There is greater abundance of space, one might almost say a greater weight of space, in the chord than in the single tone, just as the spatial abundance is greater in a pictorial composition involving many figures than in a portrait; although in both cases the space might be equally full, even in the portrait no particle of space might have been left empty. Incidentally, auditory space can even be overcrowded—as when two pieces of music are played simultaneously, or in the case of similar fortuitous combinations in which mutual relations between the tones are no longer audible. To be sure, even under such circumstances the tones still "interpenetrate," but no form becomes manifest and hence no spatial order. The chord becomes noise. The situation is much the same here as in visual space, where a fortuitous distribution of points on a surface, though presenting juxtaposition, does not for that reason afford an idea of spatial order.

SCALE

In our attempt to evoke a being whose experience of the outside world should correspond more or less with Faraday's speculations concerning the mode of existence of bodies, we also briefly touched upon the problem of what conception such a creature could have of the phenomenon that we call *motion*. It is evident that, for a consciousness which knew nothing of places and distinctions of places, the change of place which is an essential characteristic of our experience of motion could not exist. Take, for example, the process that we call "motion of the moon in the sky"—a being that had only "dynamic knowledge" of the world will experience it as change in the dynamic state of the "without" as a whole; it will apprehend motion of bodies not as change of place or position but as change of state.

It seems, then, that the same sort of bridge that was created between the mode of existence of bodies according to Faraday and the mode of existence of tones can be created between the motion of bodies and the motion of tones. The problem of tonal motion was discussed at length in a previous section, and the conclusion was reached that it is not differences in pitch which underlie our experience of tonal successions as motions, but differences in the dynamic qualities of the tones, differences in states. We quoted Bergson: "Real motion is rather the transfer of a state than of a thing." It further appeared that tonal motion does not take place in the space in which bodies occupy places and move from place to place. The question whether tonal motion—that is, music—must therefore be excluded from space as such and condemned to a spaceless existence could not yet be posed in that earlier context. We now know—tones have taught us—that a phenomenon which does not belong to the space of places, to visible space, to corporeal space, which is transcendent in respect to that space, can still be spatial in the full sense. What is true of the individual tone will also be true of the succession of tones: tonal motion, temporal succession of audibly spatial states, will no more be space-transcendent, a purely temporal phenomenon, than is the individual tone. We now ask what tonal motion can teach us concerning the structure and order of auditory space.

It appears that tonal motion contributes an insight into the order of musical space analogous to that which corporeal motion contributes in the case of the order of physical space. In both cases the contribution consists in the fact that spatial order is broken down into temporal succession; is, as it were, unrolled before us. In general, it is a gain for our awareness to be able to resolve a simultaneity into a succession, to pass from point to point, to scrutinize datum after datum. Our ability to grasp simultaneity, to hold in our consciousness different data at the same time, in one act, is decidedly limited. To imagine a tetrahedron, a cube, is not too difficult, but the image of even a regular body with twenty surfaces generally comes only step by step to anyone not trained in geometry; he has to let the figure build itself up piece by piece in his mind. (We cite this example to obviate misunderstanding—as if spatial order, observed in temporal succession, ceased to be spatial order.)

The elementary form of corporeal motion is motion in a straight line. The straight line is at the same time the basic ordering datum, the master key, for an understanding of geometrical space. The elementary form of tonal motion is motion along the scale. Can the scale, regarded as a path of motion, give us information concerning the order of musical space?

In order to view the problem from several sides, we shall report what three eminent thinkers—a physicist, a psychologist, and a biologist—have had to say about the scale as a phenomenon of order and its relation to space. Each of the three interpretations that we shall discuss betrays the interpreter's profession. The physicist maintains that there is complete agreement between the order of the scale and the order in corporeal space. For the psychologist, the scale is the model of nonspatial order. The biologist sees in the scale a type of order of spatial events, but one basically different from the accepted order of corporeal space. His view is closest to that of the musician.

Helmholtz writes: "What can occur at one point in space can also occur at every other point in space. The same is true of the realm of the scale. Every chord, every melody that can be performed at any pitch can likewise be performed at any other pitch. . . . Different voices performing either the same melody or different melodies can move simultaneously within the realm of the scale, exactly like bodies in space. . . . It follows from this that, in all essential respects, there is close conformity between the scale and space." [4] (For Helmholtz, naturally, space is equivalent to physico-geometrical space.)

How inaccurately even the greatest scientist sees, when, from the point of view of his own area of the universe, he looks at another area of the universe! Certainly, a major triad is always a major triad, no matter which tone is its root. Certainly, a melody always remains the same melody, whatever the tone from which it starts. Certainly, several tonal motions can follow their courses simultaneously. But here the parallel ends. The space in which a body moves remains unaffected by the event; the space in which a tone sounds is affected as a whole. In accordance with the order of corporeal space, with juxtaposition, simultaneous motions of bodies need not, so to speak, take notice of one another; in accordance with the order of auditory space, with interpenetration, simultaneous tones and tonal motions cannot avoid taking notice of one another. The consequences are peremptory. Two apples falling from a tree together remain two apples. Two simultaneously sounding triads are not two triads but a discord. The same melody starting simultaneously from two different tones does not result in two melodies but in a caricature of the melody. The restriction that the order of corporeal space puts upon the simultaneity of motions is that two bodies cannot be in the same place simultaneously. The analogous restriction for auditory space is that two tones cannot be in the same state at the same time—unless the interval between them is exactly an octave or the multiple of an octave. A triad is the coexistence of three tones in the states $\hat{1}$, $\hat{3}$, and $\hat{5}$; hence a triad made up of anything except the octave repetitions of these tones is impossible simul-

4. *On the Sensations of Tone.*

taneously with it. Beethoven's melody for the "Ode to Joy" in the last movement of the Ninth Symphony begins as motion from $\hat{3}$ through $\hat{4}$ to $\hat{5}$; as soon as a particular initial tone is chosen, the same melody cannot at the same time start from another tone (because different tones cannot simultaneously be $\hat{3}$, and if the state of the initial tone is not $\hat{3}$, it is not the same melody). Expressed affirmatively, a simultaneous progress of the same melody from different tones is possible only at octave intervals. With such a melody there always comes into force a particular scale; that is, the order that confers particular dynamic qualities on particular tones keeps simultaneously sounding tones separate in their dynamic states, and excludes a simultaneous existence of different tones in the same state. Simultaneous tonal motions must comply with these specific conditions if their coexistence is to represent order and not chaos. How this can be managed in practice is taught by the art of counterpoint. In any case, we see that there can be no question of a close correspondence between corporeal space and the order represented by the scale.

William James writes: "There may be a space without order, just as there may be an order without space." And he adds the footnote: "Musical tones, e.g., have an order of quality independent either of their space- or time-order." [5]

Here speaks the psychologist, the student of sensations, for whom tone, like color, taste, warmth, is above all a sense datum, a special content of consciousness. The sense datum "tone" exhibits a particular quality that we call pitch and that each tone possesses in a definite, an audibly definite, degree. Hence it is possible to compare tones in respect to pitch—in accordance with whether they possess "more" or "less" of this quality—

5. "The Perception of Space."

and to order them in a series. This order, taken by itself, has as little to do with spatiality as an order of taste sensations in accordance with their degree of saltiness, or the order of the sensations of the hot-cold series. James does not think of denying the spatiality of tone sensation as such; maintains that *every* sensation possesses a characteristic of extension, and that this direct perception of extension is our most original space experience. But this characteristic of extension, through which, he asserts, tones participate in space, and the characteristic of pitch, which makes it possible to order them in a series, have no direct connection; his doctrine of the spatiality of tone sensation and of the nonspatiality of tonal order contains no contradiction.

So far everything seems all right. But James does not say "*Tones* have an order of quality . . ."; he says "*Musical tones* . . ."; and now everything has gone wrong. In so far as tones are considered and ordered in accordance with their pitch quality, they are not yet musical tones; in so far as they are musical tones, their order is not qualitative but dynamic, or better, an order according to dynamic, not acoustical, qualities. What makes the tone an element of musical order is not its pitch but its audible relation to other tones; differences in direction and tension, not differences in pitch, are the constituents of the musical order of tones. And this characteristic of tone sensation, its dynamism, is, unlike pitch, closely connected with the spatial component of tone sensation; we have observed in the triad how the dynamic, the musical order of tones, and not the acoustical order by pitch, leads to recognition of the order of auditory space. When James writes that the order of musical tones is independent of their spatial order, he is, to be sure, still right in his way—because, under spatial order, he includes only the order of visible space, locality, localization. The real problem—whether the order of musical tones makes it necessary to assume an order peculiar to auditory space—remains concealed in the inconsistent formulation.

The difference between the two possible tonal orders, the acoustical and the dynamic, can perhaps be made clearer as follows. Arranged in order of pitch, the tones of our music exhibit the familiar schema of the diatonic scale: alternate groups of two and three whole tones separated by half tones; every seven successive steps make up an octave. But this of course is by no means the only possible arrangement of tones by pitch. Our music has other such series: the chromatic scale, which divides the octave into twelve half tones; the whole-tone scale, with its six whole tones in the octave. Many other arrangements of this same tonal material can easily be conceived—for example, a regular succession of alternate whole tones and half tones (which would give an eight-tone scale), or of two half tones followed by a whole tone. It is possible to construct scales that no longer have anything in common with the tonal material of our music—by dividing the octave into nine or fifteen equal parts, for example, or arranging the tones at equal intervals measuring nine-sixteenth of a whole tone (which would do away with the octave), and so on. All these tonal series have one thing in common: each, like all the others, represents a qualitative acoustical order, an order of tones by pitch. (Were we to discriminate, we should have to say that the diatonic scale came off worst because of its lack of regularity.) William James could have chosen any possible scale for his example; that he chose our scale is immaterial to his considerations. His conclusion—the nonspatiality of the order upon which the scale is based—would have been the same in any case. But what does this signify if not that, in his considerations, he referred precisely to the quality in which all these scales do *not* differ from one another, or at least differ only in degree, not in kind? But we know that the diatonic scale *is* different in kind from all other tonal series: it, and it alone, is heard as *motion;* and only in so far as we hear it thus, as motion, are we justified in calling its order the order of the tones *of our music.* Regarded as a series of tones of different pitches (as James regards it), its order is certainly nonspatial, but also nonmusical; regarded musically, it is motion—a motion that, to be sure, shows no trace of the space of bodies and its order, juxtaposition of places—but this is still far from saying that it is independent of all space, is nonspatial.

Let us again consider the elementary phenomenon, the succession of two tones. In general, if two adjacent tones of an ordered series of pitches sound one after the other, the event is adequately described as a temporal succession of two qualitatively different tone sensations. Every tone, to be sure, has a spatial component, extension, but it is certainly not in accordance with this component that the two tones are distinguished in this case. But if two adjacent tones of the diatonic scale succeed each other—for example, $\hat{1}$-$\hat{2}$—something entirely different takes place. We hear not two tones differing in *pitch* but two tones differing in *direction,* two tones in different dynamic states. *This* event could no longer be adequately described as pure temporal-qualitative succession; in addition, it has yet another, clearly audible meaning: the meaning "away from," the signification of a *step.* And the characteristic that allows us to hear this tonal succession as a step is not separable from the spatiality of the tones; tonal dynamic qualities are audibly spatial states. From the point of view of the space of places, the tonal step, which does not lead from one place to another place, may pass as a purely temporal event. From the point of view of the space that we hear, the step from one audibly spatial state to another audibly spatial state is eminently an event in space-time.

Regarded as a succession of steps, not as a succession of tones, the scale offers the picture of an order that yields to none in precision and intelligibility. Arranged along the scale, the various states of tension and direction trace a course that presents in the most elementary, concise, and exhaustive way the basic schema of all tonal motions: "away-from-and-back-to." This is the course that tones follow when, so to speak, they can do as they will, are subjected to no deflection—as, in like case, a body in motion traces the course of the straight line. The order that becomes apparent in such a motion and that we read from its course (the straight line, the scale) is simply the order of the stage on which the motion proceeds—of the space of bodies in the one case, of tonal space in the other. In a previous context we made use of the scale in order to read from it the structure of the dynamic field of tones. We are only following the procedure of the physicists if we do not here make a sharp distinction between dynamic field and space. The scale demands our recognition, not as the classic example of nonspatial order that William James saw in it, but as valid testimony to the order obtaining in the space of tones.

(The prominent position that we have given to the diatonic scale in these considerations must not be understood as if tonal motion, as if music, were possible only in the diatonic realm. Our music discovered the kinetic meaning of the diatonic scale, and, through centuries of development, has revealed it and taught us to understand it in its utmost ramifications; hence all the experiences of tonal motion common to our civilization spring from the soil of diatonicism. Other civilizations may have similar experiences with other series of tones. Recently, our music too has undertaken resolute expeditions in search of a kinetic meaning in tonal series beyond the diatonic. So far it is still finding difficulty in coming to any agreement with audiences as to the success of its discoveries.)

Jakob von Uexküll begins his book with a chapter on the spatial experience of animate creatures. On the first page we read: "The scale is a model of planned arrangement, although . . . the qualities perceived by hearing are without spatial discrimination."[6]

This sounds like William James—order without space—especially since the preceding paragraph asserts that auditory space has no order. "What do these three pure sensations [hearing, smelling, tasting] tell us about space? . . . Extremely little. We learn from them neither that space has three directions nor that only one straight line can be drawn between two points. For the qualities perceived by these three senses are only referred without, but not localized. In this primitive 'located-outside-us' there are no places, no directions, and no forms. If we still wish to call this 'located-outside-us' space, we must not forget that we are here dealing with an entirely different space from that of which we commonly speak." These are almost the same words that Révész used to refute auditory space; only here the possibility of "an entirely different space" is at least left open. But the premise upon which the ideas are based is the same in both cases: order by places, localization, geometrical order, *is* spatial order; space without places is space without an order.

But as Uexküll proceeds, his negative characterization of the tonal order as nonspatial receives a remarkable turn toward the positive. He first points out that tones submit to the order of the scale by virtue of the characteristic that "immediately and indubitably establishes the relation of a tone to all other tones"; or, as we should put it, by virtue of the dynamic qualities of tone.

6. *Theoretische Biologie.*

If Uexküll judges this order of tones to be nonspatial, the implication is not that it *lacks* something without which it cannot be recognized as spatial order, but that it *possesses* something which is irreconcilable with space defined as the totality of all places. Uexküll terms this something "plan" (*Planmässigkeit*)—a type of order for which there is no precedent in the space of places, but which is of decisive significance for the understanding of biological processes. Because the tonal order represents this type of order in particularly pure form, it can function as a normative example in biological thinking.

Uexküll defines biology as "the science of the plan factor in all living things. . . . Chemistry and physics do not know plan as a natural factor. Biology consists in erecting a scaffolding of propositions that recognize plan as the basis of life. . . . Physics asserts that the natural objects of our environment obey only causality. In opposition to this, biology asserts that, in addition to causality, there is also a second subjective [7] rule, by which we order objects—the principle of plan, which is a necessary complement to our concept of the universe." Biological phenomena—the term refers to the organism as such and to the mutual relations between organism and environment—remain incomprehensible so long as we do not recognize, in addition to causality, a second, an *immaterial natural factor* in operation—plan. This new natural factor is neither physical nor psychic, but a "third factor"; biology takes its place beside physiology and psychology as "the science of the third factor, the science of plan. . . . The great advantage of biological natural research lies in the fact that in this way we learn to operate with immaterial natural factors as an independent category—without ascribing to them psychic

7. "Subjective" is here to be taken in the Kantian sense: subjective as time, space, and causality are subjective.

qualities that have nothing to do with their essential nature. . . ."

These quotations should make it clearer how music can come to serve as the pattern for biology, tonal order become the prototype of biological order. The points of correspondence are not hard to find: like biological processes, musical processes run their course in neither the physical nor the psychic world, but on the "third stage"; the factor that turns acoustical into musical phenomena, the dynamic quality of tone, is something nonbodily that comes from without, an immaterial natural factor; and in music as in biology we are dealing with phenomena whose order cannot be understood in terms of the operation of causality.

The correspondence goes deeper still. Causal chains connect events that occur at definite times at definite places. In order that an event may be understood causally it must be possible to trace it continuously in time and space, that is, at least in principle, to assign to it a definite place at any moment. Where this is impossible, causality cannot apply. Certain biological processes seem to be of this kind. The famous experiments that showed that an egg cut in two may produce two whole organisms of about half the normal size did away with the assumption that the structure of the organism was in some cryptic way prefigured in the egg: there is no traceable correspondence between the individual parts of the organism and the individual parts of the egg, however small. The causal chains that lead to the parts of the developed organism are not fastened each to its definite place in the egg. The spatial order according to places breaks down here, to be replaced not by disorder but by another order that transcends that of places. Similar thoughts might be provoked by the miraculous feats of localization instinctively performed by many birds and insects—as, for example, when the Sphex wasp, attacking a Cetonia larva, finds with its sting the precise point of the larva's ganglia that will paralyze it but not kill it. Seen in the framework of the traditional spatial order—order of places—this defies understanding. But presumably, in performing this act, the wasp no more finds a place than we, in singing a tone in a melody, find a frequency.

With great discrimination, Uexküll has recognized the unique value that must be conceded to music in this connection. Music provides the biologist with a *model*—a sensible demonstration of a place-transcending spatial order that suggests a possible way of understanding biological phenomena. That Uexküll did not pursue the path to the end, that, following tradition, he equated place transcendence with nonspatiality, is not too important. What counts is that he saw in the tonal order not the absence or the dilution or the primitive form of the order of physical space, but recognized it as a basically different type of order that might serve as a model for events in physical space. Once, indeed, he comes very close to seeing the spatiality of the tonal order; it is in connection with rhythm and, significantly enough, in a passage where he is constructing the space experience of a being that cannot distinguish places but only directions. We can conceive of such a space ". . . through music. When music takes such hold of us that we forget the origin of the tones that proceed from this or that instrument and give ourselves to the rhythm, subjective feelings of direction awaken in us, even without sympathetic motions by our bodies, and, together with the tones, seem to fill the space that belongs to them" (The "subjectivity" is again Kant's.)

Faraday's considerations bridged the gap between the mode of being of bodies and of tones; Uexküll's bridge the gap between the mode of being of tones and of living organisms. The common ground that makes these correspondences possible is the place-transcending space that we experience in tones and whose order becomes manifest in the tonal order of music.

OCTAVE

A peculiarity of motion along the scale must be more closely examined: the reversal of direction owing to the phenomenon of the octave. It draws attention to what is perhaps the most remarkable aspect of the order of auditory space.

Let us first recall the facts in the case, as we set them forth in a previous section. Motion along the scale, beginning with $\hat{1}$, first takes place contrary to the direction of the active force, has the kinetic meaning "away from . . ."; $\hat{5}$ is the turning point, at which the kinetic meaning is reversed; from here on the motion is in the same direction as the active force, has the meaning "toward . . ." The last step especially is clearly audible as arrival, as reaching the goal; and the goal reached is nothing but the point of departure itself—more precisely, the octave of the starting tone: the motion has returned to its beginning.

In this description a tone is equated with its octave. With what justification? The physical cause of the two phenomena is certainly not the same: the frequency of the one tone is twice that of the other. And this physical difference is matched by a difference in the psychic datum: the two tones are indubitably different in pitch. If we increase the interval, if we compare tones that are not one but four octaves apart, and , the assertion of equality seems almost absurd. Or let us ask a tenor if and are the same. How could he answer yes, when leaves him unruffled, whereas causes him anguish and sleepless nights; when an unexceptionable impresses no one, whereas an unexceptionable brings him fame and fortune? Yet ordinary musical parlance has but one and the same name for all these different tones, and and ; it is the tone *c* each time. And the usual way of distinguishing the different octaves of the same tone—*c, c', c''*—itself indicates that the characteristic according to which we refer to these tones as the same is the essential one, whereas that by which they differ is secondary.

What, then, is the same in the different octave repetitions of a tone?

Above all, it is the element that makes the tone a musical phenomenon, its dynamic quality. If is $\hat{1}$, then or is likewise $\hat{1}$. Whatever dynamic quality a tone has, it will, so long as the dynamic field itself does not change, have the same dynamic quality in all its octave repetitions. In other words, the constellation of force that determines the dynamic quality of a tone in a given field is exactly the same, no matter in which octave the tone sounds. The difference of octave simply is not among the data of the field that determine dynamic quality. Since it is the dynamic field that makes tones music, we must say that, in the strictest sense, the difference of octave does not exist for music; in a less strict sense, that it is a secondary element.

Music is motion of tones. Tonal motion exists because a field of tonal forces exists. As the course of the motion of bodies proceeds from place to place, the course of tonal motion proceeds from dynamic quality to dynamic quality. When, during a tonal motion, a dynamic quality is reached in which the quality of the starting tone is repeated, the course, *in so far as it is motion, has* returned to its starting point. In this sense the point of departure and the point of arrival of the scale, $\hat{1}$ and $\hat{8}$, are the same. In so far as the scale is motion, it returns upon itself; in so far as it does not return upon itself, it is not motion. The fact that I leave my house by daylight and return to it at night can in no way affect the fact of my return.

The "miracle of the octave," which we discussed earlier, lies not so much in the sameness of different things; it lies, rather, in the way in which this sameness reveals itself in the course of a motion. If we move along the scale, frequency—and with it, pitch—simply increases (or decreases) from tone to tone; yet with the eighth tone we are at the starting point again. Return as the inevitable result of a constant going away, of a constantly increasing interval—this is a phenomenon which, in the context of nature, stands alone. We mentioned circular motion, which always returns upon itself, as a similar phenomenon in the bodily-spatial realm. But circular motion is only a single, exceptional possibility of the motion of bodies in space. Tonal motion, on the contrary, cannot avoid returning upon itself; return is its necessity, its law. An explanation of the "miracle" has been sought by referring to frequencies and their relations: to the series 1:2:4:8, etc., which corresponds to the series of octaves of a tone. To be sure, this presupposes not only that we *hear* frequencies and their relations but also that our ear has a particular sympathy for the frequency relation 2 (on the basis of which, for example, it would hail 440 as twice 220, and in its delight over the beautiful frequency relation would respond to the two influences with two almost identical tone sensations)—a presupposition that would be hardly less miraculous than the phenomenon it is meant to explain. For elsewhere, after all, it is true of the ear, as it is of the other senses, that different stimuli produce different sensations and that the greater the difference between the stimuli, the greater the difference between the sensations. However this may be, the really puzzling part of the phenomenon, the emergence of the octave from the course of motion, would remain entirely unaffected by any such explanations. The departure from the starting point that is at the same time an approach to the starting point, the light that, as it were falls, from the octave ahead upon the tones that are striving toward it—an understanding of these phenomena certainly cannot be brought any nearer by reference to the relation in frequency between a tone and its octaves.

We shall now consider the following assertion: the reversal in tonal motion is to be understood from the point of view of the *spatiality* of tones. If motion along the scale follows the pattern we have described, then it is an expression of the laws of the space in which it occurs. The octave must have its basis in the order of auditory space.

Let us try, in so far as possible, to approach the phenomenon through parallels. We first seek out situations in which, in general, inequality is experienced as equality, and *validly* so—that is, after the exclusion of the so-called subjective sources of error: the imperfection of the sense organ, its limited power of distinction. A schematic picture suggests itself:

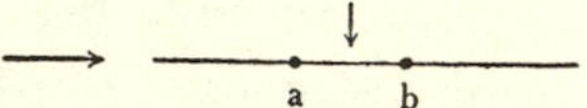

A straight line; upon it are two points, *a* and *b*. From the point of view of the arrow to the left, which, so to speak, looks into the straight line, for which the line contracts to a point, *a* and *b* are the same; from the point of view of the arrow above, which looks *at* the line, they are different. Suppose that *a* and *b* are points of light in darkness, then the arrow to the left sees one light, the arrow above sees two. If they are illuminated in succession, for the arrow to the left they are events in the same place; for the arrow above they are events in different places. If point *a* moves out of the straight line and returns to it at *b*,

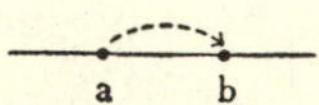

from the point of view of the arrow to the left it has returned to its starting point.

If we replace the straight line by a wave line,

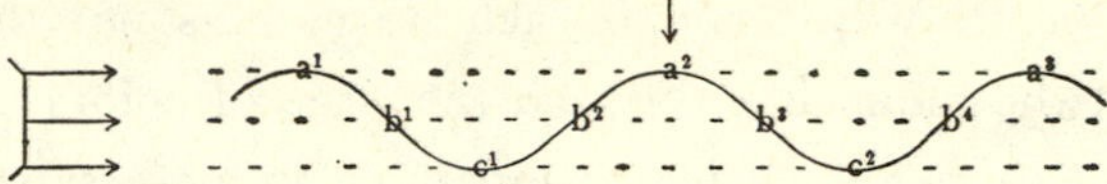

then, for the observer represented by the group of arrows to the left, all the points *a* are one point, as are all the points *b* and the points *c;* he sees the wave line as a short vertical line; motion of a point of light along the wave line is, for him, *a* repeated up and down along this vertical line, ⇃|↾. The observer above, however, will see the wave line as a horizontal straight line and the motion of the point of light as continuous progress along this line, ——→. (The wave line exists only for the reader, who looks at the page from the side.) Suppose that the point increases to a sphere and that, during its motion from wave crest to wave crest, this sphere of light goes through the phases of the moon (it need not be total obscuration; it may be only a slight dimming):

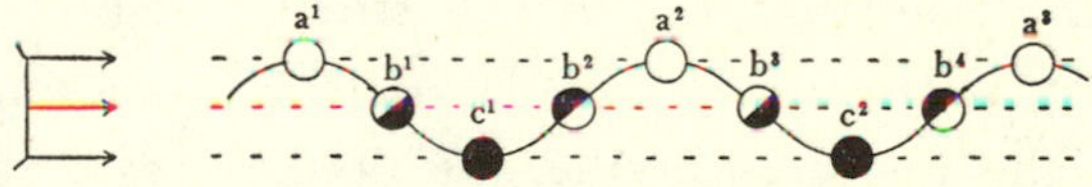

Then, although, for the observer on the left, all *a*'s and all *c*'s are the same, the *b*'s fall into two groups: all the odd-numbered *b*'s, phenomena of the descending phase of the wave, are different from all the even-numbered *b*'s, the phenomena of the ascending phase. Now we can accept the experience of this observer as a parallel to musical hearing of the scale: "away-from-and-back-to." That the intensity of illumination of the phenomenon decreases regularly with increasing distance from the observer could be interpreted as analogous to the regular change in pitch from octave to octave.

To extend the analogy to the observer above, we must change

the condition last introduced. For him, we shall have the sphere of light, on its way through each wave, pass not through the phases of the moon but through the scale of colors of the rainbow: his experience is then comparable to mere acoustical, unmusical hearing of the scale, which, on the one hand, registers only change in pitch, not dynamic qualities—motion forward in a straight line—and, on the other hand, notes the similarity of the octave repetitions of each tone—sameness of the colors at corresponding points on the wave live. This is the auditory experience of the tune-deaf person.

Or I see in the dark, at some distance, an illuminated cross; it grows dim, then bright again; this is repeated several times at regular intervals. I say: "The same event at different times in the same place." Now I start to move toward the occurrence and I find the cross and the apparatus for illuminating it. I go on in the same direction and, at some distance from the first, I find a second and larger cross, with a stronger illuminating apparatus, then a third, still larger with still stronger lights, and so on. Now I say: "Different events at different times in different places." The increases in the size of the crosses and in the strength of the lights were so calculated that, in the case of my first observation, they neutralized the difference in distance.

The problems posed in these examples are all of the same kind: they are problems of *perspective.* And perspective is a department of *geometry:* problems of perspective find their proper solutions under the laws of the spatial order—here of visual space or, more precisely, of the co-ordination between light and space. Because the path of the light ray is a straight line, because the order of the diffusion of light coincides with the order of space, problems of perspective are to be regarded as geometrical problems. So one answer to our original question—under what conditions is inequality validly experienced as equality?—could be: "Under certain *spatial* conditions." [8]

It seems risky to try to transfer these considerations from visual space to auditory space. To judge by the problems so far given, the principal elements in problems of perspective are position, magnitude, distance; and in the space of tones nothing of the sort exists.

But it is possible to think of situations in which phenomena of perspective—e.g., different things seen as the same—are not necessarily bound to particular conditions regarding position, magnitude, and distance, but occur under all conditions, regardless of position, magnitude, and distance—where, then, it is impossible to *escape* the perspective. Such a situation is presented to us by the well-known sphere of the mathematician Henri Poincaré,[9] which we are to conceive as follows: at the center of the sphere it is comfortably warm; proceeding outward, the temperature constantly decreases until, at the surface, the bitter cold of absolute zero is reached. Creatures condemned and fitted to live and move within this sphere would be subject to strange "errors" concerning themselves and their surroundings. Since, by the laws of nature, all bodies contract with decreasing temperature and, as they approach absolute zero, must also approach zero in extension, the bodies of these creatures too would necessarily become steadily smaller when they approached the surface of the sphere and expand when they moved toward its center. But since not only themselves but *all* bodies would change

8. A time perspective, in the strict sense, does not exist; temporal unequals—e.g., different phases of the metric wave, different measures of the chain of measures—can under no conditions be validly heard as equal. A problem in perspective must have at least two dimensions; time has only one. What we are tempted to call time perspective concerns the *measurement* of time, hence spatialized time.

9. Cf. his *Science and Hypothesis*.

with them in the same way, they would not have the least inkling of these variations in the size of their bodies. Just like ourselves, they would assert—and justifiably—that they and the bodies around them remained the same size; that a body does not change its size when it changes its place. Let us suppose that one of these creatures resolved to reach the surface of the sphere. It would be a hopeless attempt; for, during the course of its expedition, its legs, its strides, would become shorter and shorter, and finally infinitely short; it would have to take an infinite number of steps to reach its goal—in other words, it could never reach it. But the creature would again have no suspicion of the malicious concatenation that thus makes its project vain while it attempts to accomplish it; for the measure by which it would measure its steps contracts just as its body does—hence its steps are always "the same length." Nor would it be disillusioned by its experience; instead, it would find a formulation for it, which, by the way, has a familiar ring to us: "I live in a space whose limits I can never reach; I live in an infinite space." Because of the peculiar physical conditions in such a sphere, these creatures would, furthermore, make all sorts of observations concerning spatial relations that would appear preposterous to an observer looking into the sphere "from outside." They would call lines "straight" that the "outside" observer knows to be bent; they would assert that several equally long straight lines can be drawn between two points, that a straight line can return upon itself, and so on. In short, these creatures would have a different geometry from ours, a non-Euclidean geometry. In the last analysis, then, the problems of perspective in this world of heat and cold would again confront us with a geometrical problem, a spatial problem. The paradoxes in the statements of the "inside" and "outside" observers become reconciled upon the assumption of a space structure deviating from that of our daily experience.

We find yet another type of perspective in the "hall of mirrors." Here visual space and auditory space approach as nearly as possible. As in auditory space every tone is repeated from octave to octave, here every object is repeated from mirror image to mirror image. As, for the center of the dynamic field of tones, presence at one point in auditory space always means presence in so and so many octave repetitions as well, so in the hall of mirrors no object can be present only once; every appearance of an object at one point is an appearance of it at many places in the mirror images. As the entire dynamic field is repeated from octave to octave, so the whole space of the hall of mirrors is repeated from one reflection to the other. And as in auditory space going away from a tone is always also going toward the same tone in its octave, in the hall of mirrors too there is no going away from a place that is not at the same time a going toward the same place in its mirror image.

In view of all this, may we call the octave a problem of *perspective,* of auditory perspective? Is it justifiable to say that the phenomenon of the octave has its basis in the order of auditory space; that it is the structure of auditory space which prescribes its course (its "away-from-and-back-to") to the scale—that the law of the reversal of all movement is imposed upon tones by the organization of auditory space? May we call auditory space a *rhythmically* organized space?

We shall content ourselves with having asked these questions. What we sought here was not to solve the problems of auditory space and its order but above all to point out that *there are such problems.* For to the extent to which we become aware of these problems, we have become aware of another mode of existence of spatiality, which is neither co-ordinate with nor subordinate to our familiar spatiality of light and color, of lines, places, and physical objects, but which stands beside it as a realm of order in its own right. To this other spatiality, the eye and the hand, and the thought that they direct, have no direct access. We penetrate it through the medium of tones. Certain schematic tone patterns, the triad, the scale, can serve us as probes with which the organization of this space may be explored from within.

ENSEMBLE

It is not the simultaneity of tones in the chord, nor the motion of tones in the scale, which gives us the most complete and convincing evidence of order in auditory space; it is the simultaneity of motions in polyphony. Without this clear and beautiful demonstration of audible order, it might never have occurred to anyone that this order deserved some consideration.

In comparison with the spatial order revealed by the chord and the individual tonal motion, polyphony, to be sure, does not represent anything new in kind; but it does represent an immense difference in degree. Polyphony stands to monophony as the chord to the single tone; in the successive entrances of the voices in a fugue, for example, we experience an increase in spatial impact similar to that which we experience in the piecemeal building up of a chord from individual tones. And the space experience inherent in the polyphonic work stands to that of the chord as motion stands to the rest that precedes motion; in the chord, in which a datum that does not change is related to another equally unchanging datum, spatial order is, so to speak, only a prophecy, a promise; it unfolds when, in the polyphonic work, melodic motion is related to melodic motion, chain of events to chain of events.

We shall not go into the general problems of the mutual relations between simultaneous tonal motions. We shall only discuss one type of polyphonic music—a type that, with almost epigrammatic pointedness, exemplifies how, when tones sound, we enter a different order in the "whence of encounter and the where of relation." The type in question is the operatic ensemble, one of the most remarkable examples of musical form, and indeed of form in the arts in general.

Let us take a concrete instance, the quartet in Act II of Verdi's *Otello*. The situation is as follows: Othello, in a fit of rage, which he suppresses with difficulty, has torn up the handkerchief that Desdemona wished to bind around his head. The two are left profoundly shaken by this first intimation of the "return of chaos." Desdemona asks what wrong she has unwittingly done; Othello tries to trace Desdemona's infidelity to some cause in himself: is it his age, his black skin? The handkerchief has been dropped, Emilia has picked it up. Iago approaches her, takes it from her for his evil purpose, she makes only a feeble resistance. What in Shakespeare occurs at different times—the scene between Desdemona and Othello, the conversation between Emilia and Iago—Verdi has brought together; he makes it occur at one time. For the four voices are to sound *simultaneously;* the four melodic lines are to be woven together into *one* texture. It is not enough that the individual lines should develop, each obeying its own urgency, as the tonal symbol of the character to whom it belongs and whose most secret thoughts and feelings it reveals; the *combination* of the lines, the tonal entity that proceeds from their union, is to make audible what is happening both *between* these people and *to* them, what is about them and above them. The fluctuations in tension, the doom that is approaching from all directions, from within and without, the snares that are slowly closing, the single fate twisted from four life threads—it is this which has been transformed into the complexities of this perfect musical whole, and which we experience when we hear it.

Such a thing is only possible in opera—the drama in which

the actor does not speak but sings. No wonder that Verdi, who in general tries to follow Shakespeare as closely as possible, could find no precedent in Shakespeare for this piece. A quartet is impossible in the spoken drama, for the simple reason that no one can follow four persons speaking at once, four separate trains of thought proceeding simultaneously, and understand them. We can, of course, visually separate the figures of the four characters who stand together on the stage before us, but we cannot separate their speeches. Taken by itself, each speech may make sense; but heard together four pieces of good sense make one piece of nonsense, four orders become one disorder. And we understand why this is so. The figures belong to visual space, they are in different places, the order of visual space keeps them separate. But the speeches do not belong to visual space, are not, like bodies, kept separate by differences of place; as spoken words, they are of the audibly spatial but, not yet being tone, they do not yet share in the specific order of auditory space; as meaning—thoughts, feelings, or whatever the words express—they are completely nonspatial. Lacking an order that would keep them separate, they cannot but run together, like colors in the same place. But the four characters begin *singing* instead of speaking; and the picture changes instantly. What had run together now separates, disorder gives place to order, nonsense to sense, the meaning of each individual tonal speech appears clearly, and from the simultaneous voicing of four meanings arises, not the destruction of meaning, but a supermeaning, the meaning of a whole. How else may this change be interpreted if not from the point of view that, with the sounding of the tones, a different order in the "whence of encounter and the where of relation" opens, and now does for tones and tonal motions what the order of places does for bodies in visual space: it keeps separate things apart and relates them to one another, and thus makes it possible for ordered creations of a higher kind to originate. Without an order of auditory space, an order fully developed and strictly established, a tonal configuration of the complexity of a dramatic ensemble would be as impossible as a complex piece of architecture without an order of visual space.

Yet another observation can make this passing from one order of space to another perceptible to us. Let us have the quartet from *Otello* played to us from a phonograph record. The chains of physical events that at every instant give rise to the auditory experience all go back to the same point of origin, the point of the phonograph needle. The motions of the point of the needle are translated, through a number of technical intermediate steps, into vibrations of a membrane and thus into air vibrations. Like every material point, the point of the needle can make only one movement at one time. In the same way, each individual section of the membrane, and the membrane as a whole, can only be in vibration in one way at one time, and, consequently, only one air wave can, at any instant, have propagated itself in space. The illuminated disk of the oscilloscope shows only one line, no matter how many tones are sung into the microphone simultaneously; a second tone added to one already sounding does not appear as a second, differently shaped line but as a change in the shape of the first. Thus, regarded as physical phenomena, in the frame of the space of bodies, simultaneously sounding tones and their lines suffer the same fate that the order of this space decrees for simultaneous data not locally separated: they coalesce into one. But as soon as the physical event becomes a musical event, what has been thus drawn together separates again: what the apparatus registers as *one* wave, we *hear* as *multiplicity* of tones—and as an organized multiplicity, between whose elements complex relations play back and forth. One need only look once at the photogram of such a piece of music and realize that, in our hearing, this single visible line becomes a combination of lines exhibiting vertical and horizontal relations of the highest complexity—one will be unable to escape a feeling of astonishment. To be sure, mathematical analysis of the shape of the line permits us to deduce the individual waves that are combined in it. Yet the consideration that our ear accomplishes, effortlessly, continuously, and instantaneously, what costs the skilled mathematician a considerable expenditure of time and energy, will hardly decrease our astonishment—quite apart from the fact that mathematical analysis will tell us only what individual tones sound together and follow one another, but not how these tones are related to each other chordally and melodically. Nor does the attempt to call in the function of the organ of Corti as an explanation bring us much nearer to understanding the process. To be sure, the hairs of the organ of Corti may separate into their individual components the waves intercepted by the eardrum and spreading inside the ear. But where may we find the organ whose function it would be to bring together these separated components and again relate them to one another—the organ of musical experience? If we found the place where, on the way from ear to brain or in the brain itself, this occurs—where a whole arises from parts—the physiological process to which we wished to attribute the sensation of wholeness could again be only one; what had been separated would but have coalesced into one again. To say nothing of the difficult problem why the juxtaposition of retinal cells in the eye gives a juxtaposition of colored localities, but the juxtaposition of the hairs of the organ of Corti does not give a juxtaposition of sounding localities but an interpenetration of sounding states—which would bring us back to our first question: Why do three tones make a triad and not a triangle? No, we shall not understand musical phenomena if we approach them from the side of physical event and its order—but not because musical phenomena are subjective as opposed to objective, psychic as opposed to physical, spiritual as opposed to material. It is not because what is "wave" without is "tone" within, because the physical phenomenon is "reality," the musical phenomenon "mere appearance"—it is not for any such reason that the two views are irreconcilable, but because tone and wave, both equally real, and both equally coming from without, reach us from two different modes of being of the without; because tone and tonal events belong to another *order* of "being without" than that from which bodies and corporeal events, including ear, nerve, and brain, encounter us.

XVIII. Space as Place and Space as Force

IF WE LOOK BACK over the course that our investigation has followed in this section, we shall not be able to avoid the impression of inadequacy and incompleteness—especially in respect to the question of the order of auditory space. Yet it will not be denied that a certain amount of ground has been gained and consolidated.

1. The nonspatiality of music has been dismissed. Music as purely temporal art, a music that, as Schopenhauer has it, "is perceived in and through time, to the total exclusion of space," does not exist. The musical experience has a spatial component; he who hears music is aware of space.

2. The space experience of the ear in tones and the normal space experience of the eye coincide only in the most general sense: both fulfill the definition of space as the "whence of encounter." But whereas space is given to the eye as that which *is* without, as that which confronts it, where I am not, where things are, and are in places, as multiplicity, as aggregate of places, in which we distinguish somewhere from elsewhere, measure intervals, draw boundaries, divide and put together, the ear knows space only as that which *comes from* without, as that which is directed toward me, streams toward me and into me, as that which is given in no other way than as a boundless indivisible oneness, in which nothing can be divided and nothing measured—as placeless flowing space.

3. The placeless flowing space of our hearing does not represent a primitive stage of our space experience, as might perhaps be concluded from the negative qualification that in it no boundaries can be drawn and no parts distinguished; it is not the as yet unordered space, to create order in which would be the task of the eye and the hand and of the thought they direct. As visual space has its order, which gives the eye the visual arts and thought the art of measurement (geometry), auditory space has its order, which gives the ear the art of music. Without an order of visual space, there would be no architecture and no physics; but, equally, without an order of auditory space there would be no music. *Order of visual space,* visible-tangible order: order by places, order of "juxtaposition"; relations between positions and magnitudes, quantitative relations; order that governs the course of the motion of bodies from place to place. *Order of auditory space,* audibly spatial order: order by states, order of interpenetration; purely dynamic relations of direction and tension; order that underlies the motion of tones from state to state. Visual space and auditory space: not two different stages but two different types of order in spatiality, two equally ranking, equally justified, equally "right" modes of being of spatiality.

4. Since the eye is man's chief organ of orientation in his biological milieu; since the space experience of the eye (and the hand) becomes knowledge in geometry; since the space concept of geometry has served the science of the motion of bodies, physics, as scaffolding; since physics largely determines modern man's picture of the universe—it is not at all surprising that, in matters of space, we have gone to school to these two sciences; have let geometry and physics tell us *what space is.* Now visual space and geometrical space, to be sure, are not the same: no eye has ever seen a point, a straight line, two parallel lines. But visual space and geometrical space have the same type of order, so that

visual space can be understood from geometrical space; can be integrated into it as a special case. The same is also true of the space in which our ear localizes noises. It is *not* true of the space which encounters us in tones, the space of musical experience. The ordering principle of this space is diametrically opposed to that of geometrical space; musical space cannot be integrated into geometrical space. The dogmatic mind that, consciously or unconsciously, clings to the premise that the geometrico-physical space concept is the concept of space as such is consequently unable to admit that music participates in space; it must deny the spatiality of music. For the undogmatic observer, on the other hand, insight into the spatiality of music must destroy the validity of the dogmatist's premise: space and geometrico-physical space do *not* coincide. There are experiences of space that we owe to neither the eye nor the hand; a knowledge of space that is not geometrical knowledge is possible. The limits of the space of things and places are not the limits of space as such. The end of the space in which bodies are in places and move from place to place is not yet the beginning of the nonspatial, the psychic, the spiritual, the supernatural—whatever one chooses to call it. Beyond the space of bodies, there is still space—space that is not therefore any less real, less natural, less "of this world," because in it there is nothing to see, nothing to touch, nothing to measure. It is possible to conceive of spatial events—spatial in the full sense—that leave no trace in the space of things and places. Music is the classic example of such events.

Bergson's *Matière et mémoire* contains the following sentence: "On pourrait . . . dans une certaine mesure, se dégager de l'espace sans sortir de l'étendue." Literally translated: "One could . . . in a certain measure, disengage oneself from space without leaving extension." Since Bergson accepted the traditional space concept without criticism (as he did not the traditional time concept), "space" here means "geometrico-physical space." The word "extension," then, presumably stands for a mode of being of spatiality that the traditional space concept does not include. ("Extension," he writes elsewhere, "is not in it [space]; it is the latter that we put in the former.") Translated into our terminology, Bergson's statement would, then, read: "One could, in a certain measure, disengage oneself from geometrico-physical space, from the space of places and bodies, without leaving space as such." This is precisely what happens to us when we hear music—and not "in a certain measure," but in unqualified reality. Far from taking us out of space—as common opinion holds—music discloses to us a mode of being of spatiality that, except through music, is accessible only with difficulty and indirectly. It is the space which, instead of consolidating the boundaries between within and without, obliterates them; space which does not stand over against me but with which I can be one; which permits encounter to be experienced as communication, not as distance; which I must apprehend not as universal place but as universal force.

Thus musical experience demands that our thinking about space be as radically revised as our thinking about time, and we find ourselves confronted by a question similar to that which confronted us in the case of time. Are the two modes of existence of space to which the geometrico-physical and the musical concepts of space refer hermetically sealed from each other, as if there were *two spaces?* Is there *one space,* which presents itself differently from different approaches, from seeing and hearing? Does the space of music have a separate existence of its own? Do the space experiences of the eye and the ear exclude each other? Or do they supplement each other? Do they include each other?

We already know that the space of the eye is *not* closed to the ear. The ear is able to localize noises, that is, to distinguish the places at which bodies are, and to determine, with considerable accuracy, the place at which the physical source of the noise is to be sought. Eye and ear here work together, in the same space. One could call the localizing faculty of the ear its unmusical faculty, but we have pointed out that music by no means regards it as beneath its dignity to make use of this faculty occasionally to achieve particular ends—as, for example, when a particular spatial disposition is prescribed for individual instruments or groups of instruments, perhaps at a distance or at an elevation; or, again, in the case of the so-called antiphonal style of composition, where vocal or instrumental choirs, separated in space, sing or play to one another, as it were, in dialogue. Spatial effects of this kind are, in any case, not irreconcilable with the specific effects of auditory space; the ear is capable of both types of space experience. Is the like true of the eye?

Many people like to shut their eyes when they listen to music. Stravinsky roundly expresses his disapproval of the practice. "I have always abominated listening to music with closed eyes, without the eye taking an active part. Seeing the gestures and motions of the different parts of the body that produce music is necessary and essential to grasping it in all its fullness. Those who claim to enjoy music fully only if their eyes are closed do not hear it better than if their eyes were open, but the absence of visual distractions allows them to abandon themselves, under the lulling influence of sounds, to vague reveries—and it is these which they love, far more than music itself." [1] There is something to be said on both sides. It is certainly a valuable idea, pedagogically, to call upon the eye as an auxiliary organ in order to concentrate attention upon the kinetic character of music; and it is certainly true that closing the eyes usually serves the ends that Stravinsky so aptly describes. On the other hand, people whose

1. *Stravinsky, an Autobiography.*

attitude toward "music itself" is above question—Pablo Casals, for example—close their eyes when they play or listen. Certainly we shall not go along with those who claim that closing the eyes, the exclusion of space, is the necessary prerequisite for a pure enjoyment of the spaceless art; for it is not out of space that music seeks to take us but only out of one mode of existence of spatiality—in order to lead us all the more deeply into another. Yet it cannot be denied that the eye is the organ of our most intimate and strongest connection with *the* space that music has left behind; the corporeal things in their places, which we have before us when our eyes are open, may well block our view into the space of which music seeks to make us aware. Thus it would be strictly proper to exclude the space experience of the eye temporarily in order to entrust ourselves to the space experience of the ear all the more intimately. The question is only, Is it *necessary* to blind ourselves temporarily in order to be open to the space vision of the ear? Is the eye in this case positively and exclusively a hindrance? Can the eye only see—see things in place? Can the eye perhaps hear too?

For poets, this has never been a question. Shakespeare's lovers "hear with their eyes." Wagner's Tristan, at the highest pitch of expectation, "hears the light"—sight changes into hearing. Dante comes in Hell to a "place dumb of all light"—he hears the absence of light. Goethe speaks of the "whir" of light; light "trumpets." What is referred to in these passages is not so-called synesthesias—auditory sensations produced by visual sensations and accompanying them—it is a real perception through the eyes, but which nevertheless has the characteristics of hearing. Nor is it a matter of poetic imagination; highly sensitive persons have reported strange states that sometimes overtake them when they contemplate a thing (it can be some perfectly insignificant thing); suddenly they seem to lose themselves in the thing; the wall between person seeing and thing seen collapses; at the same time the thing itself loses its contours, expands into the world, seems to contain the whole world in itself, passes into the observer as the whole world, so that the being of the I, of the thing, of the world, coalesce into one. If the random thing I see there before me were suddenly transformed into a tone, the phenomenon would have to be described in much the same way: the limited "there" that enlarges to all space, the without that changes into a coming-from-without, space become alive, become force, directed toward me, streaming into me. Such a seeing may well be called a hearing with the eyes; only, in the case of the eye, this manner of perception is not normal, as it is for the ear: it is the mark of an unusual state, the state of ecstasy.

The observations of many psychologists on the visual sensations of infants, or of blind persons whose sight has been restored by an operation, point in a similar direction. Here the element, characteristic for normal seeing, of the localizing of the visual sensation at a particular place "out there," "where I am not," seems still to be lacking. William James, in his *Psychology*, quotes Condillac: "The first time we see light we are it rather than see it." The boundary between within and without, between the I and the world, is not yet sharply drawn; communication preponderates over distance. The function of the eye that we call its normal function—the perception of things in places—would, accordingly, not be given from the beginning; would rather be the result of a development, whose earlier stages are not so sharply differentiated from hearing as its later ones. May we assume—purely speculatively, or even fancifully—that the early stage, which is quickly passed through in the history of the individual, appeared, in the history of the race, as the distinguishing characteristic of an entire prehistoric epoch—that there was a period in which the normal function of the eye served not only local orientation in space, as it does today, but also a sort of dynamic communication with space, was a seeing of forces rather than of places? In a previous connection we referred to the instinctive performances of many animals, performances that we cannot but call miraculous if we regard them from the point of view of the space of places, but that assume a very different and much more natural complexion if one thinks of them as based on a spatial order of the type of auditory space. May we further assume, even more fancifully, that the case may have been similar with respect to the magical abilities of man, of which the mythologies of remote epochs and of the primitives tell, that they were based upon a direct seeing of space as force, a dynamic communication between within and without, whose last offshoot we should have to recognize in the hearing of tones, in the hearing of space as force? In this case, we should have in music the miraculous echo of a world that once lay open to sight. This ability, in the course of evolution and as life in civilized societies laid other claims upon sight, could have gradually been overshadowed, until today it appears only exceptionally, at unusual moments. But in this case the space of our hearing, space as force, would be *more primordial* in comparison with the space of our seeing, space as place—and not only in the temporal sense but also in an ontological sense: that of being closer to origins, more in correspondence with the primal nature of the real. Bergson must have had something of the sort in mind when he wrote (we now give in full the sentence quoted in part before): "One could, then, in a certain measure, disengage oneself from space [the space of places and things] without leaving extension [space as such]—*and in this there would be a return to the immediate.*" And elsewhere: "L'étendue précède l'espace"—in our terms: "Space as force precedes space as place." [2]

2. *Matière et mémoire.*

But now to get back to solid ground. If it remains incontestable that the principal and normal function of the eye for civilized man is orientation in corporeal space and the seeing of things in their places, it is nevertheless undeniable that the ability of the eye is not exhausted by this activity. We need not at once think of magical abilities; we ourselves, in the course of this investigation, have from time to time had occasion to speak of activities of the eye that go beyond the function of seeing a thing in a place—and go beyond it in a particular direction, which it seems natural to compare with the mode of perception of the ear. Let us recall von Allesch's researches: colors appear to possess dynamic qualities, the eye perceives in them an action of forces;[3] or Wertheimer's study of motion: to see motion does not mean to see a thing first in one place and then in another place; is in general not a seeing of "thing in place," but of "pure passing over," the perception of a purely dynamic process.[4] To attain a clearer conception of auditory space, we cited the image of the empty sky: lying on my back and gazing into the empty sky I do not see "thing out there," a blue hemisphere surrounding me; I see boundless space, in which I lose myself. The strange phenomenon of vertigo, of being drawn by space, might also be mentioned. For Gestalt psychology, seeing in general is primarily a seeing of *Gestalten,* i.e., a direct visual perception of dynamic processes. As Koffka says, both briefly and convincingly: "Visual space is a dynamic event rather than a geometrical pattern."[5]

With this reference to *Gestalt,* we have reached the point at which the ability of the eye to see space as force, so to speak, publicly announces itself: in its encounter with works of visual art. In these, the seeing of forms and colors, like the hearing of tones

3. Gustav von Allesch, *Die aesthetische Erscheinungsweise der Farben.*
4. Max Wertheimer, "Experimentelle Studien über das Sehen von Bewegung."
5. Kurt Koffka, *Principles of Gestalt Psychology.*

in a work of music, is a direct perception of acting forces. The individual form or color is no more confined to itself than is the individual tone; none is simply in its place and remains in its place, each points beyond itself, to other forms and colors, each stands to each, in the whole of the work, in a definite relation; indeed, it is only perforce of these relations that the work becomes a whole. They are spatial relations, but not of the kind that the eye otherwise observes in space and that are fully apprehended and described if the mutual positions are determined, the mutual distances measured. What the eye sees here are tensions and countertensions, harmonies and disharmonies: purely dynamic relations. Here the line, the outline, is not only the objective boundary that sets off thing from thing, thing from space; beyond that, it is a sign, a statement, in which a meaning exists, exists symbolically, as musical meaning exists in tones. The space of the picture itself, together with the things represented in it, is not simply set off from the observer; rather it opens itself to him, takes him into itself, passes into him. In another connection we discussed the unique spatial effects of Chinese painting: how a single form, a line, awakens the surrounding void to life, makes it active, makes space as such (supposedly a nothingness to the eye) visible—as space becomes audible through the sounding of a tone. We also mentioned analogous effects of architecture—the making "empty" space visible, almost tangible. But the ability of the eye that lets us perceive such things—how are we to describe it if not as a beholding of forces, of space as force? Might it be conceivable that in our visual arts the mythical ability of the eye to behold the dynamic across the corporeal still survives?

We must at least mention, if only cursorily, an amazing development that belongs in this context: it is that of the dynamization of the space concept in modern physics. Originally, as we have said, physics took over the space concept of geometry, which, for its part, drew the logical conclusions from the experiences of the eye and the hand in the space of things and places and put them together in a system. The space concept that physics today returns to geometry (but not without geometry itself having given the cue) has so changed as to be almost unrecognizable. The rigid structure, fixed for all eternity, which served physical phenomena as their absolutely dependable foundation, has become a space that bends one way or another, expands or contracts, in accordance with what physical events seem to require. Statements about space are hardly distinguishable from statements about the dynamic; the line between space and dynamic field becomes blurred like that between matter and energy. The definition of visual space just cited, which comes from Gestalt psychology—"dynamic event rather than geometrical pattern"—could also be applied to the space of modern physics. Philosophy is already drawing conclusions from this development. "All space is process," says Samuel Alexander.[6] Here we have come quite close to the musical space concept—even if we are still at an appreciable distance from it.

And now let us briefly summarize our results. Auditory space and visual space are not like two spaces; what we have said of auditory space is not true only of a definite special instance of space, but has a meaning for space in general. To be sure, the musical experience of space is basically different from the normal experience of space by the eye; but this does not make music exist, as it were, in a space of its own, shut off from everything else that encounters us as spatial. No, the space experience of the ear hearing tones is not alien to the eye, as, vice versa, the space experience of the seeing eye is familiar to the ear hearing noises. There is, then, *one* space, *the* space that encounters ear and eye

6. *Space, Time, and Deity.*

as place and force. A certain difference in rank in the two modes of existence of space is perhaps expressed in the fact that we regard the ability of the ear to localize sources of sound as inferior to its musical ability; whereas, on the contrary, we regard the beholding of space as force in works of painting and architecture as a higher accomplishment than the seeing of things in places.

Finally, it is clear that such a revision of our thought in matters of space cannot remain without consequences for the classical opposition between space and time. We need only think back to the manifestations of time that we have observed in music in order to become aware that, for the person hearing music, time and space are not diametrically opposed principles of being or of order, as they are presented in our traditional thinking and even in Bergson. Above what separates them, the person hearing music recognizes what connects them; even more, his experience forces him to recognize the connecting, rather than the separating, as the essential. He hears time as force and he hears space as force. For him, what keeps the two apart is secondary. This separating element has found expression in the two terms "juxtaposition" and "succession." What remains of it in the musical experience? Our discussion of auditory space centered itself upon a concept of a spatial order that should *not* be understood as juxtaposition; in the space that we hear there simply is no juxtaposition. The situation is not much better in regard to the musical time concept and succession. It is not the series of instant after instant which is essential in music, but the fact that the present instant contains the past instant and the future instant: an interpenetration rather than a succession. The same word by which we distinguished the order of auditory space is, then, also applicable to the order of auditory time. Space and time: not "juxtaposition" and "succession," but "interpenetration"—interpenetration of simultaneous occurrence and serial occurrence. The radical separation of the two becomes untenable in the presence of music.

In conclusion, we observe that in the case of "space," as in the case of "time" or "motion," musical experiences illuminate a side of the phenomena that, from the viewpoint and in the thinking of modern man, is normally obscured; but on the other hand, when all is said and done, music, to put it bluntly, has nothing new to tell us. We learn nothing from music that we could not, in principle, learn equally well from other sources; and the concern of the most progressive thinkers of our day is precisely to attain, from other sources, notions such as we have derived from music. This does not represent a weakness in our undertaking; it is, rather, its proper justification. Only thus does it become apparent that, in music, we *experience the world.* Were it otherwise, music would be a special province—something for connoisseurs, even a flight from the world. Its unique significance for our thinking, for our understanding of the world, does not, then, lie in its leading us to otherwise inaccessible insights. But what, elsewhere, can be made accessible only by laborious speculation, and then only uncertainly and insecurely—so that it always remains open to doubt, opposition, and rejection—music brings us patently. In music, what other phenomena conceal itself becomes phenomenon; in music, what is inmost to the world is turned outward.

XIX.

A Last Word on High and Low in Tones

We quoted a statement of Wolfgang Koehler's: "Pitches, whatever they may be, do not deserve the place hitherto accorded to them."[1] Pitch differences have been made the basis of a quasi-spatial or spacelike order of the realm of tone, and pitch differences are usually called upon to explain the kinetic character of tonal events—in both cases, as we have seen, mistakenly. It is not pitch differences which are the basis of the musical experience of motion, but differences in dynamic quality; and it is not because tones differ in pitch, but because they have different dynamic qualities, that we can speak of an order of auditory space. Since pitches as such, consequently, contribute nothing either to the musical experience of motion or to the musical experience of space, it might be concluded that they are musically irrelevant. Our relegation of pitches to the category of the acoustical (in distinction from the properly musical) properties of tones pointed in the same direction.

However, in order to silence possible objections, we stated that this negative finding did not constitute the last word on the subject of pitch. The promise thus implied we must now at long last redeem. We ask: Is it really true that pitch difference as such

1. See p. 94.

has no significance in the musical context; that "higher" or "lower" is a matter of indifference to music? To a great extent, this is true. The singer for whom an aria is too high or too low transposes it down or up, without anything happening to the music; anyone not possessing absolute pitch does not notice that a change has occurred. It is the same song that is sung by a soprano or a contralto in different keys—that is, at different pitches. A tenor sings the song in the same key as the soprano, but an octave lower. Music for the organ or the harpsichord often leaves to the interpreter the choice of octave for certain passages; the piece remains the same whether the passage sounds an octave higher or lower or in several octaves at once. The curious variations of so-called standard pitch should also be mentioned here. Every orchestra tunes by the tone 𝄞 of the oboe, but this tone is by no means the same in all countries or even in all cities of the same country. To be sure, it has the same name everywhere, A; but it is not the same pitch everywhere. Its pitch *roughly* corresponds to the frequency 440—*today*. In the past it was considerably lower, below 400, perhaps about 370. When we read 𝄞 in a seventeenth-century composition, we know what *tone* is meant, but not what *pitch*. Music would certainly not have remained so indifferent to this question if matters of essential importance were involved.

In all these cases, we are dealing with pitch differences within comparatively narrow limits. The picture changes if we take into consideration the realm of tone in its entire extent, from the lowest register to the highest. It is by no means a matter of indifference that the opening phrase of Schubert's *Unfinished* Symphony sounds in the low register and the opening phrase of his C-major Symphony in the middle register. Is the reverse conceivable—the *Unfinished* Symphony beginning in the middle register and the C-major Symphony in the low register? What would become of the A-flat aria in the *St. Matthew Passion,* "Aus Liebe muss mein Heiland sterben," written for soprano and three high wind instruments, if it were to be sung by a bass accompanied by three low winds? How carefully Palestrina, where he deems it necessary, disposes the different combinations of high, middle, and low voices—difference of pitch *is,* then, a matter of essential concern with him. And as to the effects of direct contrast between high and low, for example, in the "Funeral March" from the *Eroica* Symphony, where the soft of the violins is answered by the threatening of the basses; or in the last act of Verdi's *Otello,* when, after Desdemona's prayer ends in the highest register, the orchestra's lowest tone announces the presence of Othello? Are such differences in pitch incidental, to say nothing of reversible?

In the second movement of his Seventh Symphony, Beethoven first gives the theme

to the low string instruments, then raises it successively from octave to octave:

At the end of the movement, when the theme sounds for the last time, he does the reverse; he begins in the highest register and makes the music drop down from octave to octave. Certainly it is the same theme, the same music, that we hear in the different registers; the dynamic qualities are the same, the tonal motion always has the same meaning; hence it is justifiable to maintain that, strictly speaking, difference of pitch contributes nothing to the musical meaning of the succession of tones—is garment, not essence. But on the other hand, can we, in such an instance, disregard difference of pitch without affecting the whole, and even destroying it? Let us imagine the movement beginning not in the lower but in the middle register and remaining in the middle register through its entire course; or beginning in the higher register and, instead of the step-by-step ascent from octave to octave, giving us the contrary, a descent. Who could maintain that this was still the same piece of music? It would be a different composition made of the same music—if the expression be permissible.

Difference in pitch, difference in register, *has,* then, a place, a function, in the musical whole. It might seem possible to clarify the formula "a different composition made of the same music" by a comparison with the different visual forms that can be built up from the same basic formal element—for example,

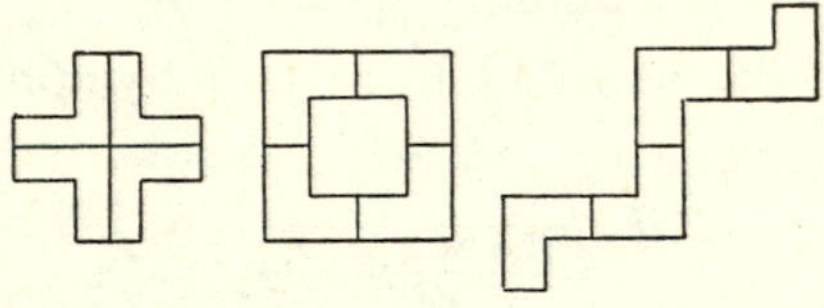

from . But here the whole is the direct and exclusive result of the different arrangement of the component forms, whereas in music the whole does *not* result directly and exclusively from the arrangement of the components or groups in different registers. Difference of register and pitch may have a function in the musical whole; it is not the essential, the decisive function.

Another comparison with a phenomenon in the visual realm suggests itself: comparison with the function of color in the whole of a painting—especially where color and drawing can be separated without violence, where we can think away the color without completely disorganizing the context of the picture. An engraved reproduction of such a picture, a black-and-white photograph of it, the negative of such a photograph, *are* the same picture only in a rather abstract, nonartistic sense. For artistic experience, they are different pictures made of the same pictorial material, in the same way in which decisive changes of register make a different composition out of the same musical material.

Further pursuit of the comparison is opposed by the fact that, in the parallel between painting and music, the place corresponding to color is already occupied by another quality of tones, "tone color," as it is justly called. Tones are not simply high or low; they are high flute tones, violin tones, celesta tones, low bassoon, cello, or trombone tones. Each of these instrumental names stands for a perfectly definite, unmistakable quality, "color," of tone. It is true of tone color too that it contributes nothing to the musical meaning: the melody remains the same, whether it is played on a flute or a violin, just as it remains the same in different registers. In this respect, then, tone color and pitch are on the same level: neither of them is able to determine musical meaning, as are the dynamic qualities of tones. Yet the functions of tone color and pitch in the whole of a musical work are far from being of equal value; if we called pitch a garment, then tone color is an overgarment. Changes in the realm of tone color are far from having the same decisive consequences that changes in the realm of pitch can have. The second movement of Beethoven's Seventh Symphony can be reorchestrated; we can change the tone color, can even eliminate all differences of tone color, reduce it to one color, as happens when the movement is played on the piano. The change will be noticeable, we shall observe an unmistakable weakening of the general effect; but we shall not say—as we did in the case of alterations in the arrangement of registers—that it is no longer the same piece of music. The functions of pitch and tone color affect the over-all structure of the composition in very different degrees.

But the painter has another quality besides color at his disposition—luminosity. Differences in light and shade, of chiaroscuro, have their particular sphere of effect, which is not to be confused with the sphere of differences in color. And to do away with differences of chiaroscuro is a far greater violation of the over-all structure of a painting than the omission of the colors: a mere outline drawing of a painting is certainly farther from the original than a black-and-white photograph of it. So the parallel can, then, be pursued. In painting, as in music, we have to do with a *pair* of qualities, with luminosity and color in the one case, with pitch and tone-color in the other. Thus pitch differences in the audible would correspond to chiaroscuro differences in the visible.

In this form, the comparison takes us a step forward. The two pairs, that is, exhibit a remarkable kinship, a kinship in their relation to *space*. Colors and tone colors are indifferent to space; chiaroscuro and register are not. More accurately, space is indifferent to differences of both color and tone color; it is not indifferent to differences of chiaroscuro in the visible, of register in the audible.

Let us take two colors, red and green, and arrange them one above the other in space. Red above, green below—green above, red below; one is as good as the other. Let us take light and dark and arrange them likewise. Light above, dark below—dark above, light below; here one is by no means as good as the other; another distinction enters into play than that of pure spatial arrangement. We might say that the one is right, the other is not right; light *belongs* above. Let us take two tone colors at the same pitch, horn and cello: horn sounding from above, cello sounding from below, or the reverse; one is as good as the other. Let us take a soprano voice and a bass voice: soprano sounding from above, bass sounding from below. That is right; the reverse is not right. In the Grail Scene from *Parsifal,* could Titurel's voice come from the summit of the dome; the soprano melody "Der

Glaube lebt" emerge from underground? What musician in his senses, composing the closing scene of *Faust,* would write the Pater Profundus for tenor, and Doctor Marianus—"in the highest, purest cell"—for bass? (Could the "purest" cell be the lowest?)

Now let us forget tones and pitches for a moment; let us inquire into the meaning of "above" and "below" as spatial definitions, as designations of a difference in place.

The space in which bodies are in places and move from place to place is distinguished by the characteristic of homogeneity. That is, every place differs from every other place only through a single defining factor, through its *location.* Except for difference in location, there is absolute uniformity between place and place. Nothing is true of one place which is not equally true of every other place. Whether a thing or a process is located or occurs at this place or that place in space, whether it is transferred from one place in space to any other place in space, makes not the slightest difference to the thing or the process. In respect to what occurs in it, the space of places is completely neutral.

In order to orient ourselves in the infinite uniformity of homogeneous space and define the location of a place in it, we think of space as organized in three particular directions, dimensions. Put concretely, in the words of our everyday language, they are right-left, before-behind, above-below. Any place in space, then, lies so and so far to the right or left of me, before or behind me, above or below me. The little added word "me" is essential; it is self-evident that orientation by right and left, before and behind, above and below is only possible and meaningful if I at the same time state *from what point* it is undertaken.

The correlative words "above-below," then, designate one of the three particular directions according to which we organize space. Since in homogeneous space there are no other differences than those of location, the difference between above and below can mean nothing but a difference of location, or, more accurately, a difference of location in relation to a point of orientation, an observer. What "above" and "below" mean, then, is exclusively a question of the position of the observer; space itself, if we may say so, does not show the difference. The same section of space that I now call "above"—when I am in a valley, for example—will later, and equally rightly (from the mountain top), be called "below." The two words are interchangeable at will; there is no sentence, no statement, in which, instead of "above," we could not *equally rightly* say "below"; and nothing has to have changed except the position from which—in reality or in thought—the statement is made. "A light burns above all night"—"A light burns below all night"; both statements can be right, equally right, as accounts of the same fact.

But we also meet with statements in which the situation with regard to "above" and "below" is entirely different. For example:

> Ye move above in the light . . . ye blessed Geniuses!

Does this "above" designate a place in homogeneous space, the situation of a stage in respect to an observer? If so, one would only have to imagine the observer looking at the spectacle from another position, and instead of "above" the reading would be "below." An absurd idea! The place does not exist from which this "above" could become a "below." "Ye move below in the light . . .": something besides the position of an observer has changed here; the validity of the statement has changed; the statement says something that is *not true.* The exchange has turned truth into untruth. There is no longer any possibility of interchanging "above" and "below."

The untruth arises from the collocation of "below" and

"light." This light does not belong below; its place is "above." Not as if there were never anything but darkness below:

> Life thou dost seek and seek; and fire divine
> Springs, brightens, toward thee from the deeps of earth.

But there is no fire without smoke; it is not in firelight that the blessed geniuses move. Nor is it as if there were never anything but light above:

> Too long has thy power hung over my head,
> Thou in the dark cloud, O thou God of Time! [2]

But is not this clearly the statement of a condition in which something *is wrong* ("Too long . . .")? The wrongness finds expression in the "dark above." Darkness belongs "below," as light "above."

"A light burns above all night"—"A light burns below all night": both can be right, because here "above" and "below" are indications of locality in homogeneous space. An "above" that cannot be interchanged with a "below" without altering the meaning of the statement cannot be a place in homogeneous space. Noninterchangeability implies that the space to which it applies cannot be the same "above" as "below." It is a space which has other differences besides those of place; in which it is not a matter of indifference at what place an event occurs; which exhibits an interdependence between certain places (e.g., "above") and certain data (luminousness). Here the difference between above and below means more than a difference of spatial location; it signifies a difference in spatial *quality*, we might almost say in spatial *value*.

Let us return to tones. Is it not a gross contradiction when, after having carefully established that pitch differences have

2. Quotations on pp. 356–57 are from the Hamburger trans. of Hölderlin.

nothing to do with differences in spatial location, we now suggest that there might be a definite correlation, a mutual affinity, between high tones and a spatial "above," between low tones and a spatial "below"? No contradiction is involved here. The first statement refers to local differences in homogeneous space, the second to qualitative differences between regions of space. In the first sense, the difference of register is spatially indifferent; in the second sense, it is not. High and low in tones, and "high" and "low" as place-defining factors in homogeneous space, are connected by no ascertainable relation; hence the attempt to understand tonal motion in the sense of a motion from place to place in homogeneous space is doomed to failure. On the other hand, there is a clearly ascertainable relation between the difference of high and low in tones and the spatio-qualitative difference between "high" and "low," "above" and "below"—the relation on the basis of which tones *belong* in definite regions in qualitatively differentiated space: high above, low below. The place of the high tone is "above," that of the low tone "below," in the same sense that "above" is the place of light, "below" the place of dark. In an earlier context we said that no material necessity dictates the choice of the correlatives "high-low" to designate the characteristic difference between tones; that instead of high and low tones, we could just as well speak of light and dark tones. We see now why this exchange of terms would be possible; the audibly high and low, the visibly light and dark, have in common their relation to qualitatively differentiated space, to the qualitative spatial order.

So, after all, pitch does bring space into play. Our question concerning the function of pitch differences in the structure of a musical work can, therefore, receive a general answer: their function is a spatial one.

But how are we to conceive this spatial functioning of pitch concretely? It certainly cannot be a question of high tones being heard as coming from above, low tones from below. In the space that we hear, there is no distinction of high and low; all tones are heard as coming from the same place, from all places, from everywhere. (The inconsistency between saying, as here, that all tones are in the same place, in all places, and saying, as we did a moment ago, that the place of high tones is different from that of low tones, is "above" not "below," need trouble us no more than the paradox of an omnipresent God "in heaven." Light too spreads through all space; yet its place is "above.") How, then, are we to grasp the undeniable difference of the space experience in high and low tones; how are we to describe it in greater detail? Musical psychology speaks of a difference in *volume;* deep tones are held to have more volume—that is, to occupy more space—than high tones. We cannot admit this interpretation. No tone occupies more space than any other tone; every tone occupies the same space, i.e., all space. It is true that high tones sound *narrower* than deep tones; shall we say that space as a whole contracts in high tones, expands in low tones? But then, on the other hand, high tones seem to come from far away, low tones from nearer, so that one might speak of a greater transparency, rarefaction of space, in high than in low tones. One might almost feel tempted to assume different densities in auditory space. Yet against all this remains the fact that we can hear high and low tones at the same time, but that auditory space cannot very well be narrow and wide, transparent and opaque, rarefied and dense, at the same time. A possible interpretation is suggested by a phrase of Révész's, which we quoted earlier: "The space that becomes alive through sound." May we perhaps venture to say that space is *differently alive* in high and low tones, and that these different modes of spatial aliveness are related to the spatial qualities "above" and "below" in much the same manner as high and low tones, light and dark, the divine and the elemental, seemed to be? In the simultaneous sounding of all registers, then, space would encounter us in the totality of all possible modes of aliveness. In a melody of Bach's, quoted earlier, a melodic step taken first downward, then upward, made us think of the bowing and raising of the head in prayer; the difference between above and below that here entered in we called a difference in levels of existence: "Where God is"—"Where I am." The "up" of music, then, would mean directed "toward God," and the spatial meaning of this "up" would not be mere metaphor—would, rather, have a real basis in the qualitative difference between different regions of space.

Two notes might be added here, one ethical, the other historical.

We must beware of reading any moral meaning into this discussion of a difference in quality, or even in value, between "above" and "below." To belong above, to belong below, are anything but synonymous with good and bad. The seed that belongs below, that belongs to the dark, is not worse than the flower in the light. The high tone is by no means necessarily the voice of Good, nor the low tone of Evil. To be sure, operatic convention prescribes a baritone or bass for the role of the villain, a tenor for the role of the virtuous hero. But Zarastro is a bass, the Queen of Night a very high soprano, Monostatos a tenor; and Mozart knew his business. Desdemona's prayer hovers in the highest register, the lowest tone sounds at Othello's arrival—but, musically considered, this is not because Desdemona is innocent and Othello a black demon. It is perfectly easy to imagine the music sinking lower and lower as Desdemona falls asleep, and a very high, soft tone indicating the opening of the door. The change would not make Desdemona a sinner and

Othello innocent—though it would make both of them different people from what they are in Shakespeare's tragedy, in Verdi's music. They would be a Desdemona whose sleep wás troubled by dark presentiments, an Othello who dissimulated, a hypocritical, perfidious Othello. The noninterchangeability of high and low has, though not a moral, a characterological meaning.

(Here again, as so often before, we have language against us. There is no word to indicate the kind of difference that is in question in all this. Our languages know quantitative differences [differences of magnitude, location, direction, which can be measured and counted], qualitative differences [as red-green, flute timbre–violin timbre], and value differences [good-bad, worthy-unworthy]; the difference between high and low in tones falls in none of these three categories. It is not a quantitative difference, nor does it have the value-neutrality of pure qualitative differences; and it is free from the black-white attribute of values in the strict sense, which are always either positive or negative. For the value difference between things of equal value, things equally good, there is no word. We have referred to "above" and "below" now as space qualities, now as space values; we were forced to; neither of the two terms is correct. In this case language shows itself to be the complaisant handmaid of a traditional mode of thought: quantity-quality-value corresponds to the threefold division of human capacities into thinking-feeling-willing and their goals into truth-beauty-goodness. Our aesthetics run aground in the vain attempt to fit *art* into this godforsaken schema.)

For the historian, the following observation should be of interest. Direction upward is, if the expression be permitted, the normal direction of our music. In playing or singing scales, we always begin upward; the degrees of the scale are counted upward; the alphabetical order of the letters for tones corresponds to the upward direction. When intervals are mentioned, the upward direction is always meant unless the contrary is expressly stated. All this is neither based upon the nature of things nor to be explained as pure convention, determined by habit; for it was not always thus. Indeed in antiquity the situation was precisely the reverse. With the same naturalness with which, for us, everything in music normally goes upward, for the Greeks and the Romans it went downward. In their books of theory the scales appear directed downward. The alphabetical series starts at the top and goes down. The same is true of intervals: "a fourth" in those days was understood to be "a descending fourth" as unhesitatingly as today we take it to mean "an ascending fourth." The change must have taken place during the centuries of the decline of antiquity, during the same period in which the art of painting bears witness to a radical change in the feeling for space, in the picture of space. In any case, with the end of the sixth century, in Gregorian chant and in the tonal system upon which it is based, the upward direction is already the undisputed norm. (The contrast can have nothing to do with the different way in which antiquity and our own day interpret *numbers* in relation to tones. We think of frequencies; the ancients thought of string lengths. For us, as for the ancients, 3:4 is the numerical symbol of the fourth. If one thinks of frequencies, the second of the two tones is higher than the first; the interval is ascending. If one thinks of string lengths, the reverse is true. But in the sixth century no one had any inkling of frequencies.)

XX. Summary and Prospect

It has been the intention of this study to outline what may be called a musical concept of the external world. The attempt seemed worth while for its own sake as well as for the sake of a possible contribution to one of those permanent discussions that mark our intellectual history: that in which the concept of reality is at issue. This discussion has lately become quite active. An established notion of reality, which is allegedly backed by the authority of science and which has taken hold of the minds of men, is being challenged from many sides—science itself among them. The discussion is not purely theoretical, since human behavior is to a large extent shaped by beliefs and assumptions, mostly inexplicit, concerning the ultimate nature of reality. Critics of our civilization have long been aware of the danger of a situation that assigns to the human mind almost exclusively mechanical, technical tasks. They have also recognized the important function reserved for music in this context. This function, however, was for the most part understood in a sort of remedial sense: music should provide nourishment for those functions of man which the one-sidedness of modern life threatens with atrophy; the dream of a better and purer world, a world of ideal beauty, might give at least temporary release from the bonds of a purely material reality. This is well intentioned but ineffectual. The moment music becomes the voice of the "other" world, musical experiences can no longer challenge our concept of reality: where there is no connection, there can be no conflict. Hence the first and most important thing to do is *to bring about the clash.* Only when it can be demonstrated that musical experiences are *not* experiences of "another" world, of an "unknown ideal life"; that the audible and the visible belong to the *same* reality; that motion of tones and motion of things take place on the *same* stage; that *one* space, *one* time embrace the world of visible event and the world of audible event—only then is a critique of our concept of reality from the point of view of music possible.

In this light, we might sum up the results of our investigation as follows:

1. The world of music, the tonal world, appears as the work of forces that act in obedience to laws and whose action is manifest in the order of tonal events, in the precisely determined relations of tones to one another, in the norms that govern the course of tonal motion. Law assumes different forms according to the different types of tonal events: one law regulates the succession of tones in melodies; another, chords and their succession in harmony; yet another, the succession of tones as events in time, as metrical and rhythmic phenomena. The formulation of these laws will be modified by the differences between tonal systems. But one thing all these laws have in common: their manifestations are of a *purely dynamic* nature; they refer to states, not objects; to relations between tensions, not between positions; to tendencies, not magnitudes (there is nothing to measure in them). The validity of these laws extends as far as the tonal world extends; tones apart from these laws are mere fragments of a possible world, chaos. Unlike the laws of nature, however, the laws of the tonal world do not prescribe the course of events; they allow for freedom under the law. What the law

determines with the force of necessity is the dynamic state, the tendency, of a tone; what it leaves free is the choice of the way, the "when" and "how" of the progress from tension to release, from unbalance to ultimate balance. The law does not determine the individual step; it determines the dynamic meaning of the freely chosen step.

2. The forces that act in the tonal world manifest themselves *through* bodies but not *upon* bodies. They need the physical event—air in vibration, stimulation of the sense organ, excitation of the nervous system—in order to appear in action. But the physical event is here only the conveyor of the action; it is not itself the action. This distinguishes purely dynamic from physically dynamic event. The physical world, too, is the work of forces acting under law; but here the force is one with its physical action, it expends itself in its physical action; and we are justified in talking about forces only in reference to physical manifestations. A force whose action reaches beyond bodies, whose presence is not manifested in the behavior of bodies—in the context of the physical world these are empty words, as meaningless as "nonmeasuring measure" or "angular curve." But in music, one of our senses meets a whole world of dynamic events that, to be sure, require a physical link in order to produce the encounter, but of whose presence the physical world is, so to speak, otherwise entirely ignorant. The forces acting here leave no more trace in the physical event that serves as the conveyor of their action than does my gaze in the windowpane through which I look.

3. The encounter with the tonal world includes the three fundamental experiences of motion, time, and space. If we try to formulate concepts of motion, time, and space in accordance with musical experiences, and compare these concepts with the concepts of these three things which are commonly held today and

which are derived from our encounter with the physical world, from the experience of the seeing eye and the touching hand, a striking discrepancy will appear. Motion, time, and space in the musical and the physical worlds seem not to have much beyond their names in common; we might well be tempted to assume that the two worlds are sharply separated, or rather that the tonal world forms an isolated precinct outside of the only real world, the physical. On the other hand, science, which has been the principal agent in developing the notions of motion, time, and space that are commonly held today, has itself been engaged, for over half a century, in redefining these fundamental concepts—and precisely in such a direction that a surprising similarity to the corresponding musical concepts takes the place of the former discrepancy. "Motion in its pure state seems to refuse to enter our space-time framework"; [1] a musician might have written that; an atomic physicist did write it. The critique of the traditional concept of time, with the formulation of such a concept as "living time," could have arisen from observation of musical phenomena; it actually arose from observation of physiological and biological phenomena. "Space is process, space is dynamic event"—not musicians but scientists and mathematical philosophers are saying these things. If motion, time, and space, seen in the light of the physical world, are so similar to the motion, time, and space with which the world of tone has made us familiar, they must have more than their names in common. The two worlds—that of bodies and that of tones, that of physical (physico-dynamic) and that of purely dynamic events—have the same foundation. The wall that tones pierce does not separate two worlds, two degrees of reality, but two equally real, interpenetrating modes of existence of one world, of *the* world that encounters our senses. We do not need, as it were, to change place in order to pass from

1. Louis de Broglie, "Jenseits der Physik."

one to the other. It is simply that tones open a view that bodies obstruct.

4. On the question, What is *nature?* we have long—and quite understandably—turned for information to those who might be expected to know, to the professionals of the "natural sciences"; to those, then, for whom—equally understandably—nature is that of which science furnishes (or could furnish) knowledge: the visible-tangible-measurable, the physical. As formulated critically by Heidegger, the answer is that Nature is "the closed kinetic context of mass points in space and time relations. This scheme of nature, as assumed, contains, among others, the following determinants: Motion means change of place. No motion or direction of motion is distinguished above any other. Any place is equal to any other place. No moment of time has superiority over any other. Every force is defined by, i.e., is nothing except, its effects in terms of motion, i.e., of amount of change of place per unit of time. . . . Any phenomenon, if it is to be conceived as a natural phenomenon at all, must preliminarily be determined as spatio-temporal kinetic magnitude. Such determination is effected in measurement by the aid of number and calculation. . . . Every event must be seen within this basic schema of nature. A natural phenomenon becomes recognizable as such only within the horizon of this schema."[2] This schema of nature is too circumscribed. One of our senses perceives events that occur in space and time, that exhibit forces acting in accordance with laws—must we call these events "supernatural" simply because they transcend the physical, elude measurement? *Music, too, is nature.* There are natural phenomena that can be defined as motions in space and time, though not as *magnitudes,* not by measure and number; that do not acknowledge an equality of all directions; in whose space there is no equality of places, nor,

2. Heidegger, "Die Zeit des Weltbildes."

indeed, any plurality of places; phenomena whose time knows no equality of moments of time, which exhibit an action of forces that are not "defined by, i.e., [are] nothing except [their] effects . . . in terms of change of place," in terms of physical event. Nature includes the purely dynamic, the nonphysical, the nonmeasurable. The immaterial is a genuine element of nature.

5. It has been said that inner and outer world meet in melodies. It would be more to the point to say "penetrate each other"; a "meeting" of inner and outer world occurs in any experience of our senses. The *mode* of the meeting is different, however, when it occurs between physical things and our eyes or hands, or between tones and the ear. Eye or hand keeps the physical thing that I meet away from me, makes me conscious of distance, reinforces the separating barrier. Tone penetrates into me, overflows the barrier, makes me conscious not of distance but of communication, even of participation. Our current schema "inner world–outer world" is derived solely from one type of encounter—that brought about by the eye and the hand. William James warned—and he had anything rather than music in mind—" 'Inner' and 'outer' are not coefficients with which experiences come to us aboriginally stamped, but are rather results of a later classification performed by us for particular needs." [3] The needs are those of so-called practical life, our active and passive encounter with the physical world. Only in this encounter do "inner" and "outer," I and world, face each other like two mutually exclusive precincts on either side of an impassable dividing line. But if what we encounter is nonphysical, purely dynamic—as it happens to be in the case of musical tones—the quality "out there" is replaced by the quality "from-out-there-toward-me-and-through-me." Instead of setting off two precincts from each other and presenting them as mutually exclusive, this encounter

---

3. "Does Consciousness Exist?"

causes them to penetrate each other, participate in each other. The distinction between "inner" and "outer" has by no means disappeared; it has been transformed in a manner best expressed by a diagram: "inner" | "outer"; two precincts separated by a dividing line become 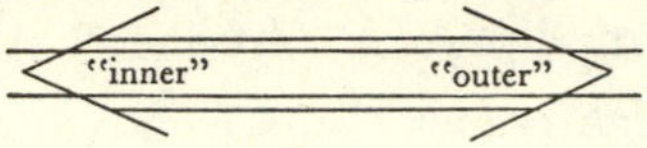 "inner" "outer", direction and counter-direction of an encounter.

5A. Merely as a note to the above: The difference in the mode of the encounter cannot but decisively influence our mode of *knowing* the thing encountered. If the encounter is of the type that emphasizes the dividing line, my knowledge of what is encountered will be knowledge of something on the other side of the dividing line, "out there," existing "independently of me," "in itself." Turning toward it, I turn away from myself; I shall know it the better the more I disregard myself (the "subject"), the more I know it "objectively." If the encounter is of the other type, if the thing encountered is of a purely dynamic nature, the mere idea of "objective" knowledge becomes meaningless: an encounter characterized by an interpenetration of I and world cannot produce an "object," that is, something existing "independently of myself." It does not follow—as is often asserted—that knowledge comes to an end at this point. It merely follows that the purely dynamic will be known in a different way from the physical. We can learn this lesson from physics itself, which has recently had some astonishing experiences concerning the "object existing independently of the observer." It appears that the existence of such an object is a function of the magnitude of the phenomenon observed; if the object is small enough, "independence of the observer" disappears, together with object and objectivity in the old sense. Have the physicists concluded that with this the limit of the knowable has been reached? Certainly not; they have altered their concept of knowledge to fit the new situation.

6. The statement above—that "inner and outer world meet in melodies"—is, however, capable of being interpreted otherwise than in the light of the current concept that equates the "inner" of "inner world" with "in me" and the opposition "inner world–outer world" with "psychic-physical." After all, it is not only the physical which comes to us from without: tones come to us from without and, in them, something which is nonphysical. Indeed, it is the unique distinction of music that it alone, of all that comes to us from without, confronts our senses with something nonphysical, that in music alone—in the otherwise completely material circle of the outer world—something that exists immaterially presents itself to us. The immaterial, then, does not exist only "psychically," does not only come "from within." The voice of music testifies against interpreting the "inner" of "inner world" as synonymous with "in me." The place of this "inner world" is just as much outside me as in me; the inner world extends as far as the world itself; the world itself is divided into an "inner" and "outer." The boundary is not vertical, running between self and world, but horizontal, running through both; as a psyche, I belong to the great context of the world's within, neither more nor less than, as a body, I belong to the great context of the world's without. Thus the absurdity of the psychological interpretation of music becomes evident. It is not because music expresses or reproduces psychological experiences that we recognize in it the voice of our "within," but because music brings to expression the mode of existence of the world that is of the same nature as my "within," my psyche. And as, in our encounter with bodies, we experience not only bodies but also ourselves as the physical organ of the encounter, so, in our encounter with tones, we are conscious of our self as immaterial living being.

7. "Impossible that this should be nothing but tones!" Who

has not at some time heard this or a similar exclamation from a listener who has just been deeply stirred by a musical experience? Nothing but tones! Of course, when we have been taught that tones are "really" only vibrating air, a physical phenomenon, that hearing is "really" an excitation of sense organ and nerve, a physiological process, we feel—and quite justifiably—that an experience which so profoundly moves our whole being cannot be accounted for merely on the basis of physical and physiological processes. Such an effect, we tell ourselves, must have other causes; something else must have come into play here, something "higher," something to which the tones, as simple intermediaries, merely point, but which itself lies infinitely beyond all tones and all that our senses perceive. Hopeless confusion from beginning to end! Certainly, music transcends the physical; but it does not therefore transcend tones. Music rather helps the thing "tone" to transcend its own physical constituent, to break through into a nonphysical mode of being, and there to develop in a life of unexpected fullness. Nothing but tones! As if tone were not the point where the world that our senses encounter becomes transparent to the action of nonphysical forces, where we as perceivers find ourselves eye to eye, as it were, with a purely dynamic reality—the point where the external world gives up its secret and manifests itself, immediately, *as symbol.* To be sure, tones say, signify, point to—what? Not to something lying "beyond tones." Nor would it suffice to say that tones point to other tones—as if we had first tones, and then pointing as their attribute. No—in musical tones, being, existence, is indistinguishable from, *is,* pointing-beyond-itself, meaning, saying. Certainly, the being of words could be characterized in the same way; but *we* have created words to the end of saying or signifying, *we* have given them their meanings; whereas, in tones, saying, meaning, exists *by nature.* To be sure, if we want to ask *what* tones say, *what* they mean or signify, if we want to know what specific meaning, expressible in words, attaches to a specific piece of music and to every part of it, we are asking an empty and almost childish question. We ask it from the viewpoint of our verbal languages, in the light of our world of things and its distinctions. In the world of tone, where every link with the world of things and its characteristics (and "things" here includes "feelings") has been severed, such questions have no application. Tones, which refer to no things, can never mean *something,* say *something*—some definite individual thing, expressible in words and distinguishable, as the meaning of one composition, from some different meaning of some other composition. In the terms of the verbal languages, we should have to say that all music means the same thing: no-thing—which in this case would not be the same as nonexisting, nonreal; it is as real as music itself. Because they are audibly meaningful by nature, tones hold up for our perception, as real, a dimension of the world that transcends all individual distinctions of things and therefore all verbal language. We can circumscribe it with words; but when it comes to *naming,* words drop out, tones alone can name it.

8. Force is not an "operational concept" [4]—something that we, as thinkers, add to the observed phenomenon in order to explain it, in order to satisfy our desire to understand. The validity of such a concept (the "ether" is a good example) has exactly the same limits as its usefulness; it lays no claim to represent a reality in its own right. It is not impossible to describe the phenomena of the physical world without introducing the notion of force. But in music, there would be hardly anything left to describe if force had to be excluded from the discussion. Force is as real as music itself. Thus it appears that though, strangely enough, the reality of force can be doubted in a physical

4. Cf. P. W. Bridgman, *The Logic of Modern Physics.*

world, it is certain beyond any doubt in a world that contains, besides bodies, tones.

The idea of a world in which nonphysical forces play their part together with physical things is familiar to us as a product of the poetic imagination. The novelist Adalbert Stifter wrote, for example, a hundred years ago, of an event "which will appear miraculous so long as the human mind has not explored those great, diffused forces of nature in which our lives are bathed, so long as we have not learned to bind and unbind the tie of love between those forces and our life." This is *beautiful;* it may or may not be *true.* It is a different matter when, fifty years later, one scholar, Bergson, writes of another, William James: "According to his view, we bathe in an atmosphere traversed by great spiritual currents." Here we have cognition, not fiction; the intention is truth, not beauty. "The powerful feelings," he goes on, "which stir the soul at special moments are forces as real as those that interest the physicist; man does not create them any more than he creates heat and light." [5] A doctor [6] has raised the question whether *thought* should not be regarded as a form of energy, comparable to other known forms of energy, a basic constituent of the structure of the universe, overlooked by the physicists yet more important even than light. The immaterial—"spirit," "soul"—breaks through the artificial barrier of the enclave "inner world"; the distinction between the material as the real and the immaterial as the unreal is gradually reduced; the area of contact is named "force."

9. Does not all this represent a decadence, a disintegration of knowledge, a relapse into prescientific modes of thought? Was it not precisely the lack of a clear distinction between ma-

5. Bergson, "On the Pragmatism of William James" (*The Creative Mind,* ch. VIII); originally the Introduction to the French edition of James's *Pragmatism.*

6. Alexis Carrel, *Man the Unknown.*

terial and immaterial that characterized primitive man's idea of the universe? And did not the sharp separation of the two, assigning its own territory to each, represent a sort of primordial separation of light and darkness on the road of thought? It is true that the musical concept of the external world—nature pervaded by immaterial forces, the purely dynamic transcending the physical, space without distinction of places, time in which past and future coexist with the present, experience of the world in the mode of participation, the external and the inward interpenetrating—much more nearly resembles the magical and mythical ideas of primitive or prehistoric peoples than it does the scientific conceptions of modern man. But why should we assume that, in such a development, we are losing rather than *regaining?* There are two ways of bringing back into sight something that has dropped below the horizon; and one of them is *ascent.* To be sure, there must be no faltering in direction; the goal remains knowledge, understanding. We do not propose to go back to the primitive state of wonder. We continue forward; we continue to question. We raise music to the dignity of a problem for the questioning mind. Those who hear nothing in music but an encouragement to stop questioning, to turn from knowledge, to give up thought, have heard only half its story. The light that music holds up for thought is precisely what concerns us here.

The musical view of the universe differs from the religious view in that it is attained not through faith and revelation but through sense perception and observation. The purely dynamic, the nonphysical element of nature, which we encounter in the musical experience, is not God. Yet no such abyss separates the two as separates the religious and the scientific views of the universe, especially in the traditional and commonly accepted version of the latter. To think of the musical view of the universe as a bridge between the scientific and the religious views is not sheer nonsense. No pantheism is implied here, no idea of nature as the visible incarnation of the invisible Deity: the invisible is no more divine than the visible. The ideas at which Goethe arrived in his old age are closer to what we mean: they were pansymbolic rather than pantheistic: all that is, is significant, all being has meaning, *is* meaning. Goethe's idea of "productive truth"—frequently misinterpreted as pragmatism—also points in the same direction; "productive" in this context does not mean "useful" but rather "leading onward."

Have we been talking about music?

Yes and no. We have talked about forces that are active in tones and tonal systems and whose reality makes music possible. Man has not created these forces; he discovers them. Tonal systems are discoveries in the realm of the audible; they are not inventions. We have talked about the music that our ear discovers, as our eye discovers the great phenomena of heaven and earth. We have talked about music as a phenomenon of *nature.* About music as *art,* created by *man,* the manifestation of *man's* power in tones, we have not talked.

Nature knows no distinctions of rank. Art cannot but establish distinctions of rank. Since the greater part of what we have said concerned music as a natural phenomenon, almost all of it is valid without any distinction of rank; is as true for the most vulgar or sentimental popular song as for the most sublime of masterpieces. For the sake of decorum, we preferred to choose our examples from masterpieces; but any tonal rubbish would have served our purpose equally well. The dynamic qualities of tone, the phenomena of tonal motion, the dynamics of time and space, can be observed in works of the lowest as of the highest rank. How music is possible at all; how musical events differ from physical events—it is this which we have attempted to understand. How the *art* of tones in the true sense is possible; how the tonal work of high rank differs from the tonal work of low rank; how man is able to become creative in tones—upon these problems we have not even touched.

Konrad Fiedler has written: "We must seek the beginning of the history of art precisely at the point where, within the so-called practice of art, a tendency toward cognition arises, and with it artistic activity in the true sense. People can paint, sculpture, make poetry and music for a long time before there can be any question of art in the true sense. . . . A history of art in the true sense, that is, a history of the cognition communicated by art, remains to be written." [7] To be sure, the traditional philosophy of art teaches that the arts are concerned with forms, not concepts, with beauty, not truth; that truth remains the exclusive concern of philosophy and science. Yet a mere glance at the scanty results of this line of thought will tell us what may be expected from it. Art does not aim at beauty; it *uses* beauty—occasionally; on other occasions it uses ugliness. Art—no less than philosophy or science or religion, or any other of the higher endeavors of the human mind—aims ultimately at knowledge, at truth. Of course art has its particular approach to truth, which is different from those of philosophy or science or religion. Heidegger has tried to find the right term for it: he calls it "working-itself-out of truth." [8]

Man in his artistic creation aims at truth. His imaging is a way of knowing; the intellectual process that leads to an image or a form is a way of thinking. In tones and tonal forces man discovers an original and infinitely fruitful material for his creation of images and his thinking in images. The same material can be

7. Konrad Fiedler, *Schriften über Kunst.*
8. Heidegger, "Der Ursprung des Kunstwerks."

used for entirely different purposes too. But to the creative artist, it opens one path to truth. Thinking in tones, forming in tones, he tries to let truth work itself out.

What is truth that we approach through tonal images? What are we who seek for truth in tones? What is a thinking, what a knowing, that works not with concepts and judgments but with images—tonal images that have no object? If, with tones, being is saying, when is what they say true? How can I distinguish truth from untruth in tones?

At the end of our road, as we see, we arrive at a new beginning. We face new questions, no less exacting, no less disquieting, than those which initiated this investigation. The fruit of our endeavor is a new task. Our epilogue becomes the prologue to a new study.

LIST OF WORKS CITED

LIST OF WORKS CITED

ABRAHAM, OTTO. "Tonometrische Untersuchungen an einem deutschen Volkslied." *Psychologische Forschungen* (Berlin), IV (1923).

ALEXANDER, SAMUEL. *Space, Time, and Deity.* New York, 1950; London, 1951.

———. *Spinoza and Time.* London, 1921.

ALLESCH, GUSTAV JOHANNES VON. *Die aesthetische Erscheinungsweise der Farben.* Berlin, 1925.

AUGUSTINE, ST. *Confessions.* Translated by William Watt. (Loeb Classical Library.) London and New York, 1912.

BAUDELAIRE, CHARLES. "Rêve parisien." In: *One Hundred Poems from Les Fleurs du mal.* Translated by C. F. MacIntyre. Berkeley and Los Angeles, 1947.

BELAIEW-EXEMPLARSKI, SOPHIE, and JAWORSKY, BOLESLAUS. "Die Wirkung des Tonkomplexes bei melodischer Gestaltung." *Archiv für die gesamte Psychologie* (Leipzig), LVII (1926).

BERGSON, HENRI. *Creative Evolution.* Translated by Arthur Mitchell. London and New York, 1911.

———. *The Creative Mind.* Translated by Mabelle L. Andison. New York, 1946.

———. *Durée et simultanéité.* Paris, 1922.

———. *Essai sur les données immédiates de la conscience.* (Bibliothèque de philosophie contemporaine.) Paris, 1908.

———. *Matière et mémoire.* Paris, 1896.

BERKELEY, GEORGE. *A Treatise Concerning the Principles of Human Knowledge.* In: *The Works of George Berkeley, Bishop of Cloyne,*

Vol. II. Edited by T. E. Jessop. (Bibliotheca Britannica Philosophica.) London and New York, 1949.

BINGHAM, WILLIAM VANDYKE. *Studies in Melody.* (Monograph Supplement No. 50 of the *Psychological Review.*) Baltimore, 1910.

BOLZANO, BERNHARD. *Wissenschaftslehre.* Leipzig, 1929–31. 4 vols.

BRIDGMAN, P. W. *The Logic of Modern Physics.* New York, 1927.

BROGLIE, LOUIS DE. "Jenseits der Physik." *Wort und Wahrheit* (Vienna), V (1950).

BROWNE, SIR THOMAS. *Religio Medici.* (Everyman's Library.) London and New York, 1931.

CARREL, ALEXIS. *Man the Unknown.* New York, 1935.

FARADAY, MICHAEL. "A Speculation Touching Electric Conduction and the Nature of Matter." In: *Experimental Researches in Electricity,* Vol. II. London, 1839–55. 3 vols.

FIEDLER, KONRAD. *Schriften über Kunst.* Munich, 1913–14. 2 vols.

GENT, WERNER. *Die Philosophie des Raumes und der Zeit.* Bonn, 1926.

GIDE, ANDRÉ (ed.). *Anthologie de la poésie française.* New York, 1949.

GOETHE, JOHANN WOLFGANG VON. *Maximen und Reflexionen.* (Gedenkausgabe, Vol. IX.) Zurich, 1949–54.

———. *Zur Farbenlehre.* In: *Naturwissenschaftliche Schriften,* 1. (Gedenkausgabe, Vol. XVI.) Zurich, 1949–54.

GUNN, J. ALEXANDER. *The Problem of Time.* London, 1929.

GURNEY, EDMUND. *The Power of Sound.* London, 1880.

HANSLICK, EDUARD. *The Beautiful in Music.* Translated by Gustav Cohen. London and New York, 1891.

HARTSHORNE, CHARLES. *The Philosophy and Psychology of Sensation.* Chicago, 1934.

HEGEL, GEORG WILHELM FRIEDRICH. *Vorlesungen über die Aesthetik.* (Sämtliche Werke, Vols. IX, X.) Leipzig, 1931.

HEIDEGGER, MARTIN. "Der Ursprung des Kunstwerks." In: *Holzwege.* Frankfort on the Main, 1950.

———. "Die Zeit des Weltbildes." In: *Holzwege.* Frankfort on the Main, 1950.

HELMHOLTZ, HERMANN LUDWIG FERDINAND VON. *On the Sensations of*

Tone as a Psychological Basis for the Theory of Music. Translated by Alexander J. Ellis. London, 1875.

[HÖLDERLIN, FRIEDRICH.] *Hölderlin: His Poems.* Translated by Michael Hamburger. New York, 1952.

HORNBOSTEL, ERICH M. VON. "Die Einheit der Sinne." *Melos* (Berlin), IV (1923).

HUME, DAVID. *A Treatise of Human Nature.* (Everyman's Library.) London and New York, 1911. 2 vols.

HUSSERL, EDMUND. "Phänomenologie des inneren Zeitbewusstseins." *Jahrbuch für Philosophie und phänomenologische Forschung* (Halle), IX (1928).

JAMES, WILLIAM. "Does Consciousness Exist?" In: *Essays in Radical Empiricism.* New York, 1912.

———. "The Perception of Space." *Mind* (London), XII (1887).

———. *Psychology: Briefer Course.* New York, 1920.

KANT, IMMANUEL. *Critique of Pure Reason.* Translated by F. Max Müller. London, 1881. 2 vols.

———. *Prolegomena.* Translated by Ernest Belfort Bax. London, 1891.

KATZ, ADELE T. *Challenge to Musical Tradition.* New York, 1945.

KLAGES, LUDWIG. *Vom Wesen des Rhythmus.* Kampen auf Sylt, 1934.

KOEHLER, WOLFGANG. "Akustische Untersuchungen." *Beiträge zur Akustik und Musikwissenschaft* (Leipzig), IV, VI (1909).

———. *Gestalt Psychology.* New York, 1929.

———. *Die physischen Gestalten in Ruhe und in stationärem Zustand.* Erlangen, 1924.

KOFFKA, KURT. *Experimental-Untersuchungen zur Lehre vom Rhythmus.* Leipzig, 1908.

———. *Principles of Gestalt Psychology.* New York, 1935.

KURTH, ERNST. *Grundlagen des linearen Kontrapunkts.* Bern, 1917.

———. *Musikpsychologie.* Berlin, 1931.

LECOMTE DU NOÜY, PIERRE. *Biological Time.* London, 1936.

LEIBNIZ, BARON GOTTFRIED WILHELM VON. *Leibnitii epistolae.* Edited by Christian Kortholt. Leipzig, 1734.

LIPPS, THEODOR. *Psychological Studies.* Translated by Herbert C. Sanborn. (Psychological Classics, Vol. II.) Baltimore, 1926.

LOCKE, JOHN. *An Essay Concerning Human Understanding.* (Everyman's Library.) London and New York, 1947.

MEUMANN, ERNST. *Untersuchung zur Psychologie und Aesthetik des Rhythmus.* Leipzig, 1894.

MEYER, KATHI. *Bedeutung und Wesen der Musik.* Vol. I: *Der Bedeutungswandel der Musik.* (Sammlung musikwissenschaftlicher Abhandlungen, Vol. 5.) Strassburg, 1932.

MORGENSTERN, CHRISTIAN. *Palmström.* Wiesbaden, 1950.

MURSELL, JAMES L. *The Psychology of Music.* New York, 1937.

NIETZSCHE, FRIEDRICH WILHELM. *Human, All Too Human.* Translated by Helen Zimmern and Paul V. Cohn. (The Complete Works, Vols. VI–VII.) Edinburgh and London, 1909–23.

PALÁGYI, MELCHIOR. *Neue Theorie des Raumes und der Zeit.* Leipzig, 1901.

———. *Wahrnehmungslehre.* (Ausgewählte Werke, Vol. 2.) Leipzig, 1925.

POINCARÉ, JULES HENRI. *Science and Hypothesis.* London and Newcastle-on-Tyne, 1905.

PRATT, CARROLL C. *The Meaning of Music.* New York, 1931.

RÉVÉSZ, GÉZA. "Gibt es einen Hörraum?" *Acta Psychologica* (The Hague), III (1937).

———. *Grundlegung der Tonpsychologie.* Leipzig, 1913.

———. *Introduction to the Psychology of Music.* Translated by G. I. C. de Courcy. London and New York, 1953.

SALZER, FELIX. *Structural Hearing.* New York, 1952.

SCHELLING, FRIEDRICH WILHELM JOSEPH VON. *Philosophie der Mythologie.* (Sämtliche Werke, Part II, Vol. II.) Stuttgart and Augsburg, 1856–61.

SCHENKER, HEINRICH. *Das Meisterwerk in der Musik.* Munich, 1925–30. 3 vols.

———. *Neue musikalische Theorien und Fantasien.* Vienna, 1906–35. 4 vols.

———. *Der Tonwille.* Vienna, 1922–24. 9 vols. in 3.

———. *Harmony.* Translated by Elizabeth Mann Borgese and edited and annotated by Oswald Jonas. Chicago, 1954.

SCHLEGEL, AUGUST WILHELM VON. *Vorlesungen über dramatische Kunst und Literatur.* Bonn, 1923. 2 vols.

SCHOPENHAUER, ARTHUR. *The World as Will and Idea.* Translated by R. B. Haldane and John Kemp. London, 1883–86. 3 vols.

SEARS, CHARLES H. *Studies in Rhythm.* Worcester, Mass., 1902.

SESSIONS, ROGER. *The Musical Experience of Composer, Performer, Listener.* Princeton, 1950.

SPENCER, HERBERT. "On the Origin and Function of Music." In: *Essays on Education.* (Everyman's Library.) London and New York, 1911.

SPENGLER, OSWALD. *The Decline of the West.* Translated by Charles Francis Atkinson. New York, 1927–28. 2 vols.

STRAUS, ERWIN. *Vom Sinn der Sinne.* Berlin, 1935.

STRAVINSKY, IGOR. *Stravinsky, an Autobiography.* New York, 1936.

STUMPF, KARL. *Tonpsychologie.* Leipzig, 1883–90. 2 vols.

UEXKÜLL, JAKOB VON. *Theoretische Biologie.* Berlin, 1928.

WAHL, JEAN ANDRÉ. *Vers le concret.* (Bibliothèque d'histoire de la philosophie.) Paris, 1932.

WERTHEIMER, MAX. "Experimentelle Studien über das Sehen von Bewegung." In: *Drei Abhandlungen zur Gestalttheorie.* Erlangen, 1925.

———. "Untersuchungen zur Lehre von der Gestalt." *Psychologische Forschung* (Berlin), IV (1923).

WHITEHEAD, ALFRED NORTH. *The Concept of Nature.* Cambridge, 1930.

WOLFF, ERICH, and PETERSEN, C. *Das Schicksal der Musik von der Antike zur Gegenwart.* Breslau, 1923.

INDEX

INDEX

T

U

V

Victor Zuckerkandl

Victor Zuckerkandl was born in Vienna on July 2, 1896. He studied music theory and piano in Vienna, conducted operas and concerts there and in other cities, and received his Ph.D. in 1927 at Vienna University. From 1927 to 1933 he was music critic for newspapers in Berlin and taught music theory and appreciation in Vienna during the years 1934 to 1938. Dr. Zuckerkandl came to the United States in 1940, and for two years was a member of the music department at Wellesley College. In 1942-44 he worked as a machinist in a Boston defense plant. He was on the faculty of the New School, in New York, teaching courses on music theory, during 1946-48. Under a grant-in-aid from the American Philosophical Society, Dr. Zuckerkandl developed a music course especially for the liberal arts student. Instead of being a technical, survey, or appreciation course, it dealt with the nature, structure, and significance of the tonal language which had been used by great composers of the past. After he joined the music department of St. John's College (Annapolis, Maryland) in 1948, the course was adopted as requisite for liberal arts students at the College. Dr. Zuckerkandl's book *The Sense of Music* (Princeton, 1959), presented this approach to a larger audience.

Dr. Zuckerkandl twice held a three-year Bollingen Fellowship. The first award enabled him to write the present work, *Sound and Symbol: Music and the External World,* first published in 1956. A second volume, *Sound and Symbol: Man the Musician,* which he finished before his death, will be published subsequently in Bollingen Series. Under the second Bollingen Fellowship, Dr. Zuckerkandl worked on a study of the creative process in music as exemplified in the Notebooks of Beethoven. His other publications included contributions to the *Harvard Dictionary of Music;* a book, *Vom musikalischen Denken* (Zurich, 1964) ; and articles in British, German, and Swiss journals.

Beginning in 1960, Dr. Zuckerkandl was an annual lecturer at the Eranos Conference held each August in Ascona, Switzerland, and his papers appeared in the *Eranos Jahrbücher* (Zurich) . From 1964, when he retired from St. John's College, until his death on April 24, 1965, he resided in Ascona and lectured at the C. G. Jung Institute in Zurich.